Southern Appalachian Storytellers

CONTRIBUTIONS TO SOUTHERN APPALACHIAN STUDIES

1. *Memoirs of Grassy Creek: Growing Up in the Mountains on the Virginia–North Carolina Line.* Zetta Barker Hamby. 1998

2. *The Pond Mountain Chronicle: Self-Portrait of a Southern Appalachian Community.* Edited by Leland R. Cooper and Mary Lee Cooper. 1998

3. *Traditional Musicians of the Central Blue Ridge: Old Time, Early Country, Folk and Bluegrass Label Recording Artists, with Discographies.* Marty McGee. 2000

4. *W.R. Trivett, Appalachian Pictureman: Photographs of a Bygone Time.* Ralph E. Lentz II. 2001

5. *The People of the New River: Oral Histories from the Ashe, Alleghany and Watauga Counties of North Carolina.* Edited by Leland R. Cooper and Mary Lee Cooper. 2001

6. *John Fox, Jr., Appalachian Author.* Bill York. 2003

7. *The Thistle and the Brier: Historical Links and Cultural Parallels Between Scotland and Appalachia.* Richard Blaustein. 2003

8. *Tales from Sacred Wind: Coming of Age in Appalachia. The Cratis Williams Chronicles.* Cratis D. Williams. Edited by David Cratis Williams and Patricia D. Beaver. 2003

9. *Willard Gayheart, Appalachian Artist.* Willard Gayheart and Donia S. Eley. 2003

10. *The Forest City Lynching of 1900: Populism, Racism, and White Supremacy in Rutherford County, North Carolina.* J. Timothy Cole. 2003

11. *The Brevard Rosenwald School: Black Education and Community Building in a Southern Appalachian Town, 1920–1966.* Betty J. Reed. 2004

12. *The Bristol Sessions: Writings About the Big Bang of Country Music.* Edited by Charles K. Wolfe and Ted Olson. 2005

13. *Community and Change in the North Carolina Mountains: Oral Histories and Profiles of People from Western Watauga County.* Compiled by Nannie Greene and Catherine Stokes Sheppard. 2006

14. *Ashe County: A History; A New Edition.* Arthur Lloyd Fletcher. 2009 [2006]

15. *The New River Controversy; A New Edition.* Thomas J. Schoenbaum. Epilogue by R. Seth Woodard. 2007

16. *The Blue Ridge Parkway by Foot: A Park Ranger's Memoir.* Tim Pegram. 2007

17. *James Still: Critical Essays on the Dean of Appalachian Literature.* Edited by Ted Olson and Kathy H. Olson. 2008

18. *Owsley County, Kentucky, and the Perpetuation of Poverty.* John R. Burch, Jr. 2008

19. *Asheville: A History.* Nan K. Chase. 2007

20. *Southern Appalachian Poetry: An Anthology of Works by 37 Poets.* Edited by Marita Garin. 2008

21. *Ball, Bat and Bitumen: A History of Coalfield Baseball in the Appalachian South.* L.M. Sutter. 2009

22. *The Frontier Nursing Service: America's First Rural Nurse-Midwife Service and School.* Marie Bartlett. 2009

23. *James Still in Interviews, Oral Histories and Memoirs.* Edited by Ted Olson. 2009

24. *The Millstone Quarries of Powell County, Kentucky.* Charles D. Hockensmith. 2009

25. *The Bibliography of Appalachia: More Than 4,700 Books, Articles, Monographs and Dissertations, Topically Arranged and Indexed.* Compiled by John R. Burch, Jr. 2009

26. *Appalachian Children's Literature: An Annotated Bibliography.* Compiled by Roberta Teague Herrin and Sheila Quinn Oliver. 2009

27. *Southern Appalachian Storytellers: Interviews with Sixteen Keepers of the Oral Tradition.* Edited by Saundra Gerrell Kelley. 2011

Southern Appalachian Storytellers

Interviews with Sixteen Keepers of the Oral Tradition

Edited by SAUNDRA GERRELL KELLEY

CONTRIBUTIONS TO SOUTHERN APPALACHIAN STUDIES, 27

McFarland & Company, Inc., Publishers
Jefferson, North Carolina, and London

LIBRARY OF CONGRESS CATALOGUING-IN-PUBLICATION DATA

Southern Appalachian storytellers : interviews with sixteen keepers of the oral tradition / edited by Saundra Gerrell Kelley.
    p.   cm. — (Contributions to Southern Appalachian studies ; 27)
    Includes index.

ISBN 978-0-7864-4751-0
softcover : 50# alkaline paper ∞

    1. Folklore—Appalachian Region, Southern. 2. Storytelling—Appalachian Region, Southern—Anecdotes. 3. Storytellers—Appalachian Region, Southern—Anecdotes. I. Kelley, Saundra Gerrell, 1948– II. Title. III. Series.
GR108.15.S68   2011
398.20975—dc22   2010038385

British Library cataloguing data are available

© 2011 Saundra Gerrell Kelley. All rights reserved

No part of this book may be reproduced or transmitted in any form or by any means, electronic or mechanical, including photocopying or recording, or by any information storage and retrieval system, without permission in writing from the publisher.

Cover images © 2011 Shutterstock

Manufactured in the United States of America

McFarland & Company, Inc., Publishers
   Box 611, Jefferson, North Carolina 28640
      www.mcfarlandpub.com

Contents

Preface 1

Sheila Kay Adams 5
Lloyd Arneach 16
Marilou Awiakta 32
Gary Carden 47
Jo Carson 61
Angelyn DeBord 80
Elizabeth Ellis 93
John Thomas Fowler 109
Linda Goss 120
Rosa Hicks 138
Ted Hicks 144
Dot Jackson 148
Charlotte Ross 162
James "Sparky" Rucker 180
Betty Smith 193
Jerry Wolfe 205

Index 211

Preface

The impetus for this book began with a serendipitous meeting with the Appalachian author of *Refuge*, Dot Jackson. At the time, I was in graduate school at East Tennessee State University in Johnson City, Tennessee, working on my master's in education with a storytelling concentration.

Coming from a social sciences background gained as a student at Florida State University in Tallahassee, I was interested in ethnography and had done graduate level coursework in oral histories and learning how to interview people in order to really hear what they had to say. By the time I got to ETSU and began work with a medical communications grant with the School of Medicine and the Storytelling Program, I had developed strong communication skills that I honed even further in my interviews with numerous cancer patients.

All of the interviews for this book were done in an oral history format, with the interviewer's voice removed from the final transcripts. Individual styles of speaking were retained as much as possible, and very few changes were made in the language each person used when engaged in conversation with the interviewer; none were made without their approval. No constraints were put on the teller—these were their personal journey stories and time and space were allotted to accommodate what they wanted to say about who they are as individuals, and their life's work.

One of the great benefits of the ETSU Storytelling Program is exposure to the very best of what the storytelling world has to offer. I met storytellers from all over the world there, including a number from Appalachia, but it was what Appalachia was telling me that called me to do this collection of interviews.

It is an old place—mountains ancient beyond memory, with stories embedded in the rocks and soil; those ancient stories are also bred into the substance of the people who trod there, from the first to those of today. I soon found myself enthralled by Appalachian storytelling and the stories of the American Indians who continue to live and tell their stories on ancestral soil in those mountains; when I began to meet the tellers, I knew there were stories in their personal life-journeys that made them unique to this place. I had to know more, and I found myself called to collect the stories of the storytellers themselves.

It was when I was invited to the home of Billee Moore in Crumpler, North Carolina, to meet a writer named Dot Jackson that the story unfolded and I began to understand the work ahead. When I arrived, the storytelling was already in full swing. There were four of us: Billee, Dot, her cousin Linda Bowie, and me. The first evening we told stories until two in the morning. I grew excited by what I was hearing. This was not formulaic stage performance storytelling—it was spontaneous and it was the stuff of real life.

These were Appalachian voices recounting the stories of battles fought, nightmarish realities and warm memories, all told around the venerable kitchen table, but it was Dot and her stories that captured my imagination. It seemed to me that everything that fell from her mouth was noteworthy. Trying not to be too obvious, I found myself running back and forth to my room to record as much of it as I could; when I left Crumpler, that notebook was packed with quotes.

I was captivated by the images and themes Jackson wove, and I could see them as though they were my memories, too. She told in the traditional mountain way sitting on the edge of her chair (she is barely 4' 11"), the only movement that of her animated face and the sound of her voice, but it was enough to weave a liminal quality around the time we spent there.

The theme of her life and that of her written work is the deep elemental longing for the Southern Highland Mountains, and her life-task was to reach that place in Appalachia that her ancestors called home, Pickens, South Carolina, and to stay there forever. Some time after that initiatory weekend, I interviewed Jackson, and her life journey in story became the capstone of my master's degree at East Tennessee State University. During over thirty hours of conversation with her, it became evident that she was the nexus of an extensive network of Appalachian writers and storytellers.

Two names in particular appeared often in our conversations—ballad singer and author Betty Smith and oral tradition storyteller and folklorist Charlotte Ross, but she also knew many other significant personalities whose journey stories demanded a hearing. It became evident that tapping into that network of acquaintances could lead to some valuable information about storytelling in Appalachia, and what it means to call the Southern Highland mountains "home."

The body of work which grew organically from my conversations with Jackson, and then with Smith and Ross, eventually led to this collection of interviews. All of these tellers of story have interests that vary widely, but for every one, the love of place—Appalachia—plays a significant role in their lives.

There is an earth-based mystical quality to the stories these people tell about their lives "on the mountain," reminding me of a quote from the ancient philosopher Dogen:

> Because mountains are high and broad,
> The way of riding the clouds is always in the mountains;
> The inconceivable power of soaring in the wind comes
> Freely from the mountains

There are several people without whom this collection might never have come together. I would like to especially thank Billee Moore, whom I consider to be the godmother of this project, for it is she who introduced me to Dot Jackson and her cousin Linda Bowie.

Joseph Sobol, Ph.D., coordinator of the Master's in Storytelling program at East Tennessee State University, provided much appreciated guidance as I worked to shape the list of storytellers that eventually comprised this collection. Roberta Herrin, Ph.D., director of the Appalachian Studies program at East Tennessee State University, also assisted with contact information for some of the tellers in this book, as did Fred Sauceman, assistant to the president of ETSU and editor of *Now and Then, The Appalachian Magazine*.

I would also like to thank my daughters, Katherine Kelley Draa and Kristy Noel Kelley for believing in me; their support of this journey has allowed me to travel far, far from home to listen to the sounds and stories of another place. Appreciation also goes to my good friend, wise counselor and traveling companion, Marjorie Shaefer, who was always ready to listen and to respond to my late night calls with unerring honesty and constant support, and her husband Harry, who contributed crucial editing assistance.

Two people come to mind as I think of the next generation of Appalachian storytellers—not that they are younger than the others, but rather that they are now coming to the fore as they seek to perpetuate the legends of Appalachia through balladry and traditional oral storytelling, and they are Judy Rhodes and Libby Tipton. To hear Judy line-sing or Libby talk about her father finding her and her husband on a mountain in the black of night is to go places you never thought to see or hear. It is my hope they will lead others to the top of the sacred mountain where the soul can fly.

Sheila Kay Adams

The product of seven generations of western North Carolina storytellers and ballad singers, teacher, author, storyteller and ballad singer Sheila Kay Adams is one of the story-keepers of her people.

She learned the English, Scottish and Irish ballads brought to America by her ancestors in the 1700s at the feet of her great-aunt Dellie Chandler Norton, and her cousin Cas Wallin, and she has continued to sing them as she learned them.

Adams' recordings, *Loving Forward, Loving Back* and *A Spring in the Burton Cove*, contain traditional ballads, banjo tunes and her own compositions, and she has earned recognition and awards for her drop-thumb style clawhammer skills on the five-string banjo.

Her childhood in the mountain community of Sodom, North Carolina, is featured in the story-performance tape *Don't Git Above Your Raising*. Her book *Come Go Home with Me*, published by the University of North Carolina Press, won the North Carolina Historical Society's award for historical fiction in 1997. *My Old True Love*, published by Random House, is based on a true family story.

Adams has traveled and performed in England and is a frequent performer at the International Storytelling Festival in Jonesborough, Tennessee, and at festivals around the country. Her focus is on her family's stories both in performance and in her writings; she released an anthology CD of stories and songs recorded live over a nine year period at the Festival in Jonesborough in October 2007.

Adams received the prestigious North Carolina Folklore Society's Brown-Hudson Award in recognition of her valuable contributions to the study of North Carolina folklore in 1998; she was elected the Mars Hill College Alumni of the Year in 2003. In addition, she was a finalist in the Southeastern Booksellers Association's 2004 Book of the Year Award and the

Appalachian Writer's Association 2004 Book of the Year Award for her novel *My Old True Love*. That same year she released a CD entitled *All the Other Fine Things*, comprised of fiddle tunes, ballads, and shape-note hymns that complement the stories in the book.

Sheila Kay Adams and her family still reside in the county in which she was born. She has three children and is passing the family traditions of storytelling and balladry on to them. As her great-aunt once said, "She might not always know where she's going, but she sure knows where she comes from."

The Interview

My name is Sheila Kay Adams and I come from Sodom, which is in Western North Carolina, right across the mountain from here, about an hour from Jonesborough, Tennessee. My people have been there since 1731. They came to America from different places, but the majority of them came out of White Haven, England, from the border country. Some of them came from Northern Ireland, but the majority of my people, all four families—we ain't got no tree—it's a wreath that keeps going round and round, they all came over here together. Granny said they's keepin' the line pure.

Granny said when you go to the old country; you look to see if there ain't mountains. I'll bet you a nickel to a dollar they is. She was right. I went and there is, and I got to see Hadrian's Wall which Daddy referred to as Harrigan's Wall—we've been gone three hundred years, you know.

The only thing I can figure is that Amos Norton, who is my grandfather's four greats-back grandfather, headed out over here in the late 1600s. It was late 1690 or something and he died in Bermuda, but he had some boys and their wives and they came on over and came into Jamestown. A couple of them didn't like it there, so they came on down—one of them was named Amos as well, and they got part of the land grant from Blount in what is now East Tennessee. It was all one area then. That's how the Nortons came to be there, and they were the first family on the land, but they were McNaughtons. I found that out from my aunt Almarie, who will be ninety this year.

I didn't know I was telling stories in the beginning. Actually I've sung stories all my life, you know, ballads—the love songs, 'cause they literally called it "singing a story." I can sing a story, too, they'd say, but it was just talkin', you know, that's the way we do it.

I was sitting in a classroom at Swannanoa getting ready to teach, when all of a sudden it just struck me how odd it was ... here was the room full of people just hangin' on every word, and had this look of adoration on their faces, and I thought, they ought to just come and have lunch at Mom's on Sunday—they'd see it's exactly the same way it is here. Nobody called it storytelling. I don't think I ever heard anybody over at home say "set down here and listen to this story," it's just one of the things we tell often. They would talk about somebody, or they would say "Yeah, I 'member that time me and your uncle Wayne..." but it was never "Sit down sweetheart, I'm going to tell you a story." No, they wouldna' done that—it was just talking. As a result, a lot of family history got passed down, because it was kind of their entertainment, or as my daddy would say, the "quarosity" of your neighbor, who just happened to be your first, third, fifth, double-sixth and seventh cousin. Instead of saying queer, strange or odd, he would say, "quarosity."

A lot of it, too, has to do with a sense of humor. Espe-

Sheila Kay Adams

cially the women had it, and Daddy had it, too. He would get to thinking about something, and just have to set down and lay his head down and laugh until he cried. It's a really sophisticated sense of humor—you wouldn't think so from people like my granny, who said, "I went six years to school to the free school." But she had a beautiful handwrite and she knew more about anything than anybody I have ever encountered in my entire life. And she was convinced that somebody had taken all that money that they give to the space program and put it in their back pockets and filmed all that stuff out there in Arizona. That was her.

She was also the one—they were thinking about putting a nuclear repository over there in Madison County [North Carolina] in Haywood, and it would have gotten a little bit of the southern corner of Buncombe County, too. Granny called it a "nucler suppository." Now she was right on the durn money. We all started usin' that "nucler suppository" because that's what they were going to do—poke it in the ground and forget about it.

Granny aggravated me from the time I was in college until she died, and she died when I was forty-five, because I was trying to tell her what kind of singing I done and I told her it was a cappella and she, in front of a packed room of folks over at Western Carolina State University, said "Now Celie [Sheila] here told me what kind of singin' it is, and I'm going to do one of them ole love songs my grand-pappy told me, and I'm gonna do it just like she said—Acapulco!" And not long before she died, we were sitting out on the porch in the dark and she said, "I betchu didn't know I knew that big word." And I said, "What big word?" It had tortured me all my life, but she hadn't told me. And then she said, "Ah, that ole big word, *a cappella*. I heer'ed that all my life. You also call it fa-so-la singin'." She knew exactly what the word was, but no, it was Acapulco!

Aunt Inez was hell on wheels. She had one of the best senses of humor—she could tell a joke like nobody's business. She could take an ordinary joke and personalize it and make it happen in Sodom ... so I thought all this was happening in Sodom! When Granny was talking about Erica one time, taking all these men and been married seven times, and I said, "My God Mama, who in the world is this Erica who has moved in here?" And she said, "What?" I was tellin' her what Granny said, and Mama finally figured it out and she said, "Aunt Bell is talking about them stories—them soap operas!" She was talking about it like it happened right there in Sodom. Well, things like that had happened right there in Sodom!

There was this fella in church settin' there next to the women. He looked out and he saw this other fella coming down the road who was the community tippler, and he had tippled quite a bit till he had just about tippled over, and all of a sudden the man in the church jumped up and balled his fists—he was a big man—and ran outside the church and just beat the snot out of this man because he was wearing a pair of his wife's underwear on his head! You know what Daddy's comment was? "Well, they is some other man in the congregation didn't recognize it as being hers." But they were that quick—just like a snake and honest as they could be.

You know, I've got a couple of cousins who are still that way and I spent some time with one of them last week. He's just as honest as he can be. He asked me if he could smoke in the house, and I said "Yeah," cause if he don't smoke, well, that's fine, he'll get up and leave. My cousin had said the same thing to him—"Don't smoke in the house," and he took up and left. She didn't see or hear from him for two weeks, because he said, "I'm going to smoke wherever I am; If I cain't smoke, I ain't going to sit here and be miserable either." Just as honest as can be, and so there's a few of them left, but not many. A lot of 'em have conformed to the nicety, and making nice and pleasing. By the way, I'm over that. I'm goin' to be me now ... as soon as I figure out who me is [laughter]—I think maybe it might be the gypsy queen.

You know, you meet people in your life, and some people just kind of pass through and there's others that really stick. I've been really lucky 'cause I've made some really good friends. It's funny, because I know me and her are going to be part of one another's lives, just like me and Sharon—my cousin that I'm living with now, 'cause I moved back to Sodom.

Moving back I felt the first peace that I have felt in probably twenty years. It's magic there—I don't know how else to explain it. I can feel the difference in the air—you know, holding my arm out the window of the car. It's like heavy and humid and then it lightens up when I get in Sodom. Energy stays in a place. There's some bad places over there and you can feel 'em. It's kind of like you know something bad happened right there, and you know. Granny called it "havin' the shine," which was having the sight. That kind of got phonetically passed down in the family, too, and a lot of them saw things.

My mother's sister Fran saw what she called a "haint" that hopped like a grasshopper. Hit had to be eight feet tall, and she grabbed a shotgun and run it down the bank and over into the graveyard, and said it hopped up onto a tombstone about midway through the graveyard, and turned around and looked at her, and she said its teeth had sharp points and it had eyes that was that big around [holding her thumb and forefinger together], and no eyelids. And she said, "I decided that shotgun wasn't going to help me one damn bit so I run back inside [astonished gasp] and I slammed the door and I got out my cross and I stood back from the door holdin' that cross sayin' 'come on, come on now, I ain't got no shotgun, I got somethin' better!'"

Later on, a cousin of mine saw it, same thing, yeah, right down the road from my house. I'm not scared of it—it's been around a long time and hasn't bothered nobody yet, but I saw it when I was probably about seven. My mother had a blind cousin, his name was Little Bob, because my granddaddy's name was Bob—Little Bob was bigger—it was age, you know, that's how they do it. I ran back in the house and told Mama that Little Bob was outside. Mama said, "Well, Lord, what's he doing out at seven o'clock in the morning?" and she went out—there wasn't nothin' there. Then she asked me where I saw Little Bob, and I pointed to the barn. She said I didn't see anything, but I said, "Yeah, I did," and then she said, "No, you didn't, and I'll whip you if you say you did!" I said, "Okay, I didn't see a thing." It's because she could see things, too.

All those religions around home are pretty adamant that if you knew things, if you were different in any way—then it was all of the evil one—Satan. Granny was not that way. That older generation—not my Mama and Daddy's generation, but Granny's generation, used to see the wee folk and the animals. She put cream and honey and honeysuckle out for them. I can remember helping her fix it as a child and every now and then she'd pour some wine in one and she'd say, "Now they'll have a good time tonight," cause her wine was about like drinking rubbing alcohol.

Her mother taught her all of this. She took all our nail clippings and hair and threw it in the cook stove 'cause you don't want no witch getting a single thread or a single fingernail 'cause they'll saddle you and ride you off just like a horse, only she said, "harse," and ride you all over Sodom and you'll just wake up with your nose a-bleeding in the morning. But they didn't talk about it all the time and they weren't afraid, 'cause they felt like they was things they couldn't explain every day. This was just one of 'em. They couldn't tell you how a light bulb worked or even how their body worked. They just know that's how it worked and I think all those mountain people developed heightened sense because of that. They had to; they had to think fast on their feet and Caz Wallin, one of the love song singers, he's a good storyteller, too, who can get a little bit off-color at times ... he said that if you thought about who was going to make it over there in that border country [England], and there was fighting all the time and the raiders coming through and killing people ... he said what went on in the Civil War went on all the time over there, and they shipped a bunch of 'em off to Northern Ireland and then a bunch of 'em come over here and went through it again. The ones that survived were the most clever—the best runners and the ones that knew what to do and did it fast when they were threatened, and that's true. I think as a result, generation after generation remembered it all, and the memories are incredible.

Do you remember who you went to the prom with when you were a junior? What color suit did you wear—was it black or white? When you came out of junior high and started senior high, what did you wear the first day? And then you do things that you know are going to take a little bit of thinking; you are going to remember because it was such a profound experience that you will begin to remember. Or the first time you got kissed by a boy—everybody remembers that. You just keep goin' back. When did you lose your first tooth, do you remember that? My aunt Almarie will talk to you about dresses she wore to school when she was six! She was the one that taught me how to take people back. People will say, "Oh, I can't remember back that far like you do." It's visualizing—okay, what color of shoes did I have on? If you can get that, then it's a start. You have to focus in on something.

For some reason, mountain people have the ability to go back, and I think it's because of not being able to read and write for so long. They had to store stuff in their minds. My father's mind was amazing, and Granny could tell you stuff you wouldn't believe.

The first time Mama said she heard "Camp a Little While in the Wilderness" was in 1920, when her and her mother were walking up the road, and she heard Uncle Willis was settin' up there in the chimney corner, which would have been on the outside, and that big gray coat he wore—he was 99 years old and he froze all the time, and singin' that song. But what caught my attention from her comment was "that big gray coat." And I said, "What big gray coat?" And she said, "Well, he said he took it off a Confederate soldier in the Civil War." See, it's that curiosity. I remember Daddy telling me about the story "My Own True Love," and the strange mule it had in it. That strange mule ... what was strange about it was had the "U.S." branded on its backside. That told me these two boys were fightin' for the Union. To them and to me, it's not storytellin'. I still don't think about myself as a storyteller. I run my mouth a lot, but I do remember stuff and I've gotten now that really trust that I'm going to be able to file it away with all the other "shit" that's up there, but what I do is I will make a note of it. If somebody says something I'll say, "Wait a minute, I'm going to steal that." And I swear, it's all the time.

There's one distant cousin of mine, if he can ever get to Jonesborough, I don't know if they'll let him go home or not. He comes up with some of the craziest stuff: he told his sister when she was a little girl that when she was born she had a tail. Said it was about two inches long and had three feathers stickin' out the end of it. Said, "You know that happens sometimes in our family. We had it removed, but they told us it might come back," and he kept her going for ten years on that. When she had a child, and it was up four years old he told that young'un the same thing — "You know your mother had a tail just like you did when you were born." He had her really believing that. He's thirty-seven-years-old and he's got a *turn* to him; it's a turn they would call it, and Daddy always said it was the catching ear, being able to catch things with your ear and curiosity.

The best stories are absolutely the truth and I usually tell 'em in the voice of the person who told me. If I told them it wouldn't be near as good. What I do is basically repeat the story — I allow them to tell their story. Those are the best kind, that's why I kind of go into "their" voice whenever I tell a story. Some of them are mine, like when we went to New York for our junior and senior trip — that's my voice, but the majority of them are told in the voices of the fine people I grew up with back home.

I love old country music and I know just about every song George Jones, Tammy Wynette, and Loretta Lynn and Dolly, too, have ever sung. It's amazing how you remember those songs and the ballads. They are beautiful songs. I had the opportunity to talk to George Jones some, and he said his grandmother was a ballad singer, that's where he gets that little quirk he's got that nobody else has; that's where it comes from.

In February of '58 I would have been four, fixin' to turn five in March, and that's when my grandmother died. Daddy's mother died when she was fifty-one — had a stroke, but Mama's mother was still living and I stayed a lot with her and Granddaddy. They were moving a cook stove and it started to tip back — it was one of those cast-iron Home Comforts, and Maw ran in to try to steady that stove to keep it from falling and it hit her at the top of her thighs and just raked down the top of her knees and probably formed a blood clot. My cousin Sharon and I were there the day she died in February, and so I was left without a grandma. Granny and her both lived up at the end of the holler—they could holler at each other literally and have conversations back and forth standing on the porch.

The last thing my grandmother said was, "Poor ole Ross and Delly. I reckon they're really missin' Tete,"—that was their boy who had died from carbon monoxide poisoning. That was the last thing she said before she died and she was looking out the window there in the kitchen up toward Granny—the woman that became my granny, and my grandfather's brother, Ross. And then she died and I went right on up the road to Granny's.

She said, "Well, she showed up. Some of our family died and I ain't been able to get shed of her since." I loved spending time with them mainly because of these old songs. Granny used to say "Sweet Betsy from Pike" or "Red River Valley," that was what she called modern songs, but the long ballads she called the 'love songs.' That was what she called the broadside ballads and they would usually start off with "come-all-ye." Them's the shortened versions of the love songs, because they started to writing on little pieces of broad-scrap paper and selling them in the big cities in the old country, but a lot of them came straight from those long ballads. There was one called the "Knoxville Girl" that I found out was "The Oxford Berkenshire Tragedy," dependin' on who you talk to. The tune "Streets of Laredo" was an old love song, just different words, and then there was one more—"Pretty Polly" was really the "Cruel Ship's Carpenter." The bluegrass version, which says "come ride away with me," never made any sense to me—why would you jump on a horse with a feller you didn't even know after you just finished telling him, "I'm a-feared of your ways," and then get on a horse with him? That's stupid. A lot of those songs came over here that way.

Inez said it this way, "I sing eiter what I hear on the radio—that Carter family done some pretty stuff—you know he took 'Little Birdie' and it's 'Sweet Fern' now." Once radio came in, it started to change things, but in my family Granny sung "The Little Farmer Boy." Burzill, her sister, sung the "Cruel Carpenter" and Cass sung "The Demon Lover." And they were virtually all three the same song, just three different versions. They just chose the version they liked best.

It must have been that summer, and I would have been five, that I started to singing. They had been working in tobacco, and there was lightning bugs out which would have been about now, but there was no lightning bugs so they must have been topping it, but they might have been pulling worms off—back then they didn't put all that spray on it, but anyway, family would show up to help you. Uncle Ross was sick by then—my guess is it was strokes—

he was quite a bit older than Granny, and he had already gone to bed, but they was still a big crowd sitting on the porch. I was falling asleep—I was bump-rocked a lot. They didn't have a rocking chair, so bump bump, bump bump—the rhythm itself would put you to sleep and that sound.

Then Dillard Tanner started singing. Nobody was saying a word. They were wore out. When you work in tobacco, it's nasty, nasty work sticky, but there's a smell that lingers, almost like a spice. They were all a-settin there, they'd had supper and it was right at dark and Dillard started singing. I was five years old and I wanted to learn it, and I wondered if there were any more of those songs because it was just magic. My cousin Larry lives in that same house. He sings, too—he has the best voice of all of us. He leans toward country-western, but the thing is me and him learned these country-western songs early, early. If you put us together with a couple of beers, then we'll sing every song George Jones ever sung. [Chuckle] We did it this past Sunday night, sang maybe three hours, me and him rememberin' words setting there on the couch. Stuff like that is still happening back home and that's why I wanted to go back home.

I don't ever remember a time when there was not music. Out of all my first cousins, all of them play. The music took all sorts of forms—old fiddle tunes like "Cumberland Gap" and "Cripple Creek." Johnny Horton's "The Battle of New Orleans" is set to the melody of "The Eighth of January," and then bluegrass invaded—that's all I'll say about that.

And then there's country and western—some of the early stuff was great—Patsy Cline and Hank Williams. I was telling a young feller about him. He died when he was only twenty-eight years old; "Your Cheating Heart," and "I'm so Lonesome I Could Cry"—he wrote all those songs before he was twenty-eight. He was a short time here and a long time gone; he had a lot to do before he went at twenty-eight, and he did. Patsy Cline couldn't sing until she had scarlet fever and went into a coma for two weeks, and when she woke up, she sung five octaves. It's just weird stuff like that.

They told me I wouldn't have a voice by the time I turned fifty because I sang full-voice; I didn't know how to use my voice. I remember the doctor asked me if I had smoked at one time and I said, "I am a smoker now!" and he said, "You can't be. There is absolutely no sign in your lungs that you have ever smoked! They are as clean as a sixteen year old's." Well, that and being a changlin', as my granny called it.

The music is a big part of my memory and it brought people together. Folks would just pull up and blow the horn after I got home and holler, "What are ye doin'?" I had forgotten all of that. My cousin Jenny rode her lawn mower all the way up the hill and mowed my yard. That's the way it has always been—they enjoyed company and they enjoyed each other's. They spent a lot of time together and they spent a lot of time wandering around in the woods by themselves. Granny said anytime you'd forget who you are, all you had to do was find a little patch of woods, go out and set down a minute.

Larry told me two years ago, "Come home. That's what your heart's a-wanting and that's where you'll find peace. The world out yonder ain't fit to live in. Come home." When I came home, he came to the house and played music just like he promised.

They looked at me as not necessarily a traitor, but just as somebody who left home. And I remember Larry sayin' to me, "You're supposed to come home; you can't be right and stay out there all the time 'cause they'll change you." And he was right—you can't help but change, because there are certain expectations from us when we are away from home.

He said that when you are out in the big world, you will change for them, that's why you need to come home. When you need to be somewhere other than "out there," it needs to be here. He was right. I've been the happiest since I went home where I was born and raised. It hadn't changed all that much 'cept the old folks are gone. My grandson is there ... and my cousin; go down the road a little bit and there's my cousin Keith, a new generation. We've had people move in but they are good people.

There are clichés about just about everything—blondes, African Americans, Chinese Americans ... pick a group—women in general—and there's gonna be somebody who has something negative to say, or they romanticize which is equally as bad. For me, there's no better people in the world than mountain people. It's true, some of them are mean or racist, but show me a community that's not. I used to get mad when somebody called us hillbillies until I found out it came from the border country in England and Scotland. "Hillbilly" was a positive thing—it meant a lot of the men were named William and they lived in the hills—some of the most beautiful parts of England and Scotland. It's not necessarily about the mountains—it's just people.

It just so happened that the people I grew up with were always honest or tried to be and they helped if they could, and they truly and honestly loved you. They wouldn't accept stupid, crap behavior and you didn't get no second chance, because they grew up in a time when all they had was their word. They were insulted if you asked them to sign a contract—"I gave you my word!" That was like giving you their firstborn son to hold. Granny used to say, "This generation a-comin' up now, they don't know what givin' your word means." That's why when I tell my grandson something, or anybody, I try my best to make it happen. In hard times, it's hard to keep all your promises, but I figure the ones that really love me will understand.

I'm livin' with my cousin Sharon now in one of the houses that Mama and them had and I'm just as happy as I can be. That little blond-headed boy across the road has something to do with it. He's within hollerin' distance now—I don't have to drive nowhere, and he watches like a hawk for that car to get there when I do have to leave. Everybody that picks him up at daycare says he throws the awfullest fit there ever was, but when I come to the door with his little lunch bag, he says, "Let's go, Gegee." He knows everybody in the graveyard back there and exactly how he's related to them. That's called "layin' a foundation," the way I look at it.

    I'm just glad to be home and the stories just keep on a-happenin.' My aunt Almarie started talking and explaining the family connections back three or four years ago; it just blew my mind because as she said, "Hell, they're all dead now, I can tell the story," and she just plastered my head against the chair with all of these stories that I had never heard from anybody. I caught them and I kept them, too. They were so fantastic, and they explained a whole lot about a bunch of stuff I couldn't ever get a handle on. Some of the things they did were just unconscionable, but we have to realize, that was a different time and a different situation. Frank Proffitt wrote a song, "Poor Man" [about how life doesn't offer much for a poor man] and it's still that way. Hopefully it will change. I think it might and I just hope I'm around to see it.

    If I was going to say anything, the people who are coming into my life right now are almost carbon copies, just in a different way, of the people I grew up with. Now that's kind of odd, but it's reconnecting the lines. Like Judy here—we met in 1973 at the Shindig on the Green, but we only knew each other that one summer, but when I met her again, I remembered her giggle—I know that woman, I told myself! We went our separate ways, and now here we are again, best friends.

    My uncle Ward called the other night and said, "Well, I finally got you by way of Buffalo, New York." And I said "What?" And he said, "I been a-tryin to call ye and I can't get you, and I finally called Robbie and she told me." And I said, "No, Uncle Ward, she's in Vermont," and he said, "It don't make no difference, she's a way north of Virginia so it's all Buffalo as far as I am concerned." But he said, "I'm callin' you by way of Buffalo," 'cause Robbie gave him my cell phone number. He's Aunt Almarie's husband and he said, "You need to come and see us," and I said, "Okay." And he said, "You need to come this weekend." So that tells me Aunt Almarie's not doin' good. So I'm goin' Sunday.

Lloyd Arneach

Lloyd Arneach was born and raised on the Cherokee Reservation in Cherokee, North Carolina, and is an enrolled member of the Eastern Band of Cherokee. A Vietnam veteran, Arneach worked as computer programming professional with AT&T prior to accepting the call to storytelling. His first mentors in the art of storytelling were two uncles who also lived on the reservation and from whom he initially learned the stories of his people. He began a side career as a lecturer on the history and culture of the Cherokee while still living and working in Georgia and added storytelling to his presentations on culture and history in 1990.

In demand as a lecturer, Arneach continues to lecture on Cherokee history and culture in schools, universities, libraries, historical societies and civic groups. In addition, he also conducts workshops on Native American storytelling, building appreciation of Native American culture, and what the stories mean to the cultures that produced them.

He is the author of two books: one of Cherokee stories, *Long-Ago Stories of the Eastern Cherokee*, published in 2008 by The History Press, and *The Animal's Ballgame* published by Children's Press in 1992, which is a collection of his favorite Cherokee animal stories. His CD, *Can You Hear the Smoke?* features stories and legends he has adapted for telling.

Arneach has told stories at the Kennedy Center; the National Folklife Festival in Washington, D.C.; the opening of the Museum of the American Indian also in Washington, D.C.; the Winnipeg International Storytelling Festival in Canada and numerous festivals, schools and universities, powwows and theaters throughout the United States. He has also acted for the past several years in *Unto These Hills—A Retelling*, which is the outdoor drama held in Cherokee, North Carolina, every summer, and has told stories on the Discovery Channel.

An avid collector of stories, his repertoire includes both the "old stories" of the Cherokee and contemporary stories he has collected. His work ranges from creation stories to "behind the scenes" stories from the movie *Dances with Wolves*, to the historical stories of various Native American tribes. Many of his stories feature Native Americans such as Floyd Red Crow Westerman; Billy Mills, who was an Olympic champion; a young Cree girl with no stories to tell; and a postmaster on the Papago Reservation.

The Interview

I've been doing presentations since 1970. I was doing Cherokee tradition and history for twenty years and in January of 1990, I started sharing stories, too, so I've got about thirty years of doing this, and I would certainly like to share with some of the young people coming out so they could pick up the ball—the rest of us are getting ready to ease out of the picture.

The way I got into storytelling was this: my late wife and I had a baby sitter who was the leader of a Girl Scout troop, and she was trying to find a book on Indians to fulfill their Indian lore badge. She didn't find such a book in the entire county library system—this was in Georgia, and she said, "Wait a minute, I babysit for Indians." So she called me and asked if I could help them, and I asked what the requirements were and then I said, "Sure, but I'm going to have to come straight from work. I won't have time to change—will that be a problem?" So on the day of the meeting, I went straight from work to her house and they looked at me and said, "I don't know where the Indian is, but he's going to be here soon." You see, I was wearing a three-piece suit. When I finally got up to speak, you could see their jaws dropping to the floor—an Indian in a suit? No!! I started blowing their misconceptions out of the window, right off the bat. When we finished, I started getting calls from all of the other Scout leaders, because they had the same problem with the Indian lore badge, and they started asking me if I could come to their groups. I started speaking to their groups, and then Boy Scouts heard of me and asked if I could come to their Blue and Gold banquet, so I started going to them, too. Soon other groups started calling including historical groups and museums, and then I was telling at Georgia State and Emory University and this was all by word of mouth. I never did any advertising.

This was in 1988 and my wife was having tremendous headaches at that time, and it got so bad I took her to the emergency room. It took about forty-five minutes and then they came out and said she's either got a brain tumor or a brain lesion, so they did a biopsy in November and discovered it was a brain tumor. No one had ever survived more than twenty months with this type of tumor. The tumor destroyed her motor skills—she couldn't walk; she was totally bedridden and couldn't feed herself, but her mental faculties were still there. She was a very intelligent person and had a very quick mind and could communicate with no problem, so we brought her home and her father, my son and I had someone with her 24 hours a day, seven days a week, every hour of the day, somebody was always in the room with her. I was working with AT&T at that point, and they were very understanding and gave me the time off I needed to care for her.

In the mid–1980s, a Dr. Burleson was teaching a folklore class and putting all the stories a student had recorded back in 1971 into a book, and he was calling all of the storytellers (I was one of the people she recorded) and asking them to come to the book signing. I said, well, let me know when the signing occurs and I will check my schedule because I was doing a lot of programs at that time. And then in '88 we discovered Charlotte had the brain tumor in November and in the spring of '89, Dr. Burleson called me back and said, "We will do the book signing in September." I said, "Let me talk to Charlotte and see." I talked to her and she said, "Go ahead and do it—you are in the house all of the time." So I said I would do it.

**Lloyd Arneach
(photograph by Dawn Arneach)**

When Charlotte passed away August 31 of '89 and I was doing everything I could to fill my time, so I went to the book signing in September. While I was there, a lady came up to me and said, "I'm Vivian Winely and I'm a member of the Circle of Storytellers and we have a storytelling festival in January. Would you be willing to come and share your stories at our festival?" and I agreed. So in January of 1990, I started sharing stories and that has taken me to the Kennedy Center, and the National Folk Life Center, and in June I was up in Winnipeg for an international storytelling festival. All of this came about because some thirty-eight years ago, our baby sitter couldn't find a book on Indians! [Laughter] That's why I say it's a complementary story there that's tied in—as I said, I had never thought of storytelling.

I had heard of the Southern Order of Storytellers but I couldn't find them, couldn't locate them. Carmen Deedy [a nationally-known storyteller based in Georgia] was a member of our group and she was my mentor for quite a while with this storytelling, and I worked with her quite a bit. One of the things I told her was that I couldn't get the audience to pay attention with the stories and she said, "Lloyd if you have 100 people in the room and one person isn't paying attention to your stories, what about the other 99 who are? Just share with them and that one will come around," and I thanked her. That has proven to be true, as I have seen people who look like they are thinking, "What am I doing here?" and I say, "Okay," to those who *are* listening to me—I'm going to tell to them.

My only regret is that my late wife didn't live long enough to hear more of my stories, but she heard many of them and she, in turn, would share hers.

I've participated in the *Unto These Hills* outdoor drama in Cherokee for six years now: I did it four years as a teenager—for two years I had a minor role and then for two years I had a minor speaking role. When they re-wrote it in 2006, I was in it again. Last year I had too many gigs going and I didn't feel comfortable being out that many nights, and told them no. They asked me again this summer and I had very few gigs booked this summer when they asked me, so I said "Okay, I will do it this summer," and was delighted to do it, and had a lot of fun with it.

It was a very powerful role to play—this particular character was funny in the beginning, and then they showed him gradually turning serious—he's got a bit of a temper there—not physically, but verbally. When the soldiers came to get his family, he protested, saying, "The Indian agent said we have permission to stay—we're not supposed to go." During this final confrontation, one of the young women is knocked down by a soldier and it turns physical. The family ends up killing two soldiers, and then more soldiers come looking for them. Tsali and his family fled into the mountains, but after much hard traveling, his wife came to him and said it was too rough—too hard for the women, and he sent them back home. Then Tsali gave himself up to be killed so his people could stay in the mountains. That was the role of Tsali.

I worked with a number of people in the play, but the fellow who shared my dressing room was a native of Alaska, north of the Arctic Circle. He shared stories with me and one is a very, very powerful story about his village. That is one of those stories that puts me close to the edge. It's his legacy, because he is alive because of what happened. He's an actor, a trained Shakespearean actor [laughter], now if that isn't a contrast—you have two Indians and one of them is trained as a Shakespearean actor! He shared his story with me during a quiet time and as he shared that story, his expression didn't change, but I saw a tear running down his cheek. When he got into the story,

I understood what it means to him and as I said, it wasn't just a story, it was his legacy. I told him, "You need to share your story. This needs to be told," and he told it. I said one thing you need to tell them is the part at the end:

> This took place at his village and they were hungry, and had a big hunt, but found no game. A young man sitting by the fire said, "I smell moose cooking," but there was nothing. He said he still smelled moose cooking and they began to smell it, too, and realized the smell was coming from the fire. Then they realized they had built their fire over a brush and underneath were two moose that had locked antlers under the snow. The two moose provided for the whole village until the hunting got better.

What is so powerful about this story was that his ancestors were among the ancestors of that village. When he said that, I understood why he was crying—you can hear it in my voice now ... he shared the story but didn't include the last part. I said, that's a very powerful story, but you must include the most powerful part that moves that story—your ancestors were among the survivors and that moose is part of every one of them. He didn't realize how powerful that final phrase was to the telling.

We did a pre-show at the drama—a couple of girls would perform, and then I would tell a couple of stories, and then the choir would sing and then we would leave the stage and the show would start. I was out that time and they had Allen come share that story and he added that final piece—the one in which his ancestors were among the survivors of that village. He said you could just hear the audience respond to that, and he said he never realized what that could mean to others, but he knew what it meant to him. I said, now you know that when people listen to you, they have an idea of what that story means to you. It was wonderful and this is what I said—stories come to me. If I hadn't been there, I would never have heard this story. Our stations were side by side and we would talk. This was my first opportunity to talk with someone from Alaska, who was born and raised there, and he said, we live by hunting. We talked about survival skills and what it meant to them and that if they do another pipeline in Alaska, what it will do to the herd migration. We talked about many things and every night, he shared something different with me.

I told you earlier about how stories come to me: I was sharing with the North American Indigenous Women's Association—which is a national Indian women's organization—at their national conference, and I shared stories about an athlete named Billy Mills, who was an Oglala Lakota [Sioux] Indian who was raised on the Pine Ridge Indian Reservation in South Dakota, and a woman came up afterwards to tell me she was his aunt! I told her, please tell Billy I am still sharing his stories and she laughed and said she would. These things just happen.

At the 1996 Olympics, we had Billy come in. It was at the opening of the festival and the lighting of the fire in Atlanta and I was the senior Native American representative. When I was bringing Billy to the stage, because he was the national honorary chairman, they played the tape from the 1964 Olympics when he won the race. The crowd was going crazy, and there was a guy sitting in front of the stage saying, "Go Billy, go Billy," instead of listening to the announcer. And then when the tape ended the guy was yelling, "Yes, yes," and dancing in circles. I thought, doesn't he know this was thirty or forty years ago? I didn't say anything and when the tape ended, I took my hat off and took Billy to the stage to a standing ovation. As I left the stage, this man tapped me on the shoulder and I recognized him right away and he said, "I'm sorry, I didn't mean to be a distraction, but you have to understand, I was in the stadium the day Billy won and when I heard that announcer's voice I was there again." I said, "Did you get to meet Billy?" and he said that yes he had, and that he got his autograph and he gave him a hug and got a picture with him.

Several years ago I was sharing over at Ft. Loudon at the Sequoyah Museum and shared this story, and we had Cherokee instructors there, and we gathered the students together—they ranged from teenagers to adults, to work with the different instructors, and when I walked off the stage one of the instructors was waiting for me. She said, "Lloyd, I was there in Atlanta, and I saw that man jumping up and down, and I didn't know why until today." So there's the story, within the story, within the story within the story. I certainly enjoy the telling and I hope do it a while yet.

I always feel when I come home to the mountains after a trip that I am returning *home*. They mean home to me: it's peace; it's tranquility for me. I feel there is so much here that we still don't know about: they are finding plants on occasion; they're finding animals that again, no one has ever seen, simply because we are going farther and farther back into the mountains, because we have more people, and more people observing the flora and fauna. As before, we traveled and looked at the beauty; now we are looking discovering more and more. Here in the Great Smokies in the summer they go out hiking and don't realize that in the higher elevations the temperature really drops, and you can still die of exposure in the summer nights here in the mountains, but it doesn't usually happen.

I feel there are spiritual elements in other places—much like going into someone's home—they are all homes, they are spiritual elements. Our people generally say we have been here forever, and yet the archaeologists can track us coming down the Ohio Valley and that our language is of Iroquois origin and some of our legends are parallel with Iroquois legends. Even in [James] Mooney's *Myths and Legends of the Cherokee* book, he has one phrase which I've never heard before, he said one elder told him that when we came to this country there was a pale-skinned people who couldn't see well during the noon day sun. We lived with them for a while, and then we fought with them and drove them into the west. Now, the phrase, "When we came to this country," is a phrase that is used to mean, "When we moved here" basically. It's the only reference I have to an old story like that, but on the other hand I've not been able to find any stories about woodland elk which were here, and buffalo, which were also here in the Great Smokies; as huge resources of meat as these animals were, I can find no references to them. Of the other animals, yes, but not those two, and this one story is obviously an old story, but it's the only one of its kind I have found. How unusual—that phrase—"when we came to this country," so here's one of the old stories that say we were not always here, and the archaeologists reinforce it, but our people still like to say we've always been here. The spiritual aspect of coming back to the Smokies is wonderful—I'm home and at ease.

Doug Lipmann held a seminar some time ago, and I attended. He wanted to come up and see an old storyteller in the mountains, so I and a lady said we'd go with him. I drove and they were interested in learning about the Cherokee. As we got into the foothills, I said, "Do you want to see what I do every time I go into the mountains?" They said, "Yes," so I eased down, pulled off the road and said watch my finger and pushed the overdrive "off" on my dash. I said I turn my overdrive off every time I go into the mountains. They nearly beat me to a pulp, but it was fun.

We went on up into the mountains, and when I saw this house I got excited. I described this house to them—just on the side of that rock, this man used to tell us stories. I remember as a youth in the [*Unto These Hills*] drama, we went up there to see an old mountain man, and I remember sitting there in the yard listening to this old fellow sitting in a rocking chair tell stories, and it was Ray Hicks. As a teenager I heard Ray without knowing who he was, and even when Doug told me who it was that we were going to see, it wasn't until I saw the house that I knew I had heard him.

It's another story, just because I would never have seen that house again, visited with him and became friends with him had I not gone up there with them that day. We stayed three days there. I slept in the van and Doug and Christine had tents that they set up in the field. It was wonderful. I had basically an "in" with Ray, because when he was young, he remembered the Cherokees who would come through and camp down by the big overhang, and his father would go down and talk with them and he got to go with him and sit and listen. He remembered me from that earlier visit when I was a teenager, and I got to know him and Rosie and Ted after that and it was just wonderful.

People identify me with my big black hat with the turquoise stone. If I want people to leave me alone, I just take my hat off so they won't know who I am—this Indian with the receding hairline. One time I went to a school and was walking to the auditorium, and the kids saw me without the hat and didn't pay any attention. I put the hat on and suddenly, it was, "Here's the storyteller, here's the storyteller!"

I lived in Atlanta from 1967 to 1993, but I would make periodic trips home, and our children would spend two and three weeks up here in the summer with relatives, so they got to know people on the reservation. As it turned out they knew more people on the reservation than I did, since I basically left in '61 to go to college, and then into the service, and I got married while I was in the service and then moved to the Atlanta area. My children have moved back, and now both of them have very intelligent children—my son has three children and my daughter has two.

I've run for councilman and chief and was soundly defeated in both cases. I was talking to someone and they said, "Now Lloyd, stop and think if you had placed higher in the running for council, you might have run again and gotten in; if you had placed higher for chief you might have won and got in as chief. Now, if you had got in as councilman what would that do to your storytelling?" And I said I would have to stop for two years. "And if you got in as chief, what would happen with your storytelling?" And then I would have stop for four years. "So do you think somebody is trying to tell you something, that politics is not where you are supposed to be?" I said, "Ah ha, I did not stop and think about that," so I've moved out of the political arena.

There are about seven of us in Cherokee who go out and tell stories, but in the family, very few of those go out and tell stories in public. It's not that the stories aren't supposed to be told in public—it's that basically, they are very shy people. I was very introverted until I met my late wife—she brought me out of my shell, but very few want to get up in front of a crowd. Most people have that aversion—they like the stories, but they don't want to get up and tell in front of a group. They will tell in a small intimate setting with family.

I recall, growing up, that the elders would meet informally, and they would start telling stories. It wasn't that anybody had asked them to tell a story, it was just in the course of conversation and they would get into the story. With my two uncles one would start the story and the other would pick it up and go on with it, but normally, when I would hear an elder tell a story, the others would nod and agree that they had heard that story too. We would have the family gatherings at my uncle George's house, and after supper, he and Uncle Dave would start telling stories; or we would be at my grandma's, their sister, and after the meal they would start telling stories. The stories in my book are the stories I heard from my uncles.

I enjoyed hearing them tell those stories, and without realizing it I was learning the stories. They would tell how the bear lost his tail or tell about

Spear Finger, and this is how I learned the first stories of our people. Later, other elders shared stories with me, and then I heard stories from other tribes and then stories would just happen—I would remember what happened and begin to tell that story, or I would see something, or something would occur, say with a rattlesnake, and that would become a story that I created.

Young people on the reservation, on hearing a story say, "That's an interesting story" rather than "that's a part of my culture," but we are going through a renaissance right now and young people are learning the dances, they are learning a lot of the old ways. We don't celebrate Columbus Day here, but we do have a day later on in the month that we call National Heritage Day and that's where they want us to come in and do the pottery, woodcarving, weaving and do the storytelling and the men dress in the ribbon shirts and ladies dress in their Tear dresses. And they come in with the young people and there's different young groups that have dance groups and go around and share the Indian dances; they play Indian ball and travel around to various locations—it's gratifying to see this coming about now, however there are very few—I don't know of any of the young people who are going about telling stories. Now let's see, there's Jerry Wolfe, Susan, Shiver, Davey, Freeman, myself, but we are down to six storytellers. There's one lady who only tells in the vicinity of Cherokee, so there are only five of us that are still going out and sharing the stories.

I would like to take some of the young people interested in telling the stories; I would like to take them under my wing and share with them what I've learned because there are so many things to storytelling. I've seen storytellers who were constantly flipping their hair or tugging at their sleeves and I said it's a wonderful story if you could just stop these mannerisms from distracting from it; or how to use a microphone. I've heard people who speak quite often in public, and yet they don't know how to use a microphone! What you're doing when you are sharing the stories, how to read your audience and see whether you have their interest or not, and if not, why don't you have their interest? You want to do this in the course of a program. At this point, I could go into any group and start telling stories and I would know after three stories what to tell to that group.

I have done training in schools and one of the things I am very proud of was in a school in Asheville. It's strange that I was asked to do it there and not in Cherokee, but that's the way it normally works. I went into a school there and I had basically three days to work with them and then there was going to be a festival. The kids were going to be sharing stories there and they wanted all the kids to be involved in storytelling. I said they were going to have to select some tellers, because there wouldn't be enough time in the festival, so I worked with three different classes. I did just very basic storytelling with them, but one of the techniques I learned in Atlanta was to get people up and sharing their stories. If I work with people who are open minded adults then I will have them telling a story off the top of their heads in twenty minutes, but it involves changing their focus from people in the audience to people on the stage with them. When they do this, you'll be surprised how it changes and the stories flow. The minute that changes, they lose focus. And then, once they are comfortable with that, moving it simply to the audience is the next big step.

And so I worked with the kids to keep their focus on the stage, and part of this was to focus on a tree and you have that person make a motion like a tree and a sound like a tree and that sound can be anything you want. You're the person doing the tree—who can tell you whether it is right or wrong? The next person is a bear—make a motion like a bear, make a sound like a bear. You remember what each person is then you tie them into a story right off the top of your head. We had one young lady—let's see, I think we had fourteen kids on the stage, and we had the audience decide what each person was going to be and the young lady who was doing the storytelling had to remember what each person was. You're a hawk or a tall bush, and tie them all into a story that she had made up on the spot, and she had to remember all fourteen (she was a fifth grader) and tie them into a story. It was a phenomenal achievement and the audience gave her a standing ovation. We had done it with three and four people who saw the technique that was being used and suddenly we had that many people on the stage and you could hear the audience saying, "Oh, my gosh!"

I love working with people on the storytelling and getting them to understand that we all have stories and getting them to recognize that *I have a story!* But I'm not a storyteller, they say. I respond with, "Ah, but you have lived twenty-two years—a lot has happened in there. What is your most memorable occasion?" They answer, "Oh, that's why it was memorable!" They need to bring that out.

There are times when I have told a story and it has been different from the one I was going to be telling, maybe to a bigger audience, and then I realized somebody there needed to hear that story. I go by these feelings quite often. Sometimes I will be going down the road and decide to turn in here—I don't need gas, I don't need something to eat, but I turn in there and something will happen that will show me yes, that's why I turned in here. It may be a story, it may be a meeting, and it may be something that I've been trying to find. When I start hearing a story in my mind and I tell it, I know someone needed to hear that story for whatever reason. I've learned not to question it, I just do it. It has been validated so many times—it's not me, it's something else sitting on my shoulder and guiding me and it's up to me to listen. Every time I have followed those feelings, it has proven that I should have listened to my feelings—I've been aware of this all of my life, but especially since I was a teenager. There's a lot out there we know nothing about, that people are unwilling to explore.

When I start sharing a story, I know there's someone out there who needs to hear that story, whether they ever come up and verify that with me or not—someone needed to hear that story for a reason. It's like, why do I want to go over here? I don't know! I've learned, don't question it, just do it, and it has proven so many times—validated; yeah, it's not me. It's something else that I would say is sitting on my shoulder and guiding me. It's up to me to make that decision, am I going to make that decision or not. Every time I have followed those feelings, it has proven that yes—that is why I needed to tell that story, or go over there or do this. It has been something I was aware of—this aspect of life—since I was a teenager: ok, there's a lot in this life that [is] out there that we know nothing about, and that most of the people know nothing about—it scares them. Or it's so far out there—oh, you're doing witchcraft. No, it's if you're willing to increase your awareness, it's all around all of us.

If you have heard the [Cherokee] story, it was not a sacred story. [Smiling] Sacred stories are not told in public: they are told in special ceremonies and normally, non-Indians are not allowed in these events. There are so few of these ceremonies that occur that I don't know of any that I've been to where stories were shared. So when people get carried away sometimes from wanting to honor our culture—believe me, ninety percent of those people who honor our stories are more respectful of our ways than we are; people say your stories are of Mother Earth—you take care of her, but I guarantee you, come to Cherokee on a Saturday night and I will show you Indians throwing beer cans out of the window just like any other community. That was an old truism. We do have a few who practice the old ceremonies, especially among the elders, and I have had people tell me that they live the old ways. And I say, well, how did you get to this event? And they will say, well, I drove. And then I will ask if they have electricity in their home and they will answer yes. Well, I don't recall having electricity in the old days. How do you heat your home? Propane. I thought they did that with wood and fire. Do you get your food at the grocery store? Yes ... you say you do this in the old way and yet you live in a modern way.

To get back to the ceremony, that's not the old way, you just do the ceremonies—there's a whole lot of difference. If you are not going out into the woods getting your food and medicine, and heating your house with a fireplace and cooking over a fire like the old ways, you are not practicing the old way. When someone tells me that, I always smile. It's like; I used to be a computer programmer. You always question when somebody asks for a program, because I am the one who has to write the program to make that work. It's fallen over to me to ask questions, and some people say, "Why are you asking questions about the old ways?" And I like to say, tell me about the old ways. We have people who are selling spiritualism and they sell Native American medicine. As soon as I hear, if you pay $500 you can come learn the Sacred Medicine Wheel of the Lakota, I say, stay away from them—our spirituality and our native medicines are never sold. We have Native Americans who make a living doing this—they are charlatans—nothing more than snake-oil salesmen.

I'm destroying a lot of myths, I know, but unfortunately, people have learned how to do this and they will sell something that people will blindly accept, because it is coming from a Native American—that means, all right, they know what they are talking about. It's like in any other community—you have those snake oil salesmen who are out to make a quick buck and get out of town.

We have those who are not Native American going around saying, this is a sacred story of the Cherokee. There's one lady who says she's Cherokee and yet she's never come to the reservation. She steers clear of the area, because she knows there are those of us who will go out and immediately question her in public, because we have so many doing this. She is supposedly teaching our culture, saying that in the old days you had to be scratched with bones made from animal teeth and they had to draw blood before you could go in and hear these stories. What she's done is mix up these stories with games. They did use combs; they did draw blood before going out to the games, but for storytelling? No! But the people don't know because she's "Cherokee." She dresses up in a white buckskin dress and braids her hair and has beadwork on and people say, "Okay, she has the costume on and the beads, and she's 'Cherokee,'" but they don't know any different. And she will tell them that in the old days these stories were not told until you had been scratched with the animal bone combs and drawn blood for a ceremony that night and were cleansed, and the next day we would share the stories with you. That is what she has written on her Web site.

What I would rather people do, instead of dressing up like a Native American to tell Cherokee stories ... some try to dress up in authentic Cherokee garb ... it all depends on what part of Cherokee history or era you are talking about ... when we were introduced to cloth, we started wearing turbans and hunting jackets and the women learned to weave yarn into belts ... before that, we were wearing buckskins. It just depends on what part of our history the story is coming from, and there are so few books on authentic Cherokee dress—I would really rather the people give a little bit of the history of the Cherokee than wear the "dress."

The problem is some people are very sincere about wanting to honor our culture and they are very sincere when they dress up, but what they think is Cherokee garb may be from other tribes. You will see some of them come in with big war bonnets which we never wore, but they thought, however they researched it, that this was authentic Cherokee headdress. They weren't trying to make fun of us or anything. That is why there is such a big misconception about the clothing we wore—just give a little bit of the history, or simply say it's a Cherokee story and continue on. We have people who, when you go to a powwow, you may see somebody with Lakota-style moccasins, Pawnee beadwork on their vests and I have a Plains Indian bustle which is combined from three or four different tribes but the other Indians know and say, "Oh, those are so and so moccasins you are wearing!" or somebody comes in with a new outfit and the people say "Go look at their outfit—they've got something from the Cree Indians in Canada," and they go around and look at it. At powwows, you know the dress, the shoe-wear or beadwork or how their bustles are made, etc.

I can tell to three separate groups, one right after another, and all three groups will have different responses, and consequently, they end up with different stories. I've never shared the same stories in a situation like that. Some people say that only Native Americans should be telling these stories, and I ask them, are you sharing these stories? If they are not, then, "Why are you objecting to people sharing these stories?" They are going to die out otherwise. I tell people that in sharing these stories, understand you will get into a situation in which there will be a Native American present, and they will give you this response. Don't argue with them, don't say anything, just continue on from that point afterwards, but don't let that deter you from sharing the stories.

When I tell stories, I don't go in with a pre-set program, because you never know how an audience is going to react. Sometimes, in the beginning, I went in with a prepared program and I got no response, and I asked myself if I had just entertained these people. Were they interested in the stories? I just didn't know. They responded, but not in all of the appropriate places and then I knew they were just being entertained, so I just shared light stories with them. Then others, they laughed and I got the appropriate reaction from them, and these were the people I wanted more time with so that I could share more intense stories with them. I feel those are the people who understand the stories and what they are telling.

When I get those audiences that are very responsive, I have a series of stories that I tell to prepare them for the more moving stories that I will share. I am also preparing myself—some of the stories that I tell, I walk on the very thin edge of control because they are so intense. I have no idea why the stories affect me this way. Chief Joseph is one that brings those feelings out in me. The feelings are very intense, and normally when I share Chief Joseph I end my program with that story, because physically and emotionally I am wiped out after telling that story. And why it does that I don't know, because it is about the Nez Perce and not even remotely connected to the Cherokee. I remember reading about Chief Joseph's story when I was teenager and I researched it.

In 2004, I planned a program in memory of Chief Joseph and rented an auditorium downtown in Asheville, North Carolina, and advertised it and had Native American dancers and singers come in and we shared with the audience. I did it in the middle of the week because it was the 100th anniversary of Chief Joseph's passing, September 21, 2004, and that was on a Tuesday. I felt so strongly about this that the Smithsonian had asked me to come up and speak at the opening of the Museum of the American Indians, and I said, I am honoring Chief Joseph on that Tuesday, but I will be able to come up the rest of the week if that's possible. And they said they wanted me to be at the opening to tell, but I said I am going to do this. Then they called and asked me to come up for Wednesday through Sunday, and I said yes, I can do that!

When I finished the program with Chief Joseph—we had the dancers on first, and then the singer and she sang in five different Native American languages. And then after we had an intermission, she sang a Native American song in Cherokee, and her mother had never heard her sing it in all the years she had been performing. My program varies from one telling to another, but as I said, I began sharing about Chief Joseph that night. When I finished Chief Joseph I was crying when I walked off the stage and the audience was silent. No one was clapping, and as I went off stage I remember the control booth calling the stage manager asking, "Is he going back on?" and I heard the stage manager say, "I don't know if he's going back on." I nodded and he said, "Yes, he's going back on."

When I had gathered myself enough to walk back out, I told the people, "It has been a dream of mine to honor Chief Joseph on this hundredth anniversary of his passing, and thank you for making my dream come true." They came up with a standing ovation; that was the kind of audience that I could share it with; it pulls so much out of me emotionally that I have to have a special location where we don't have people running in and out, or hear trucks going by. I have to have an audience that is responding and I need about an hour to prepare not only myself, but them, for the story. As a result, I've probably told Joseph less than twenty times. It's what I mean when I have those stories that I walk on the very thin edge of control with.

There's another story I tell that's not Native American and it is called the "Desks," and it's a very short story, and it is one that I use to honor veterans, and again, that is a very powerful story. Let me give you a name—it's Martha Cothren, who is a teacher at Robinson High School in Little Rock, Arkansas, and it's her story. I and others have called it the "Desks," and I think it's one every school child should hear. And I share that with veterans and it is another one that puts me right on the very edge. I am a Vietnam veteran and it is one of those stories that is very powerful for me. I can't tell you what draws me to that story other than I'm a Vietnam veteran, too, and that one hits me very hard. Chief Joseph? I have no idea. Other tribes suffered the Trail of Tears too, just like the Cherokee—the long walk of the Comanche, Chief Carlson, the Navaho ... Kit Carson is not worthy to be mentioned, and yet he's held up as an American hero, but he double-crossed the Navaho—they thought he was their friend, and he wasn't. Andrew Jackson and the Cherokee—I do not care for Andrew Jackson at all—again, he did the same thing to the Cherokee.

Wherever I go there's always interest in talking to me. I enjoy the questions and I encourage people to come up and talk—ask questions. Sometimes the programs allow me the time to answer questions and I welcome those questions and answers, but beware, because the answer can be either positive or negative to your question, because I am going to give you my answer, and it may not be the answer you like.

I think often of the story of Ishi, and this is a story that I share. He was supposedly the last *wild* Indian that was captured in California. Of course, he didn't speak any English when they found him, and they later found out he was speaking an old dialect from the Yahi. They took him to the University of California and started working with him and he started learning English, and they started increasing their knowledge of his language. They thought the last Yahi had died out decades ago, and when they finally got his story they couldn't understand his fear when he heard dogs barking, and he told them when they saw white people there were always dogs barking, and it meant death. When they would come up to hunt them, they always brought dogs and they would hear the dogs first and they would scatter and the dogs would be used to track them down, and basically it was for sport. And every time, when they would gather, they got to be fewer and fewer, it was finally only Ishi (which is Yahi for "man") his mother and his sister. And again they heard the dogs barking and again they went three directions and he heard the guns firing in the direction his mother went, and then guns in the direction his sister went. And when he came back to the meeting place, he waited for a long time, but neither of them showed up. He was the last one.

There, it took several people to gather enough food to subsist; one person could not gather enough to keep alive and it was hunger—starvation really, that drove him down to civilization. But he learned the language, the culture and even how to wear the clothes of the people that had hunted his people to extinction, and yet he was called a savage. I thought how brave he had to be to survive when every one he had ever loved, or had ever known, was gone. And I just don't know if I would be able to accept and learn.... He was a very gentle person, and he made friends wherever he went, but he died from tuberculosis. Tuberculosis was the number-one killer among the Native American tribes for many, many years, and now it has shifted to diabetes. I know it well—I lived for two years with my great-aunt and uncle in Oklahoma when my mother was in a hospital with tuberculosis.

All of these stories are important and they must be heard. I'm a firm believer that stories are for telling—whether it's an Indian or non–Indian. Stories are for sharing, and if we don't share the stories, who will?

Marilou Awiakta

Marilou Awiakta is a Cherokee-Appalachian storyteller and poet. Born in Knoxville, Tennessee, she is the seventh generation of her family to grow up in Appalachia, principally in East Tennessee.

The triple experience of Awiakta's Cherokee and Appalachian heritages and of the mystery of the atom are closely woven into her work as a storyteller and writer, as her first book, *Abiding Appalachia: Where Mountain and Atom Meet* attests. Both *Abiding Appalachia*, and her second book, *Rising Fawn and the Fire Mystery*, were chosen by the U.S. Information Agency in 1985 for the global tour of its *Women in the Contemporary World* show.

Closely attuned to the heart of the earth, Awiakta has taken the technology of today's world and spun it together with the ancient wisdom of both the Cherokee and the Celts to produce works that are both thought-provoking and deeply introspective. Her book *Selu, Seeking the Corn Mother's Wisdom* was a 1994 Quality Paperback Book Club Selection, and the audio version was nominated for a Grammy in 1995. A quote from *Selu* is engraved in the Riverwall of the Bicentennial Capitol Mall in Nashville, Tennessee.

Awiakta's poems were chosen for the 1997 winter issue of *Poèsie Première*, a French literary journal, which published a 35-page retrospective of her work as a poet, and her poetry was recently featured at the International Congress of Poetry in Brussels, Belgium. Her poem "Motheroot" is inlaid in the Fine Arts Walkway at UCLA, Riverside.

Awiakta's life and work were profiled in the *Oxford Companion for Women's Writing in the United States*, which included her essay "Grandmothers." BeMe.com, a British Internet magazine for women, commissioned an essay which became "Sunrise in Cyberspace" for its millennium issue.

She has been featured in three public broadcasting productions and was recently featured in *Built for the People: The Story of TVA*, which was produced by Fine Film Productions. In addition she spoke at the World Wilderness Congress in Alaska, and also at West Virginia's Peace Tree Ceremony and Diversity Conference. For thirty years she has spoken at colleges and universities where her work is taught.

Marilou Awiakta graduated magna cum laude from the University of Tennessee in 1958 and received an honorary doctorate in humane letters from Albion College in Michigan. Other honors include the 2000 Appalachian Heritage Writer's Award (Shepherd College) and the award for Outstanding Contribution to Appalachian Literature from the Appalachian Writers Association in 1991, and the state-juried Distinguished Tennessee Writers Award from the Tennessee Mountain Writers Conference. She was awarded the Meritorious Contributions to the American Indian People from Northeastern State University in 1999; the Award for Educational Service to Appalachia, Carson Newman College, in 1999; and from the Center for Appalachian Studies at East Tennessee State University, recognition for Contributions to the Cultural Life of Appalachia.

Marilou Awiakta

Awiakta resides in Memphis, Tennessee, with her husband Paul Thompson (and two Corgis). Their two daughters and grandchildren live in Knoxville, and their son is in Nashville, Tennessee.

The Interview

I am the seventh generation of my family to grow up in Appalachia, principally in East Tennessee. My Cherokee and Scots-Irish family has lived in the mountains as a "designated family" since 1730. Especially in East Tennessee, as science would put it, I have the mountains in my blood—they are in my cellular memory. I think most people who grow up in the mountains are deeply rooted to the place where they live, especially to its spiritual nature.

I love to quote what a truck driver said. I was on my way to Nashville with two other poets some time ago. We had stopped at Hud's Truck Stop off of I-40, and we overheard a cross-country truck driver who was from Appalachia talking to another truck driver. They were having coffee—and he said, "You know, I drive cross-country, but I'm from the mountains. Everywhere I go, I got the mountains inside of me; they help hold me steady, and when I'm coming cross-country on I-40, I just keep pushing as hard as I can through Memphis, and on out, looking east, because I know the exact spot when I see the first blue line of the mountains rise up, I'm home! Still 300 miles out—but home's in sight."

I know the exact spot he means—the Birdsong Exit. I put that quote in *Selu: Seeking the Corn Mother's Wisdom*, because I think that's poetry. Here is a fifty-year-old truck driver talking to another one, but he's saying poetry—he's saying, "Got my mountains inside of me everywhere I go; they help hold me steady," and then, "The sight of them—I know I'm home." Now that's not a literal-minded person. It's when you get in sight of your home ... I feel that I always have my mountains inside of me, and that's a major, major influence on me.

I laugh when I say I was born in a web of stories and just picked up the threads, and went on with them. I was born in Knoxville during the greatest snowstorm in decades, and I was premature—only weighed four pounds and six ounces. My grandfather, my mother's father, came to "pronounce"—you know the way elders come to pronounce—I was the first grandbaby. He was teasing my mother, saying, "Why she looks like a little possum." Tears came up in Mother's eyes, because I was her first baby, and my grandfather laughed and said, "Oh, I'm teasing you, I'm teasing you," and he said three things: "She has a good head of hair, she likes her dinner (nursing) and she has a lusty cry. She ought to thrive and do well." He was a judge of stock, so that hair meant strength. I think there was three and a half pounds of blue-black hair and one pound of me. [Laughter]

Mother said she thought I came early on purpose so I could be born in the homeland. Daddy was temporarily assigned to Nashville, so she was in Knoxville visiting her parents. She said I did it on purpose and that "it would be just like you to come early and be born where you want to be born!" I think I was very fortunate to grow up on the home ground of my ancestors, because the earth has memory; East Tennessee was once part of the Cherokee nation—the "Overhill" part.

In the summertimes we went barefooted, so I was growing up on my home ground where all the memories were, where people told stories daily about the culture. Stub your toe ... I have a poem, "Mother's Advice While Bandaging My Stubbed Toe"—you know how bad that hurts when you're barefooted—stub your toe. Just in that incident, something so small as to stub your toe, the culture was saying you were supposed to take your knocks, bind up your toe and go your way again. It's related to the Cherokee heritage and of course the Appalachian and Celtic heritage.

I want to add something I believe is very important to a storyteller: it is important to go barefooted, to touch the ground and feel the energy the earth is sending up through the feet. If I were the president of Harvard University, I would have everyone go barefooted for a month in September—every student and every professor across every walk and every lawn and gravel pathway, and every floor, because there is something to be learned from contact with the earth. If you walk on something barefooted, you get a different knowledge of it.

The story was always told about how my grandfather, when he dislocated his shoulder, had it set with no anesthetic and did not cry out. I screamed every time I stubbed my toe because they poured iodine on it, but I didn't get that gene of not screaming. I tell this little story to illustrate how in a person's life, culture and teachings just flow naturally with everyday life. Nobody sits you down and says you have Cherokee or Celtic heritage, and here are the things you are supposed to know. Instead, they say, "When you go into the forest, respect everything there as a relation. Don't pick blackberries without taking a long stick; make noise, sway the stick over the grass because copperhead snakes like to curl around blackberry bushes. But they don't want to see you; be respectful and let them know you are coming and they will leave, but if you sneak up on them, they'll bite you." Then they might say, "People are like that, too."

The family was a great influence on me. I was born just as Hitler was coming to power, and I heard the elders talking about war coming. The voices I heard on the radio or Victrola were all we had for entertainment, so the earth, the woods and the forest and the people were what we directly connected with. I grew up in a duplex during the war until I was five. My daddy was working for the government, and they assigned him from Knoxville to Nashville. Jobs were at a premium as they are now, so he had to go where the work was, so he went to Nashville until the secret project, the Manhattan Project, began, then the government transferred him back to Knoxville. Then he worked at Oak Ridge, which was a top secret installation, unlike anything we could imagine now. It was locked down and no one knew what the government was doing. People said, "They're pouring millions in there and they've got a fence around it, so it's something big." Go figure! My daddy couldn't even say what he did.

Finally, we got a house and it was—and this is where the storytelling really begins, as a child, an Appalachian child of the mountains, you were proud of the culture, proud of your heritage as a mountain person, because that was taught to us. You know, we're independent; we do for ourselves or we do without; we give full measure for value received; when you do a job, you do it well, and you respect your elders—respect your family.

My maternal grandmother was born at Ebbing and Flowing Springs, near Jonesborough, Tennessee, and my great-grandfather helped build the church, which is still there, and the school. When I came to East Tennessee State University in 2007 for the Distinguished Lecturer Series, Paul and I came a little early and went to see Great Granddaddy's church at Ebbing and Flowing Springs, and I stood in the spring where my grandmother had stood so long ago. The school house is still there, and there was a woman there who had taught in the school house. I made that part of my stories to tell in my lecture at ETSU as an illustration of how, here we are in the 21st century in hard times, but one-hundred-fifty years ago, our ancestors with axes, brooms and spinning wheels were surviving. I told about standing in the spring that ebbs and flows and thinking, they built something of value here, something that would last, and there was no electricity, no wells though they did have the spring. I also told how we went to the Cherokee memorial on Long Island to pay respects to our people who suffered the removal of 1838, yet had the strength to survive. It gives a person strength to know the stories of the ancestors, even though there may be tragedies, and it's always good to know the whole heritage.

I was always the kind of a person who had a webbed mind—one who wove things together; because that's the way my family told things and lived things—not in little compartments. My mother used to say, "Don't kill those honeybees because they are helping make the apples." I heard things like that over and over—you'll upset the balance of nature if you kill a species, or overkill a species like the deer for example, and I was told the stories and read to a lot and grew up in the oral tradition.

I like to say I am a poet-storyteller, because I tell stories through poetry. I put the story into a poem, or if I'm writing a journalistic piece, like "Tellico Dam vs. the Cherokee," I use the poet's perspective. I tell historic stories and current stories, too. Oak Ridge is now a historical story, but I lived it when the atomic frontier came to Appalachia, and I was right inside that secret world.

To me, poetry is not just a literary form. It's a way of living; a form of storytelling. Growing up, I was always read to aloud—fairytales and Bible stories. Hans Christian Anderson was a great influence on my life [pointing to her childhood collection of storybooks on the shelf] and I was read to from an excellent translation. It was not Disney; it was not simplified, then later in my life, I discovered he was the first Danish writer to write in the vernacular, as people speak. I'm very drawn to the way people speak and to the words they use to tell their stories, and I listen carefully.

Many of my stories come to me, like "What the Choctaw Woman Said," which was told directly to me by the Choctaw woman. I didn't change any of the words, she just talked to me for forty-five minutes and I took the key lines just as she said them, but I asked her if I could do it. Some people want to tell their own stories and some people would like someone to tell their stories for them.

The oral tradition is so strong, and the oral tradition cannot be erased. Though the Internet fail, though the tsunami come, the earth opens; radio and TV fall silent, someone will go and tell the story. Like the messengers in the Book of Job, they will recount what has happened, saying, "And I alone escaped to tell thee." I work in that oral tradition. Some things are done in stories, some are from history, and some are like the songs of the troubadour who went from town to town. Storytellers are people who are very hard to stop. You can use surveillance all you want to, but somebody will sing the story over the wall. It's a long, powerful tradition—storytelling!

I think what might be clearest about me is my poem "Where Mountain and Atom Meet," which is on page 56 of my book *Abiding Appalachia, Where Mountain and Atom Meet*. It is the first of my mature work; I had written maybe seventeen hundred to two thousand articles and poems, but it was only after experiencing forty years of life that I sat down to write [the book] *Abiding Appalachia*, I had to live and work abroad, have children and family, and you know how it is when you have three children—there wasn't a lot of time to write the deep things of my heart that I liked to do.

When I reached forty, the time opened up: the children were grown and Phyllis Tickle, the publisher at St. Luke's Press, approached me and said, "Would you like to write your heart?" and I thought, sure! I want to weave together the Cherokee, Appalachian, Celt, and the atom which became part of me deeply, as a constant—atom itself, as it exists in nature, and the whole experience of a bridge and weave that together and show how it webs together. And she said, "Lou, that will fall apart!" and I said "Phyllis, do I look like I'm falling apart?" And she said, "No, you're all together, so I guess the book will hang together." That book has been in print since 1978—constantly, and went into a new edition in 2006, and it has been taught in many schools and universities.

This story is very important: when I said I wanted to be a poet, I was a little girl (maybe four or five years old,) and my mother said, "That's good, but what will you do for the people?" So right there the tradition was ingrained in me that whatever work you do should contribute to the whole. Maybe that's why I've received many awards, but the reason they make me so happy in my heart is that every one of them have come from organizations made up of the people of Appalachia, professors, writers, students and other readers.

If your own people read your work and give you honor for it, then it is true honor, because you know you have written truly of them, and of the traditions. The last lines of "An Indian Walks in Me" [express what is] the best I know about who I am inside, and why I write—to seek the whole in strength and peace and not allow anyone or any institution or anything, to split my soul and tell me who I am. That, I think, is so important for every person who lives.

Each person has the birthright to tell their story of who they are as they see themselves and feel themselves and not have "hillbilly" laid on you, or any other kind of word that stereotypes you, or you live in a little cabin like we did and therefore you can't think, because your house is too small. Who would think that somebody who lived in a cemesto house (something like Sheetrock) would be thinking these things?

I bring this to the attention of my students a lot about making or accepting judgments about the quality of people's thinking by their exteriors. For example, right across the street from us, in a cemesto house, lived the assistant director of the Institute of Nuclear Studies. What kind of thinking was going on in that house? It was a modular, "cemesto" cabin like all the others in Oak Ridge.

I grew up in what was later called a "classless community," where everybody lived in the same kind of house, and you only got your house by how many children you had. Everybody had a house built of cemesto, and they were modular, and you could only get a three-bedroom cemesto if you had children of the opposite sex. Families with two children of the same sex had to have two-bedroom houses. If you went beyond three children, you got a D house that had four bedrooms. It was a young population—the average age was thirty—and there were children everywhere! The secret part was so far away we never saw it. The government owned the property, and there were lots and lots of woods to roam.

We had excellent teachers and there was a wonderful feeling of openness without "class." Gradually Oak Ridge changed after the war and became stratified, but my senior class at Oak Ridge was said to be the last to graduate that was "classless." That kind of environment, getting along with all kinds of people who were able to work things out when it was necessary—one was a professor from the University of Chicago, another was a carpenter from Kingston—to see them all work together in the church and at different things became a growing conviction to me: it's good, and it's very difficult for different kinds of people to respect the differences, and to work on what is harmonic for the good of all the people—all kinds of people.

Another thing: there were no servants at Oak Ridge—everybody did their own work, just like up on the mountain with my great-great-grandmother—everybody had chores and we couldn't go out until we got our chores done. You couldn't finish them? It's your own doing ... make your own bed, you sleep in it! You could have gone to the movie this afternoon, but you didn't do the rest of the ironing; it had to be done, it wasn't shouted at you, just a matter of fact. The chores got done or you didn't play. We had a radio, phone and a record player, but not the Web or text-messaging; we went out to the trees and ran the ridges. So I grew up in this very high-tech world and yet, on the other hand ran bare-footed in the forests just like our ancestors.

It was very much like the communal culture of the Indian or pioneer. That is where I got this little "d" of democracy—of the people, by the people, for the people and I'm the people and you're the people. I don't like people to take a high hand with me, or I won't do anything.

Where God puts you down is where you grow up, so here I was with this Cherokee-Appalachian background, I was nine or ten years old when we moved to Oak Ridge—it was 1945, after Hiroshima. Sometimes people think I write about Oak Ridge, but Oak Ridge was a phenomenon that moved into Appalachia, my ancestral home. What I am writing about in *Abiding Appalachia* is through the eyes of an Appalachian person about what this atom meant, and what this strange configuration of a city, which was fenced in with barbed wire at the top, and you could only get in with badges, meant. None of us knew what our fathers did. One family was moved out in twenty-four hours because somebody broke security, and everybody knew the story; the FBI was everywhere—"loose lips sink ships"—so you didn't ask. It wasn't like the "don't ask, don't tell" policy; it was just "don't ask about *anything* to do with the plants" [laughter].

A Cherokee-Appalachian characteristic is to be very reserved in what you say anyway—don't tell more than you are asked and keep your own counsel about a lot of things. My Celtic relatives are also very big on keeping your own counsel—tell what you're asked and don't talk about family outside of family. What happens in the family stays in the family. I'm talking about private things. You don't talk finances or quarrels or anything like that—that's family business; silence on family matters. So silence on government matters didn't bother me. Some of the first words we learned when I was five, after Pearl Harbor, were "surveillance, sabotage, spies, FBI, the draft, rationing"—even sugar was rationed. I have a suggestion about the current issue of obesity in America 2010—just bring back sugar rationing! Ration people, ration corporations, ration just like in the war, and take snack machines out of our schools. Eat what is put before you when it is time, and you don't eat anything until you get home and eat whatever your mother will let you have. We were told, "Don't spoil your supper. Don't load up because supper will be served at 5:30 when your Daddy gets home."

Suddenly, seventy-five thousand people were brought in there from every region in the United States and put in there in this big fence to create a community. There were no churches, so people had to share the church—you used the buildings that were extant. We went to Sunday school in the high school building—the Methodists, and then we went down the hill to the Ridge Theater to church—it was air-conditioned and had soft seats ... and then the Baptists, Catholics and Jews worked out a schedule of who would go at what time—it was ecumenical. Everybody didn't go together, they kept their denominations, but the denominations cooperated in their activities with the buildings that were already there. See, it was a frontier—the atomic frontier. You worked with what you had; the streets weren't paved and there were no sidewalks and there were rocks in the yard that had to be swept up everyday until you could get enough soil to grow grass.

The mothers mostly were at home, but most of them were college-trained like my mother. The men went into the plants, but the women had to create the community. They had to create and support the schools and churches; a woman started the newspaper. And there were no private clubs; everything was an interest club like books, photography or hiking. There was no good or bad side of town and everybody was living in the same kind of house. It was a burglar's paradise if they wanted to face the FBI—the house plans were the same give or take a bedroom or two. There was a marvelous kind of energy—high energy and people working at something that was vital for America when my daddy went there in 1943. We had to wait two years for a house at Oak Ridge.

We found out later that the Germans were building a nuclear reactor, and the [U.S.] government was acting on the recommendation of Einstein, trying to get a reactor active before the Germans, so it was built in a race in time against the Nazi regime; that is how Oak Ridge started. It was built there because of the mountains—good cover, and the Tennessee Valley Authority—water—energy, and I have heard it said that the government wanted to employ a lot of people who were native to the area, because the mountain people were known to take pride in their work and give full measure for value received, and were not overly talkative. The government also wanted to look thirty or forty years in the future and put a national laboratory in the South with the idea that after the war it would be connected to the University of Tennessee and other schools. It would serve as a source for technology—looking towards the "high-tech corridor" with national funding right there—and so it came to pass.

One of my great dreams as I grew up was to go to France, so I studied the French language. In my senior year at college I won a scholarship to the Sorbonne, and in the same month Paul proposed to me. He said if I would delay my dream until he finished his medical training (seven years of it), he would see that I got to France.

I asked Mama's advice. She said, "You are a writer and you are determined to be a writer. There aren't too many men that will put up with that. If you think you have found the right person, consider that Paris will be there for centuries. If you go to Paris at this age at twenty-one and stay a year, it could be that when you come back you won't be the same person, and he will have changed and you won't have changed together. It you go together and live it, then that's a different story." I gave it some thought and decided it was reasonable. I trusted his word because he had always kept his word—

we'd gone together three years, and so I gave up the scholarship. That was in 1957.

In 1964, he volunteered for the Air Force, and that's how we got to France. He went to Washington and asked to be assigned to a French base because I was French-speaking. It worked out that we went to the north of France for three years. We lived in a trailer and we called it the "yellow submarine," because I painted it yellow. It was not a mobile home—it was a tin government trailer, but Paul went first for two months and wrote back that he'd had a lean-to put on it and that it was "wonderful." [Laughter] Well, here we are, true to the Appalachian pioneer: we crossed the Atlantic and had a trailer with a lean-to on it; we lived there for two and a half years.

My children went to French schools because I didn't speak any English to them as they were growing up. I wanted them to be bi-lingual if I could do it, because I knew we would be going to France, so Aleex, who was four, went straight into French school near the base (Audrey was not old enough—she was only two). It was like a kindergarten, with this exception—the French don't believe in printing. Imagine this: a classroom of thirty four year olds with their little smocks and inkpots. The teacher says, "Here is your notebook; here is your staff pen, and inkpot. Do not blot your notebook," and so the students wrote in cursive. You can imagine the discipline. Can you imagine thirty American four year olds with pots of ink? We are a different culture!

Our son Andrew was born after we were back in the States, in 1969. When we went to kindergarten, the teacher announced the little ones would not be taught to print because psychologists said it would inhibit them. I laughed to myself, having just come from a country where everyone would laugh at that idea [since the French had long been teaching their children to write in cursive, instead of printing their work].

I also worked as a civilian interpreter and liaison for the United States Air Force in France and also, unofficially, as a scout for the base commanders to listen on the street to what people were saying, because it was during the NATO withdrawal. My "scouting" doesn't appear on any official record, but that's what I was supposed to do, and I did. What French people were saying on the street about kicking the Americans out—it was a bad time—it was the Gaullist–Vietnam period and the French were very angry. I would just stroll along with my toddlers and my sack of groceries, and listen and report to the base commander.

It's said you know children by their games.... When I was little, Tarzan was a big movie. When I was visiting my grandmother Marilou, my namesake, I had two friends there. We were eight or ten years old and we played Tarzan up in the tree, and we had a rope. You could be Tarzan, Jane, Boy or Cheetah. I always wanted to be Cheetah, because he carried the news! So, when the base commander told me he wanted me to go out on the street and bring back the news, I said, "Sure, I'll do it."

Understanding of my own heritage deepened during that time—I've never written very much about my French experience, although I consider those years in France the watershed of my creative life, first, because, being away from Appalachia, things became clear to me of the beauties of the Cherokee-Appalachian philosophy, and I could see a contrast—the French think this way, and I think this way and yet not all Americans think this way, but coming from Appalachia gave me a perspective. Also, living and speaking in French sharpened my ear to the beautiful cadences of our mountain language. You know, when you are living in it all the time, you don't always hear the language as it is, but it was like hearing it afresh when I came back from France.

My concept of working for peace, and the whole, and strengthening world peace was reinforced by my working as an interpreter and living and working in France with people who think completely different from Americans—360 degrees on some things. I think my mature work, which I date from the age of forty, comes out of a whole life experience of a certain kind where I was much grounded in the pride of my own culture—the mountain culture of Cherokee and Appalachian culture. At the same time, because I always lived with diversity after the age of ten, I developed the respect for nature that I was taught, and for people that were not mountain people. Then I saw that principle of respect meant getting along with people of different cultures, and different points of view and the importance of it—of showing respect. That's not to say you should let people run over you, but respecting that other people have their stories and they tell them in a different way. It wasn't important how I perceived the French—it was important how they interpreted themselves to me and expressed themselves to me.

I have lots of stories I haven't told about that and it may be something I do in the future, but *Selu, Seeking the Corn Mother's Wisdom* and *Rising Fawn and the Fire Mystery* were written along the same line. *Rising Fawn* was written with the permission of two families to use their family stories in the book. That's a very important distinction—in doing the kind of writing I do—with respect to an American Indian value system versus American publishing rules. In America, if something is in the public domain, and anything that has been spoken is in the public domain, it is fair game. Even a person's story—you don't have to get a person's permission to write a family's story or write about them, but you can't do that with an American Indian's story. That's the value system—appropriate a family's story and your name is mud. I didn't write a word of *Rising Fawn and the Fire Mystery* until the families gave me permission to use family writings for background, so I knew what people said. I said I will not tell the story of your family and they said, "Good, because we want to tell the story, but you can have facts surrounding the story." The other family gave me permission to use the storyline about the little girl saved by the soldier. I couldn't write one word of the story until the family reviewed it. They inquired person-to-person with people who knew me, to see if I was a person who kept my word or not; had I lived that kind of life or not? That's not a bad principle, is it? That's kind of a mountain way, too, isn't it? Who are you and what is your business? That was the ancient challenge of the mountaineers to anyone who approached, and stopped, until the man came out on the porch and said who are you and what is your business.

In '91 my first two grandchildren were on their way and I wanted to create something for them specifically geared toward the 21st century where they would be living their teen years and adulthood. I chose the Cherokee traditional story of *Selu: Seeking the Corn Mother's Wisdom*. For the Cherokee, everything in nature is a relative—there's no dominion. You have equal standing with the honeybee and the bear—they are all relatives and what you are supposed to do is live in balance and harmony with all your relatives including humans. Of course, like human nature everywhere, people don't do it all the time but it is an expectation and a standard one strives for.

The story of Selu belongs to the Cherokee nation; it is a sacred story and is one of the deep traditional stories. In the Cherokee, Grandmother Corn signifies the Life Force. I had to be very careful what version of the story that I used. There are many versions of Selu that are equally authentic, from the east and the west, but there are also many adulterated versions. There's a bad habit of people that are non–Indian—they appropriate Indian stories and they change them, and they change central elements to the story and adapt them to their own culture—white European culture. I went to the story I liked, which was published by the Cherokee as told by the Cherokee storyteller who spoke the story in Cherokee to a couple, Jack and Anna Kilpatrick, who were full-blooded Cherokee, Cherokee talkers and college-trained linguists and folklorists. Here you have a Cherokee man telling a story to Cherokee who are trained to gather story and translate, and they put it into English in their book. That is the story I requested and I went to their son, not just the publishing company.

It gets wild and wooly here, because we couldn't find him and I didn't know what to do, so Chief Wilma Mankiller helped me locate him. I only used material in this book that the Cherokee Nation had published itself; there are no ceremonial words in this book—no intrusion into ceremony. *Selu: Seeking the Corn Mother's Wisdom* is not my book at all. It is our book. It is Cherokee-Appalachian, but it is also the artists' and the reader's, because I ask the reader to become a companion directly, in the storyteller fashion, which is kind of rare in a book. The storyteller always addresses the audience directly, so I wanted to speak directly to the reader and say I would like you to be a companion in this book. Mark the book however you want, recall your roots and traditions that strengthen you. At the end, gather seed thoughts and keep the ones that are in harmony with you and sow them. Leave the others.

Selu is the first woman in the Cherokee creation story. In America, everybody knows about corn, but they don't know what corn teaches—the story of the spirit of the corn, or the life force of the corn. The word for corn in Cherokee is *selu*; it is Grandmother Corn and teaches many things: it teaches cooperation—it takes cooperation to grow corn and to harvest it; it teaches respect for variety—it is speckled, and it teaches democracy. [Taking up an ear of multicolored corn, Awiakta taught from the corn she held in her hand.] See, this particular ear has all of the colors. One must live in harmony, one doesn't say, "You have to be black or I'll kick you out, or you have to be white, or I'll kick you out," so you have an ideal visual democracy, and it's in a circle so nobody is above anybody else.

If you know the story of Selu, her grandsons showed her disrespect. When she shut the door of her cabin, they peeked in and saw her rubbing her body and the corn was coming off her body into a pan. Of course, she was born from the corn to begin with which is a point to remember. She realized they had been disrespectful by spying on her when she specifically said "No;" their spying on the mystery is very hard to get across in the 21st century. They did not have the right if their grandmother said, "The door is closed." They did not have the right to spy on her and the mystery of the life force. Remember, she said, "I know you have spied on me in disrespect, so I'm going to die *to* you, not *for* you—I'm dying to you, but if you show me respect and take my body and bury it in a respectful way, and keep the watch for a certain amount of time, and when you see a plant growing and you see the silks come out like my hair, you will know I have returned. Remember this, corn is a woman."

And so the boys showed her respect, and they harvested the corn as she instructed, and saved some and planted more and more and more until corn went all over the world, but when the Europeans came, they saw corn only as a grain, an "it." Because they didn't know the story, they didn't get the message that was out there before them: democracy, and of strength and cooperation, and that what happens when you do not show respect to the earth and to people is death. That's the same message of Little Deer, another traditional guide story. The people were killing too many deer and the animals got together to see what to do about the people. That's an interesting concept you don't often find in European folklore—the animals gathering to see what to do about the people.

Little Deer, the Spirit Deer, came up with the idea that if the hunter showed respect, and only took what he needed and did a ceremony of respect that was acceptable, he would be blessed. But if a hunter didn't do it, Little Deer would track him to his home and cripple him so he never could hunt again, which would mean death. The principle of respect is the major principle here and in *Selu*, and I think it's the major principle with the atom and that's why I put Little Deer in the atom orbit as the logo of my life and work, because the atom itself is present in nature and if it's used with respect, it does so many things. It helps heal cancer, it helps grow things, and it helps heat—if it's used with respect. The same reactor that split the atom for a weapon made isotopes for cancer research at Oak Ridge.

Having spent so much of my life and thought with the atom, I felt it was mysteriously fitting that when I had breast cancer in 1998, it was radiation therapy—in addition to chemotherapy and surgery—that came to help heal me, as it does millions of people in the world who have cancer. Not many people think—because it hasn't been brought to their attention, I believe—that the same reactor that can make a weapon can also heal; the difference is in the human that directs the hand. Nuclear energy is not evil in itself. Actually, the sun is a natural nuclear reactor, which can also heal or harm.

As I looked at the trends going towards the twenty-first century, I thought that through cooperation and trying to bring about peace through negotiation instead of war was possible, but it's going to be very important, as America becomes even more diverse, for people to respect one another and live by the principle of respect.

I can't help telling stories; I've always loved stories, and on a deep level, the stories I've published contribute to my strand of the web of keeping the story of our mountain people going, our cultural story. I believe mountain people of every race, including Appalachia, have been overlooked as part of the American mainstream. We have a philosophy of life—I'm speaking of all races because the mountains teach us things. If you don't respect the mountain it will kill you; if you don't respect the black bear it will surely tear you up. It's very much a philosophy of doing for yourself in order to be self-reliant and to sustain the earth.

When the big companies like timber and mining came in, some also came to "civilize" us. It angered me for a long time, so much that I didn't write about it, because I kind of froze up. I didn't want to hurt the feelings of the people who respected Appalachian people and tried to learn and appreciate the culture. It took me thirty-five years to reach a balance where I could see how to tell the truth about both sides and about what it had done to me and others. I consider the essay "Honor to the Founding Elders of Oak Ridge," in *Selu: Seeking the Corn Mother's Wisdom* to be a spiritual triumph for me, of being able to work through years and years of being ambivalent about how to say it, how to tell the story about the people of good will, but at the same time tell the story about the people who wanted to stereotype Appalachian people, and what it did to me and how I reacted.

We must have our stories. If we lose our stories we are lost. If we lose the roots of who we are, and the knowledge of our history as an individual, or a country or region, if we lose that, we will be adrift. The stories, the traditional stories, the cultural stories, and the journalistic stories—the stories help keep us steady and even, but a story/poem needs a listener. One of the great needs of people now is to take more time to listen to the spoken word. I'm not against the "e-world" or Twitter or any of those things, but to keep technology in balance with a space of quietness to listen to what other people are saying, to listen to nature and to assimilate what happens is crucial to survival.

My father passed away in 1989. The recent passing away of my mother is taking me some time to assimilate what that means in my life, and what her life was, what stories need to be preserved of her for her descendents. I haven't stirred about this year much and have been thinking it through. I call it "stump setting" sometimes. Old timers used to say when they needed to think deeply about something, "I'm going to set on a stump for a while," meaning, like a hen sets on her eggs, I'm going to set on my thoughts until they are "hatched out,"—quiet and patient. Now, you don't often hear that said, and when you stop hearing it, it's not being done so much.

We storytellers and poets can help call people back to listening to the spoken word and to the stories and to their own lives and their own stories. That will help. Listen to our blood, listen to our stories and go on with our work.

Gary Carden

Gary Carden was born in Sylva, North Carolina, where he continues to live in his family's farm house to this day with a dog named Jack, a feral cat and a flock of chickens.

A storyteller, a playwright, a fiction writer, teacher and artist, Carden attended Western Carolina University and taught for many years in the public school system before turning to storytelling and writing full time.

A speaker for Elderhostel for many years, Carden also conducts workshops and seminars on a variety of subjects, including Appalachian folklore and humor, mountain culture and tradition, the work of Joseph Campbell, the history of the Cherokee people, Southern literature and the Brothers Grimm.

He was awarded the Peace Pipe Award for outstanding contributions to grant writing for Native Americans by the Economic Development Office in Washington, D.C.; the University of North Carolina Award in Drama; the North Carolina Arts Council Playwright's Award; Appalachian Writer's Association Book of the Year Award for *Mason Jars in the Flood*; Kansas City Drama Festival Award for "Land's End"; North Carolina Language and Life Award, North Carolina State, for the preservation of mountain heritage; Key West Drama Festival Award for the "Raindrop Waltz," and the North Carolina Society of Historians Award.

His list of books, productions, videos and CDs include *Mason Jars in the Flood*; and *Belled Buzzards, Hucksters and Grieving Specters*; *Blow the Tannery Whistle*; *Mountain Talk*; *The Raindrop Waltz and Other Plays*; and *The Prince of Dark Corners*.

The Interview

I've lived here basically my whole life. Technically, my history is my own life; that's what I talk about in my plays and stories. It's all personal.

The first time I ever told stories as a "professional storyteller," I was terrified! We were broke; I had lost my job and I was feeling very guilty, and my wife was sick. So I said to myself, okay, I'm going to try to make it as a storyteller. So I wrote some letters and I got a job telling stories at a storytelling festival in Macon County, and another one at the John C. Campbell Folk School.

I went to both of them with my story written out and I read it, and it was awful. In Macon County, I did the same thing, but who should be there but Richard Chase? He was in a motorized wheelchair and was near the end of his life—bad things were happening to him, even though it didn't seem possible that a man that talented could end up that way. He had no place to go, and there he was in that wheelchair; he had those wonderful eyebrows and huge eyes.

When I finished reading my story, here he came in that wheelchair, and got down to the speaker's platform where I was, and he looked at me and said, "Thank God I never learned to read." And I quit reading my stories right then; from then on it was whatever came out of my mouth. I think that is the secret to storytelling. Sometimes there are things hid in your head that you wouldn't even know were going to be there!

I don't believe in memorizing; storytelling should be spontaneous. You tell stories and you don't know what you are going to say next—I believe that gives the story an energy that it loses when people memorize. I have no idea how long my story's going to be when I start it—forcing stories to conform to a time frame is something I don't understand, because I don't always know where a story is going to go when I begin it. When I start telling it, if the audience likes me, it may be forty-five minutes. If they don't like me, it's amazing how quick I can get off of that stage.

Something happens between you and an audience—there's a mutual exchange of something, and that's great storytelling—that's when it is at its best: you are telling a story and they are listening and they want you to be good. They knock themselves out helping you to be good. The worst storytelling I've ever done in my life was down at a resort in north Georgia—they must have done a computer search to get those people—they were so unresponsive! You couldn't move them; they were determined not to be impressed. But, 99.99 percent of the time, audiences are wonderful.

There's something curative about storytelling—at least the kind I am interested in. I got a job teaching at Elderhostel's and soon learned that it was an ideal setting for telling stories—I did it for thirty-five years. Storytelling is flexible; it can be anything. So, I taught Appalachian history, Cherokee history, and Joseph Campbell. I taught Jack tales, King Arthur—I could teach anything I wanted to, but it always involved storytelling. One of the best things you can do is to take folklore from other countries and then convert it to Appalachian settings.

Also, what became routine for me was to tell the story about my grandmother going to the nursing home, and her desperate fight to stay out, and her final defeat, and her going to the nursing home and me going to see her. She refused to speak to me when I went, because I had let her down, because she always told me, "You owe me. Don't you let the family put me in a nursing home." I told how she created a fantasy world in that nursing home. There was a day when I went to see her and when I opened the door, she said, "Come in, John Lyndon (that's my daddy). Sit down, Arthur will be back in a minute. I think Albert will be coming over from Brevard."

She was talking about people who were long dead—died in the seventies. The only one that wasn't dead was Asbury and she treated him like he was eighteen years old and still working in the paper mill. Asbury asked her doctor—we still had a family doctor and he came to the nursing home—if she had lost her mind. The doctor said, "Well, no. I guess you could say her mind has gone back to 1937. She's picked her a day, and it's in June (the doctor said he had heard her talk like this many times), and it's a Sunday and everybody's home, nobody's died yet, even that little baby she had that was a "blue baby"—it's still alive. She's going to live that day over and over and over. She's always talking about hearing the cow's bell coming down to the barn and the rooster crow—none of that is here now. There's nothing outside this nursing home but an interstate and a train track, but she's gone back to live that Sunday over and she will do that for the rest of her life." So we would go to the nursing home and sit with her on a Sunday in 1937.

Sometimes she would tell me about the dress she wanted to be buried in and the music she wanted, but there came a day when I started to leave, and she came over and hugged me and it scared me, because she had never done that in my whole life.

I asked her, what's that for? And she said, "Well, I thought I'd go on." I said, "Go where?" and she said, "the other side." And I laughed when I said, "Ah, Mama, I'll see you next Sunday," but two days later she was in the hospital, and two days after that she was dead. And the Jameson Quartet came and sang. The preacher was new and mispronounced her name and didn't really know who she was.

When it was over they told me I needed to go by the nursing home to pick up her effects. They were tied on the door in a little plastic bag; she was eighty-six and that was what her life had come down to: her glasses with one arm broken off; a dental plate with one tooth missing in the front—she always covered it with her hand when she laughed, and there was eighty cents in dimes tied in the corner of her handkerchief and a picture of that "blue baby" that had died in 1938.

When I told that story, I would see people crying all over the Elderhostel. It wasn't because of my storytelling; it was because they had all done what I have done—put their mother in a nursing home. That's what storytelling is. It's like some incredible purgation, guilt and bad feelings about it—shouldn't have done it, but it's a shared experience: we all do it. We all die. As Queen Elizabeth said, "We all must turn our face to the wall." She sat on her death bed for two days with her thumb in her mouth.

Storytelling is a communal thing. The thing that fascinated me when I was working for the Cherokee as a grants writer was a story the old tribal members told sitting by the fire on cold winter nights. They scared themselves silly with it. It's called "The Uktena." I told that story, usually at Thanksgiving and Halloween and scared kids. Then I wrote a play, *The Uktena*, and it went to Atlanta and played there three weeks, then I got the theater to bring it to Cherokee and perform it at the Cherokee High School. After that, I knew it would probably never be done again—it was too elaborate with special effects, elaborate sets and a cast of about twenty-five, including dancers.

To me, there's a natural progression from storytelling to theater. Every play that I have written has started as a story I told. It always seemed a natural step to turn it into a play. Storytelling is very close to theater anyway. It's like Jack tales—I think that's where I found that out. I once saw a woman on the stage, Cheryl Oxford, and she took a Jack tale and she read it and she tells a class of high school seniors, "This is already a play." She assigned roles to kids in the audience and put those kids on the stage with their lines and they did "Jack and the Devil" as a play. She said, "It's already there, you just fill in the gaps."

I think that good storytelling lends itself to the theater. If developed enough, it's just like moving across a faintly marked boundary—it's as simple as moving from "he" to saying "I." To be honest, that is the "mission" that I failed to accomplish—to create a link between storytelling and drama. It's just logical—instead of telling the story about my granny sitting on the front porch, it is a simple thing to put that porch on the stage and put my grandmother on the porch on a rainy night saying, "Oh, if you could have heard your daddy play!"

Great stories, I think, are not always about squeaky clean people doing the right thing. Maybe they are ignorant, flawed people who stumble into a crisis and have to find their own way out.

I don't have any family left. They are all gone. I was born ... I used to say in this house, but my grandmother used to correct me when I said that. She said I was born over there [pointing across the street] in that field; there used to be a little shack over there. But I grew up here, so I'm still obsessed by the idea that I was born in this house. I love it, but I come close to freezing to death in it in the winter. For years after I moved back, I was using my granddaddy's little fireplace as my only source of heat. It was so cold that my breath would fog while I was reading. Finally, I got a little soapstone wood heater. It has helped a lot.

My father was a mountain musician, and apparently was a good one, very popular; a good natured fella, and they nicknamed him Happy. I grew up being "little Happy," course you get a little tired of that by the time you turn forty [chuckle]. I grew up in this town, largely with the people that knew my father. He'd had a band called the Smoky Mountain String Band and they told me about it endlessly, and told me, "You orta heard yore daddy play the 'Raindrop Waltz.'

Gary Carden

Of course, I ended up doing a play called *The Raindrop Waltz* which was about him and my grandmother.

My father was killed when I was two and my mother was so horrified at the prospect of taking me home—her family was composed of some dangerous people—she left me on the porch of this house. Then she walked down the road to the highway; she flagged a bus and she went to Knoxville. I was two and a half by that time.

I ran away immediately and went looking for her, usually without any clothes on. I'd get up early in the morning before anybody missed me, and I'd go. This was all pasture and cows [ironic laughter as he spread his arms to indicate the surrounding houses]. There was an old woman who was always working in her garden. Her name was Granny Painter and she would catch me. She was arthritic and couldn't stand anymore, but she would work in her garden, getting around on her hands and knees.

She would be out weeding her tomatoes and she would come over saying, "little boy, little boy," and she would grab me and hold me saying, "Let's wait. Agnes will be here after a while." And she was right—after a while my grandmother came looking for me. I didn't know where Knoxville was, but I was going to find my mother. I only knew it was Knoxville, because I had learned to spy as a child. I lay in bed listening to my grandparents talk. I heard them talk—that's how I learned about my mother and Knoxville.

I did eventually find my mother—she came to see me graduate—just came out of nowhere, and she bought my class ring or I wouldn't have had one. She came to this house, but my grandmother wouldn't let her come in. She said, "She's yore mama, you go on over there and talk to her in the road."

It was a little dirt trail and it made a big circle around this cove. We walked and talked for three hours. I got up the next morning and told my grandmother that I was going to see my mother at my other grandmother's— and it broke my granny's heart, and she said "Don't you go over there." But I did, and I stayed with her until she left.

My mother wanted me to go see her in Tennessee. She had married a man and had a son. I rode the bus to Columbia, Tennessee, and was supposed to stay a week, but I lasted one afternoon and they had to put me on the bus. Her son had a screaming fit when he saw me, and her husband would not speak to me.

I didn't see her anymore until I wrote a book, *Belled Buzzards, Hucksters and Grieving Specters*, and I sent her one. She wrote me a note and asked me to forgive her. I got in the car and went to Tennessee. Her husband was dead and my half-brother had married and moved away. I stayed two days. We yelled at each other a lot and she cried the whole time. When you are a storyteller you are tempted to make the past ideal, but it was not. We all do it and I sometimes consciously do it—if you can't live with your past, you make up another one—the one where you are a better person. She said she did not abandon me and had every intention of coming to get me, and that she even came to visit me once, which was a fact, but I don't remember it. I always took my granny's word for it. I think that finally, my mother and I made an uneasy alliance.

She wrote me after that and I wrote back; we had a correspondence, but it was remote. She wanted me to come down there and live and I wouldn't. I saw it wouldn't work. On the way back home, I remember that I pulled off the road, and even though I'm not religious, I said, "Thank you, God, for letting my grandparents raise me."

My grandfather always knew that his children would give me a hard time all my life, so when I was little, he went down to the courthouse and legally adopted me. My grandmother and grandfather were old Scot-Irish and my grandmother always said, "We ain't huggers and kissers" when I wanted a hug. That's just the nature of the Appalachian culture.

Every time I became a problem to my grandmother, she'd take me out on the porch and point to a place over there and say, "I found ye right here. You didn't have nothin' but a brown paper bag with some clean underwear in it. An' I took ye when nobody wanted you. Now you owe me."

I called her "Mama," but I called my grandfather "Grandpa," and I would ask her, "Mama, what do I owe you?" Sometimes it would be a load of wood, and later it got to be, "Don't you let them put me in the county home," and our county still had one. Those things are gone now, but she was terrified of ending up in the county home. She said it meant that no one loved you enough to keep you.

There was always a lot of resistance from my uncles and aunts about my going to college. I went to Western Carolina University—the first in my family to attend college, but it was resented by my uncles and aunts. After I graduated, my uncle Asbury always called me professor, but it was said with contempt. I had an aunt who used to take me aside when nobody could hear us and say, "You're trash, GarNell" and then she'd walk off.

When I came back from teaching for fifteen years, I asked my uncle Asbury, "What's going to happen to this old house?" He told me the fire department had already asked to burn it, and he was thinking about letting them do it. I asked him, that if I could borrow the money from the bank, would he sell it to me. In the back of my mind, I always knew that if this were a good and fair world, this would be my home. Nobody wanted it—it sat here abandoned five years.

The roof had fallen in, the windows were knocked out and a couple of druggies had moved in and sold drugs out of this house! He told me, "Professor, now I always knew you didn't have a lick of sense, and you've gone and proved it. That's the stupidest thing I ever heard of. This house has one light bulb in it and the wiring is shot and the plumbing is gone and you'll freeze to death in the winter, but if you want it, I'll sell it to you." So I moved back home. Sat on the same porch my granny sat on. I'd saved enough from my last year of teaching at Brevard College in 1989 to fix the roof and plumbing.

Asbury used come by every once in a while. He would tell my aunt Tink, "I gotta go see GarNell, and he will say something stupid that I can tell you later." One day he drove by and saw I had built a deck on the side of the house. He stopped and asked why I had done that, and when I told him it was so I could watch the sunset on the Balsam Mountains, he said "God damn, you gawn freeze to death this winter with no insulation, and you build a deck!"

When they did my play, *The Raindrop Waltz* in Key West—I knew they weren't going to understand either the language or the culture that was depicted in the play.... They obviously knew nothing about Appalachia, because the cast continually hugged and kissed one another. Southern; they talked slow and lazy like warm molasses in the play. The Appalachian dialect was totally missing.

There is harshness in the Appalachian language, a nasal twang that you never hear in the South. I taught school down in Cartersville, Georgia, for five years and they were wonderful people, but they were not my people. They ate hotdogs with a fork and said things like, "Gary, can you carry me downtown?" I thought they meant that I should literally carry them downtown. Everyone had a slow, lazy drawl, you know.

There is little similarity between mountain culture and southern culture. For example, when I was in Cartersville, there were some colorful misfits and eccentrics in that town. One was a mentally deficient guy who wore a dress and carried a pocket book and wore heels. He played with little kids and did odd jobs up and down the street, and the town loved him. When they had a kiddy parade, he led it. There was another guy who didn't have legs. He sold newspapers from a garage dolly and propelled himself with his elbows. He had more friends than anybody in town—what I'm saying is, Joseph Campbell says it is a healthy community that accepts their misfits, and they are allowed to participate in a useful way. In Sylva, I have friends who have brothers and sisters who are deformed or mentally deficient; they are never allowed outside. In Appalachia, we hide our misfits; I think it is Southern to turn them loose.

There's a negative aspect to mountain culture—it's the idea that we should "stay in our place," the idea puts you in a box, and you're not supposed to get out of it. You're not supposed to marry above you—you're supposed to stay in your social caste. You are not supposed to marry a lawyer's daughter like my poor uncle Albert did and paid dearly for it.

When I went to college my aunt Elsie told me, "You forget about this college stuff. You get out there in that cornfield and help your granddaddy. What the hell you gettin' above yore raisin' GarNell? Gettin' the big head is what you're doin.' That poor ole man is down there workin' in that field and you're up there in that college."

My aunt Elsie was my granddaddy's sister and she was anti-education. There's no point in getting the big head—stay where you belong and help the family. I went to college anyway and she would not speak to me for a long time afterwards. When I graduated, she almost forgave me, but in mountain culture, you never say "I'm sorry." All you do is start speaking again. At the next family reunion she wouldn't speak to me but she said, "I see the one that's got the big head is here again."

Then, several years later, at another reunion, she said, "GarNell, have you ever heard the story about the little boy who caught a speckled trout and ran all the way home with it?" And I said, "No ma'am, I don't think so."

"Well hush," she said, "and I'll tell you. The little boy caught a speckled trout and ran all the way home with it and put it in the spring. He went out there every day and he fed it cornbread and he loved that fish. And that fish got to lookin' forward to him comin'; stick his head out of the water and look for him; sometimes get out on the bank and wait for him. One day he fed it and got up to go to the house, the fish follered him, flop, flop, flop; it had a terrible time gettin' up the steps. He loved that trout and it went everywhere with him all summer, but when the summer was over, he didn't want to take the trout to school—the boys would laugh at him, so he tried to sneak off when he thought it wasn't lookin.' Ran out the back door quick as he could, but here come that trout, flop, flop, flop. He run across the big swinging bridge and here come that trout went flop, flop, flop, and that trout flopped over the edge of that bridge and fell in the creek and it drowneded! Now, GarNell, the reason I told you that story, now that you graduated from college and you're a teacher, don't be like that trout. Don't forget where you come from."

John O'Brien, who wrote *At Home in the Heart of Appalachia*, said that many people in Appalachia have been ridiculed for so long they believe they really are inferior, and O'Brian gives his own father as an example, because he urged John to "stay in your own place. Don't get the big-head."

I had an adjustment problem when I went to Georgia to teach. I absolutely loved teaching, but I soon found out that people in Appalachia looked at the world differently. As a result, when they find themselves in an urban setting, they are aware of being "weighed and found wanting." I think that is why so much of Appalachian humor is self-effacing. You make yourself look foolish. There's logic to that and I learned it as a child, and I think a lot of mountain kids do that. It's like when my grandmother told me when I went to school, she said, "Now, GarNell"—I didn't hear anybody call me Gary Neal until I went to school and the teacher called me that—"When you get out there with them town people, you're going to be weighed and found wanting."

If you find yourself in that situation, you suddenly realize that you are in alien country. You are surrounded by people who think you are a stupid "hillbilly." The way you can diffuse this situation is to tell a joke in which you make fun of yourself. It's like having a gun fight with somebody and discovering that there's no ammunition. What is the point of attacking you if you have already surrendered? I remember my uncle Albert once telling a roomful of uptight academics and snobs about his trip to Detroit to get a job.

He said he went to a hotel and asked about renting a room. The manager led him to the elevator to take him several floors up, but as soon as the door of the elevator closed, Uncle Albert said, "I'm sorry, but I don't think I could even lie down comfortably in here." Everybody laughed. Albert had made fun of himself. He had also deflected all of the potential barbs about him being backward or unsophisticated.

Even the worst things that have happened to me, in some strange way, over a long period of time seem to have benefited me. Okay, my father was killed and I was raised by my grandparents. It was terrible, it was hard and I grew up hard. I eventually learned that my grandparents, being Scot-Irish, were superstitious. I remember grandpa—this is just one instance—"GarNell, the cows got the 'holler-tail' an' I need you to help me cure her." And I said, "All right Grandpaw, but what's the 'holler-tail'?" He said that when a cow quits giving milk, it is because she has the holler-tail. "Now, come on."

So we go over to the barn and he puts the cow in the stall and he feeds her tail through a knot hole and I go outside and hold her tail, and then he takes a knife and splits that cow's tail all the way down and she gets operatic [makes the sound of an operatic cow] then he poured Epsom salts in the cut and tied the tail up in white rags and then we opened the stall and she ran out. She ran all the way to the top of the hill and we heard her all night, but she gave milk the next day. I would have, too!

When I tell that story, it reveals my grandfather as an uneducated, superstitious farmer. But, if I keep talking about him, my audience learns that he was also hardworking, devoted and capable of a kind of tragic nobility. I sincerely believe that his flaws make him more sympathetic.

One of the most misguided concepts that my grandparents had was the one about my "bad blood." According to my grandmother, "Your mama—everybody on that side of your family, is crazy. Your great granddaddy on your mama's side shot himself and fell down the well. Yessir. It was a week before they found him. Don't that tell you something ... when they don't miss you for a week? And then, the family had to move because they couldn't drink the water."

My grandmother once told me, "You know that chubby man who lives on the back side of town and wears that big yellow duck bill to town on Saturday? He ties it on his head with a piece of elastic and he would jump out in front of cars and goes, 'Quack, quack!' Now, GarNell, that's your uncle on your mother's side. They've all got bad blood." So I grew up thinking I was different because I had "bad blood" in me. It didn't help matters any to have Uncle Asbury calling me "Runt" and my aunt whispering, "Trash! That's what you are." When I tell these things now, they are funny, but when I was a little kid, they were terrible and frightening.

If necessary, people like me design another world and move into it to survive that kind of thing. It was the Ritz Theater on Saturday for me; I was always foolish about "imaginary things," fantasy and make-believe. It was what I got from theater, movies, books and radio shows—they shaped my heroes and kept me company. And then I had one old lady who ran the library—we didn't have much of a library, we had a one-room library with maybe 500 books—and every time I would walk in the door, she would say, "Gary, I have something for you," and she'd give me *Lassie, The Green Grass of Home* or she gave me *Return of the Black Stallion* and *Beautiful Joe*. I just read everything she gave me. When I ran out of children's literature to read, she gave me *Red Pony* and *The Great Gatsby*, and the one she told me to take my time on, saying that it might take several months, was *Look Homeward Angel*; I read them all.

I had nobody else to talk to about what I read, so I talked to her. She would say, "What do you think about that green light on Gatsby's pier; or what do you think about the sign with those big glasses?" She talked to me and she made me think—nobody in my family made me think, or dream or dance.

The first time I told stories was at my elementary school. It got so the kids would ask me to tell stories at recess every day—this was a country school—and we would go to the pine thicket below the school. There were all these pine needles and you'd take your bag lunch and go down there, and I'd tell them about the movie that was on that Saturday. They would say, "Let's hear about Roy Rogers in *Shadow Canyon*," and I would say, "Why do you want me to tell it? You were there, I saw you!" "Yeah, but I didn't see the one you saw," they'd tell me, so I would sit there and tell them stories from the movies, and then it became the comic books like "Sheena, Queen of the Jungle." I was crazy about "Submarine" and "The Heap." They were both outcasts like I was. "The Heap" was about a German pilot who was so disfigured from a plane crash that he turned into an ugly bush and he had to hide all the time, but he had some sort of system that told him there was evil nearby. When he picked up on it, he went out and captured the killers. "Submarine" stayed in the ocean because he didn't like to be near people, but when they needed help, he always went. He had little fins on his feet and looked like Robert Mitchum.

I had polio when I was a child, but I didn't know it for the longest time. When I got out of high school, I was told I couldn't go to college, but the high school principal told me to tell my granddaddy there was a way I could go that wouldn't cost him anything. I told my granddaddy and he says, "I don't give a damn about that—you're still not goin.'"

About a week later I was sitting out on the porch one night and he came out and said, "I've been thinking about what you said about going to college." Well, he hadn't been thinking about it—my grandmother had told him, "Let him go!"

I told Mr. Galloway and he told me he was sending me to Bryson City to see a doctor. Bryson City was only 15 miles away, but it may as well have been Africa—I had never been anywhere. I rode the bus to Bryson City; Mr. Galloway had given me a letter for the doctor. I opened it on the way down and it said "Find something wrong with this boy." I sealed it back up and gave it to the doctor. He gave me a physical—the first one I had ever had in my life—and then said that I'd had polio.

When he wrote it down, he said, "You've had polio." I said I didn't know I had it, but he said, "You've got one leg that is one inch shorter than the other, and you have severe scoliosis; I'll write that down and you give this little slip of paper to Mr. Galloway." When Mr. Galloway read the word "scoliosis," he said, "Good, now I'm going to get you a scholarship." He sent me to Asheville and then Vocational Rehab sent me to college. Nobody in my family paid for a damn thing—not until my senior year when I lost my Voc. Rehab scholarship, when I only had one more semester—my grandfather paid for that.

When I told my grandmother about the polio, she said, "So that's what that was? You was real sick when you was 12, GarNell, for six weeks." She said that they let me sleep in their bed until I got well.

I've been losing my hearing for 44 years, but it happened very gradually. It was like the world receded; I couldn't participate before, but it was getting farther and farther away. Finally I couldn't even watch movies unless they were closed-captioned. Then, a couple of years ago captioning became commonplace. Up until then I watched a lot of Japanese movies because the captions always told you what they said.

By the time I went to Brevard, North Carolina, to teach (around 1988 and I was about 60) I began to have major hearing loss. It was seventy percent when I left to teach in Brevard and by the time I came back, it was 85 percent. I had swellings on either side of my ears that, according to my audiologist, was the result of my straining to hear in the classroom. Lots of bad stuff happened at Brevard College that I don't like to talk about ... all having to do with my hearing loss.

Deaf people are paranoid—Goya was deaf, Beethoven—many gifted people. Of course, being deaf doesn't mean that you are gifted, but it probably follows that you are paranoid. Often, when I am in a room full of people, I wonder, why are those people looking at me? Why is that one smiling and talking to the other one? I have been told by audiologists that this is a common reaction to losing your hearing.

I never learned to talk "sign." Where am I going to find people who can talk about Celtic mythology or the novel that I am reading, or my favorite poets? The only thing that signing is good for is general communication with humankind. If you wanted to talk about movies, books and folklore, it's impossible in my experience. I tried signing for a while, and I finally decided that I would prefer to struggle to communicate with the hearing world.

I have a cochlear implant now, and it has made a remarkable difference in my life. There are things that it can't do, but I am delighted with it. I can participate in conversations now, go to movies, and I am probably a better storyteller. In fact, I may actually hear too much! I never dreamed that birdsong and crickets could be irritating. It doesn't reproduce music well, but I'm pleased with what it does do.

My grandfather was manic-depressive and so am I. His episodes began when my father was killed; he would go and sit in the barn loft for an entire day.... The psychiatrists say I am not a true manic-depressive, because I seemed to have escaped into depression to avoid a lot of bad things that happened to me all at once: I lost my job, my wife left me and even my teeth fell out and I couldn't talk clearly for a long time; then my car burned in a freak accident and all of my teaching notes were in it. I almost lost this house, too. I could no longer work since I lost my car and I had maxed out on the credit card. The bank had notified me that they were going to foreclose on my mortgage. I got depressed.

I locked down for a while, but that's when I started painting. They put me on Prozac, lithium and Zoloft—I just sat there for two months in a kind of pleasant stupor. I couldn't read a book because it didn't make any sense. I'd watch a movie and I couldn't remember what just happened ten minutes ago, and I couldn't have conversations with people because I couldn't remember what they'd just said. I was just a contented fool. I wasn't depressed anymore, but I couldn't write, create or think clearly.

I told the psychiatrist I couldn't live that way and when he refused to approve my going off medication, I got another psychiatrist. The third one I found took me off the medication. He said I would have to work with him, but it could be done. He told me to find something that would eventually replace medication. Then he said, "Why don't you try painting?"

I came home and went out to Walmart and bought sixty little bottles of acrylic paint and I went down to a furniture store and cut up refrigerator boxes for something to paint on. I came home and started painting on cardboard and before it was over I did 62 paintings. When I knew it was working, was the day I realized I needed to get something to eat. I looked at the clock and discovered that I had been there four hours. I was totally focused on painting.

I also learned that you are never "cured" from depression. It will always be there. The best you can do is learn to live with it. Nobody can help you. Nobody; it's just you. And to me that's the way it's always been anyway, so when I wake up at 3 A.M. terrified and wanting to die, I get up and paint; it still works. I painted a new one three weeks ago.

You know the Kingdom of the Happy Land? It was about a group of African Americans who came together and believed God was going to take care of them in a kingdom somewhere in the Appalachian mountains, and they walked from Mississippi all the way to North Carolina and when they came up out of South Carolina, they picked up more people until they numbered 400 when they got here. They picked up stray cows and a starving horse and found an old woman who had a huge plantation with half of it destroyed. All her family was dead and gone so she struck a bargain—you come in here and help me get this place up and running again and I'll let you live here. They said, "If we live here and plow your fields and milk your cows; will you sell us some land?" She agreed and they worked for ten cents a day and saved enough to buy 300 acres. Then they moved onto that land and called it the Kingdom of the Happy Land. They elected a king and a queen and built it on the state line: the king lived in North Carolina and the queen lived in South Carolina and they created a religion that alarmed some people, for it was based on something the oldest members of the group remembered from Africa.

A lot of it had to do with nature and fertility and I painted it. Progress killed Kingdom of the Happy Land. They used to load up produce onto big wagons, take it to the highway and sell it, but when the railroad came, the railroads destroyed their livelihood. They all moved to town and became craftsmen and servants.

Another picture I painted is *Preaching to the Chickens*. When I was a child, a holiness preacher who preached in a little church near my grandparents' home used to scare the congregation to death talking about hell and brimstone. I used to sit in the woods above the church and listen, and a few times, I actually went in the church and watched the frightened congregation. One night, I came home and got the lantern when nobody was watching me, and I went to the chicken house when it was right over there [pointing out the window], and I preached to the chickens just like he did. I told them about chicken hell and scared 'em to death....

So, what I did instead of taking drugs was get my paints and start painting *Blow the Tannery Whistle*. Now I want to do a book and illustrate it myself, and that may be the one. The real tannery whistle is in Sylva—one night, it blew to signal the end of time. That is a lot different from when it blew every day for work hours at the tannery. And now, what I want more and more is to sit out there on the front porch and watch the sun set. The way my granny used to say it was, "Watch the light fade up on the balsams." It's like Joseph Campbell said, "We are all drawing from the same sources." He meant that inspiration was like water in a well. You can let down a bucket and draw up water in Appalachia or China or Russia or Cuba.... It doesn't matter, because that water is the same, and we are all drinking from the same mysterious water.

Jo Carson

Jo Carson is an author and performer living in Johnson City, Tennessee. She has published books for adults, plays for which she has won a series of national awards, and three books for children.

Carson organized the founding meeting of Alternate ROOTS, an ongoing social, activist and artist service organization that is still active after 30 years. She was an occasional commentator on NPR's *All Things Considered* for eight years, and in 1997 Emory and Henry College held a literary festival in her honor. In 2002, Jo Carson was the second artist to receive the Award of Honor from East Tennessee State University, her alma mater, for her ongoing work.

Plays by Carson include *Daytrips*, which won the Kesselring Award for best new American play in 1989, and *Preacher with a Horse to Ride*, which is published in the anthology *Alternate ROOTS: New Plays from the South, 1994* and was awarded a Roger L. Stevens Award from the Fund for New American Plays in 1993. *The Bear Facts* won a playwright's fellowship from NEA in 1993–94; *Whispering to Horses*, a play, won an AT&T Onstage: New Plays for the '90s award for the 1996-97 season.

Carson was also the recipient of a Theater Communications Group/NEA residency award to work with 7 Stages in Atlanta in 2000. The result of that residency was a new play, *If God Came Down...*, a story of shamanic healing. Carson played it in Atlanta at 7 Stages and continues to do performances.

In 2003, Carson began a project for storytellers with the Orchard at Altapass on the Blue Ridge Parkway in North Carolina from stories of the Battle of Kings Mountain in the American Revolutionary War, *What Sweet Lips Can Do*. A second piece, *Men of Their Time*, also came from that project. Both plays are published in *Teller Tales: Histories* from Ohio University Press. *A Tale of Two Charlies* played in the summer of 2009.

Stories I Ain't Told Nobody Yet, a series of monologues and dialogues, made the Editor's Choice on Booklist and was brought out in paperback by the Theater Communications Group in 1991. This work is currently being taught in Appalachian studies courses in high schools and colleges in this country and others, and is performed in professional theaters in this country. *The Last Waltz Across Texas* was published in 1993 by Gnomon Press.

Carson currently performs *Liars, Thieves and Other Sinners on the Bench,* which is also available in paperback from the Theater Communications Group. Another new book, *Spider Speculations: A Physics and Biophysics of Storytelling,* also published by the Theater Communications Group, explores how stories work in people's bodies and lives.

The Interview

You ask about what and where I come from.... I was born in Kingsport, Tennessee, in 1946, and three days later I came to Johnson City, where I grew up. My grandmother Catron had decided that my mother, Marie, couldn't have a baby away from Kingsport where they lived, never mind the natural process, so I was born by caesarian section in a Kingsport hospital but grew up here in Johnson City, Tennessee. My mother married a service man—my father was a fly-boy, a pilot in the Navy in the Pacific. My mother graduated from college and waited for him, and they married when he got back to the States from the Pacific. I tell stories of his experiences sometimes. He was at Midway, at Guadalcanal, the Solomon Islands, New Guinea, and then into the Philippines when MacArthur returned.... I can hardly imagine what all that must have been like. I have five stories. He didn't tell much until right before he died.

I spent a lot of time at my grandmother's house growing up, so I spent a lot of time with Grandmother and Granddaddy—my mother's parents. Mother had heart trouble and she wasn't supposed to have children to begin with, so she *chose* to do that—it's why I was a caesarian birth, and my brother was her second caesarian. When I was little, everyone was worried about Marie, and two children were a lot harder to deal with than one, so I (the eldest) spent a lot of time with Grandmother and Granddaddy. That woman was afraid of everything: she nailed her windows shut because she was afraid someone would try to abduct me like the Lindbergh child had been abducted, and the upstairs, where I slept when I was there ... in the summer you could crack a window just so much—maybe two inches—and it would let out only so much heat, and it was just excruciatingly hot in my room. During a thunder storm, I would have to come inside and lay down in the middle of the living room floor and be still so lightning wouldn't come in the window and strike me. Grandmother was also afraid of men. She loved her husband, but she was afraid of most men, and she was afraid of men for me. The second reason the windows were nailed shut was that she was afraid somebody would try to get me because I was a girl. I think now that the woman may have been abused. She ran away with her school teacher—eloped when she was fourteen, and then she took in her two younger sisters just after she married. She was a fourteen-year-old bride and she invited the two younger sisters into her home and they came ... that says a lot if you read it a certain way, and it could explain a lot about why she was so fearful. I think about her often—she is one of the voices I still hear regularly in my imagination, and I hope there's some joy for her now. She loved me dearly—she was crazy about me, but she'd lost her elder daughter to flu the spring before I was born in the fall, and I was her new Inez from the time I was born.

I had all four of my grandparents until I was 18. That is a real gift. Much, much later, I lived in my Grandma and Grandpa Carson's house—I inherited it—in Johnson City. I put it on the market recently and the bottom fell out of the housing market with the economy, so at the moment, I still have it. Big old house. They had a small farm originally, but everything but the house and one other lot was sold off long ago. It was still too much yard to mow and I was getting sick in that house—I've been dealing with colon cancer recently—and I'm sure I was already sick with it when I got my father's pneumonia. He died of it. I was doing my damnedest to not let him know I was sick because he didn't need to worry about that, too. Finally, I left that house, moved into another much smaller house, because I didn't have the wherewithal to take care of the big one. It was after I'd moved that I got the cancer diagnosis. A-ha. My current struggle is living through that.

About the oral history work: twenty-eight years ago, I wrote a series of monologues and dialogs that became the book *Stories I Ain't Told Nobody Yet*, and that got me the Colquitt, Georgia, gig which became the Swamp Gravy project. I wrote a show from oral histories they had collected. From that beginning, I have worked all over the country with these community story projects, not just Appalachia. Being from this area had an impact on my work mostly because Appalachia, and things Appalachian, had become objects of study and interest. My name might not have gone anywhere if that interest in Appalachia had not happened.

Harry Caudill brought attention to Appalachia with his book, *Night Comes to the Cumberlands*. He brought the poverty of the region to light, and so was instrumental in influencing the War on Poverty (you have to be of a certain age to remember any of this) and from that, the Appalachian Regional Commission started building roads here and opened things up. People found things here they hadn't known existed—there was a real culture here. I was never particularly a part of it, I never lived in a traditional romantic

Appalachian situation; my father's family was made up of educators and scientists and mathematicians. Grandpa Carson was head of the math department at the Normal School which became East Tennessee State College which became East Tennessee State University. Grandmother Catron came from that culture, from Kyle's Ford, Tennessee, down on the Clinch River. She spent most of her life trying to leave it; trying to go somewhere that she wasn't named by that heritage. She came from dirt poor people, she married her school teacher and they sent their daughters to college. My mother went to college, both my mother and her sister, which was fairly unusual at that time. Educatin' girls wasn't the fashion.

Grandmother Catron had the idea that women's feet, or those who had never gone barefoot, were long and narrow instead of short and wide, and she felt you could tell somebody who had had to go barefoot as a child by the width of their feet and by the size shoe they wore. She wore a seven-C shoe, and she forced her foot into a nine and a half double AA shoes, and her feet were wretched for all the time I knew her. They hurt a lot but she kept putting them in those long narrow shoes, because she was not going to say she had gone barefoot as a child.

Then my mother bought into the whole '50s thing and tried to mop her floors in high heels. Mother ruined her feet too, almost as badly as Grandmother did, just for a different thing. An image ... my mother, Marie, had early onset Alzheimer's, and I was her caregiver for this particular day (there were lots of these days), we had gone to Kingsport because whoever had Marie for the day went to Kingsport to be with Grandmother, who needed almost as much help as Marie did, just not for the same reasons. That way, the other caregiver (my father) got a real day off. So this day, I had the two of them. And I tried to get them to get up and move, we had errands that Grandmother had to do, and these were all time consuming because it was hard for Grandmother to walk, so we didn't walk very fast at all. Mother and Grandmother were just sitting there, working, massaging their feet, unaware of each other, and they were both sort of moaning separately: their feet hurt. I stood there watching that, and I swore that I would never do anything that ruined my feet. You don't make rash statements like that without consequences. When my grandmother fell and went into a nursing home, and Mother went into assisted living, I went out and bought a horse (her name is Kate; I still have her). Two weeks after I got her, she stepped on my right foot and broke the second toe—crunch, you could hear it. So I hobbled around for a good long time because it was a real broken toe. A couple of years later I bought a second horse, Farley. I had him about two weeks and he stepped on my left foot. This time I was wearing good boots, but he was a much bigger horse and he managed to break a second toe—the same toe, the same way, just on the other foot. I said, okay Spirit, I get the point: let me not swear that one again.

My father read to us (my brother and me). He read Br'er Rabbit and Uncle Remus stories, which we loved, but he changed the names of the characters in them so they were our names, Br'er Skip and Br'er Jo, and remade the stories to make them applicable to our lives. Didn't know Br'er Rabbit had to go to elementary school did you? Br'er Rabbit was a trickster, a tradition that fascinates me—all that trickster business—and the Br'er Rabbit cycle was originally from the Cherokee. That's just FYI. As often as my father did something like making my brother and me trickster characters, he read us Shakespeare because he loved it and he liked playing all the parts. He read poetry. Uncle Tom, my father's oldest brother, had a photographic memory. He quoted from Shakespeare; he could quote passages of poetry— Robert Burns was a favorite— and he could quote passages of the Bible, he was a literate man who enjoyed his learning. My father wanted us to be able to do the same thing, so he read to us. Tom was a scientist, a chemist, but he loved language and words and played with that.

Jo Carson
(photograph by Murrary Lee)

Now, all these brothers were storytellers and raconteurs and liars, no doubt, so I came by that inclination quite honestly [laughter] even if I didn't get the photographic memory. Aunt Sally, my father's sister, told stories, too. (She also taught mathematics.) There were five children in that family: Sally had four brothers and all of them were good storytellers. Sally, bless her heart, never knew when to leave a detail out. Her storytelling always had way, way too many details, so it was always something close kin to shaggy dog stories that you lost the point of long before she got to the end. One family dinner, Grandma Carson looked at her across the dinner table—I was a child—and said, "Oh, Sally, please ... don't ruin a good story by sticking to facts!"

I tell that story now and people assume it is Grandma giving me (or whoever was listening) permission to be exceptionally creative with storytelling. It is amusing to think that, and she was rather creative herself, but it really was an admonishment to pick your details, which is just as—if not more—important.

One story that was told on Grandma was about how she had hired a young woman, Maud, to help her with housework. I vaguely remember Maud, and I do remember some of this event. Maud locked herself in the bathroom and she was crying and wouldn't come out. Finally, she told Grandma—through the locked door—that she was pregnant. Grandma asked who the father was, and it was a boy she had been seeing for a while, Tommy. Grandma said, "Well, when are you getting married?" Maud answered, "He left town." So Grandma took it upon herself to go see Tommy's mother. She called my mother and told her to get dressed in fancy clothes. It didn't matter what they were, she just had to "look like somebody." Then Grandma borrowed a friend's new car, picked up my mother and they drove to the front of Tommy's mother's house. Grandma tooted the horn just a little when they got there, attracted the attention of all the neighbors. When they knocked on Tommy's mother's door, they said they needed to talk to Tommy. Well, Tommy wasn't there, he was out of town. Grandma asked, "When is he coming back?" Tommy's mother answered that she didn't know when he was coming back. "Well, Maud's pregnant, and he's getting married and I'm going to have the reception at my house and I need to know when to plan for it and who to invite."

So Tommy was hauled back to town by his mother, and he married Maud. I have no idea how long the marriage lasted, or whether there was any grace in it at all, but Maud was saved from the '50s disgrace of an illegitimate birth. Mother and Grandma did the reception at Grandma's house just like they said they would. This was a story my mother remembered time and time again when she had Alzheimer's—it was about when she was powerful, when she was able to do things. She and Grandma were quite a team. That's just one story. And Grandma was so different from Grandmother....

Grandpa Carson was a fisherman and I went fishing with him sometimes in the summertime; when he couldn't find anybody else to take, he would take me. Here's why I was useful: I would sit on his shoulders and pick the big green catalpa caterpillars from the trees for bait—I hadn't gotten to worm fear yet. I was not his preferred fishing partner ... in fact, he would get really mad at me—I didn't like fishing—I liked to fall in the lake, so he would have to fish me out and we'd have to move because I'd scared all the fish away. Grandpa would go out to Boone Lake and catch a mess of bluegills, and we'd have a fish-fry.

After family dinners, the adults would play bridge—Grandma and

Grandpa Carson were addicted to bridge, and so all their children played and all their children's spouses played. There were at least two tables and then there were us children. They would sit there half the night playing, and Grandma had a pile of blankets in one of the downstairs closets, and when it came bedtime we would end up curled up under the card tables, around our parents' feet, wrapped up in blankets listening to what was being said above us. Dave and Meade had five children, Mike and Ruth had three, Tom and Lib had three and my parents had two, so there were a mess of us laid out under the tables. It's a good memory.

So there were the four brothers in my father's family and they were wonderful storytellers, they were raconteurs, and they were part of their own stories. They told stories on one another and they told stories on friends and they made the stories really juicy. My father outlived all his siblings. Uncle Tom was in a nursing home late in his life and he was even deafer then than he had been during his life—there's a family inclination to deafness—and Tom had also gone blind and couldn't read anymore. It was a perfect nightmare because so many of his pleasures were gone. My father took a book of favorite verse, or the Bible or Shakespeare, and he would put Tom's hand on his chest so Tom could feel the vibrations when he spoke, and he would read to Tom. And Tom knew the material well enough that he could figure out what was being said, and he could usually understand enough that he could say the poem with his brother. So my father was at the nursing home every morning for about a year and a half, reading to Tom.

When I went to school I was a terrible student; it was boring and I hated it from the get-go, so I did everything I could to get out of it. I lied a lot and made up my own stories and spent a lot of time in trouble for that. I didn't want to be there so I made up all kinds of excuses. I've written some of these since—always look at any experience in terms of its future anecdotal value. A nightmare is what it was, for me, and I didn't do very well with it. It's fashionable to claim dyslexia these days—I'm not sure that was my situation—it was just boring and my imagination was richer, so I lived in my imagination and that continued through high school. My parents insisted I go to college. At eighteen, I looked like I had just turned eleven and behaved a lot like it, too. I was a truly late bloomer. I got to college and I looked like the youngest one there. I hated college too. I dropped in and out and flunked the stuff I didn't find interesting, and I'd go back and then I'd drop out again. I took me eight years to get a degree. But I had announced in something like the fourth grade that I intended to be a writer—that was going to be my job. I have no idea where that came from, but it was certainly part of what got me in trouble so regularly, I was writing bad poems instead of doing my homework [laughter], Pulitzer Prize–winning poems, or so I thought at the time.

I have since changed my opinion about the quality of that work. But there was always this urge to write, always. I don't know where it came from. I come from a family of scientists and mathematicians and the idea that one of the children of this family was going to go write was pretty appalling to everybody. If you're not going to be a scientist or mathematician, the least you can do is go be a teacher. David, another of my father's brothers, took me on a car ride I didn't want to go on, I was twenty-something, and he lectured me the whole time. David was big on lecturing people and he told me I was wasting my life, throwing it away on useless things and bad poems—you can hear all this if you care to try hard enough—what did I think I had to write? I was stuck in the car. I could have gotten out and hitchhiked, but I would really have been in trouble then. When we finally got back, David announced to my father that he had straightened me out [laughter]. The grace in that story is that some years later, David wanted me to write something for him ... I told him he needed to write it himself. Much later, he said, "You know, I wish I had done what you did." And I asked, "What was that?" And he said, "You stuck by your guns." And yeah, I did. I don't know where I found the courage or wherewithal to do that, but I did.

Once, I decided that if I was going to be an artist, I needed to be from New York City, so I dropped out of school (again) and hauled myself to New York City. I answered an ad in *Saturday Review* for the job I had. I was a house sitter on Fifth Avenue, which is fine and dandy except that the woman who hired me was sick and getting sicker—she had Hodgkin's disease and I ended up being a sort of surrogate family for her, for the time I was there. I spent the first six months I was there seeing everything I could spend money on and see in New York City, and then I spent some time taking care of her because she was desperate. She had a mess of daughters—the youngest one had died a short time before in a car accident, and none of those women would deal with the fact that their mother was dying. They just couldn't do it. So I helped her get her affairs in order. I came home to find my grandma Carson dying; I came home, actually, with a medical problem of my own: as a child, I had been treated with x-rays for tonsillitis. It was the fashion in the '50s to do that—nobody knew x-rays did any damage—they used them for lots of things. There was even a machine that you could look into, punched a button, and saw how your foot fit in a new shoe—an X-ray image. Well, a hotshot doctor came into Appalachia because—I suspect—he figured he could try things here. My mother believed in buying the very best she could in medical care, and she had a great deal of faith in medicine, so she took me to this man who told her the treatment for tonsillitis was x-rays. So weekly, for about a year and a half, I was getting x-rays—with no lead shield over anything—to my throat. After that, they took the tonsils out.

While I was in New York City, that doctor committed suicide. I suspect he did that about the time reports of thyroid cancer due to x-ray treatment for tonsillitis started coming out in the medical literature. Whatever other reasons, the timing there is right. A woman who had been his nurse kept up with the medical literature; she contacted my parents and said that I needed to have my thyroid checked. So I did. I had a node and it was necessary to take it out. So twenty or so years after those x-rays, I went back home from New York for what I knew would be cancer surgery. Grandma was dying, but because thyroid cancer is slow-growing, I waited until she had passed to do it. My family did not need two people lying in the hospital. And, sure enough, I had a pre-cancerous node on my thyroid.

Now, there's a bunch of that I'm just beginning to understand: I'm sixty-three. I think that man managed to do a blow to my immune system in addition to my thyroid, because shortly after that treatment ended, I got a case of German measles and it wouldn't go away. I kept catching them over and over again—had them something like five times over the course of a summer. Your body is supposed to build up immunity and you don't get measles again, but I did. Then, as German measles can, my problem turned into ear infections, which began the wrecking of hearing. I know I was slightly hard of hearing after that, so it was doing inner ear damage. So the course of the ear business started early in my life (I'm rather profoundly deaf now) but that is not what I want to dwell on. It's just a part of the story that I have been putting together—more a-ha's. I'm fascinated by these little a-ha's, how maybe you finally get old enough or smart enough to begin to put things together. We humans are narrative makers, it is how our brains are hardwired, and the story we must work on, the story we are compelled to work on, is our own.

I came home from New York and had the thyroid surgery and went back to school and finally graduated, and got a job with Broadside Television. I graduated with a degree in speech and communications, and I had figured I would go work for TV somehow. The Federal Communications Commission had just recently passed a law that said so much of TV time had to be local origination and there were a bunch of little independent television stations that popped up all over this country overnight like mushrooms. There was new technology—it was a portable reel-to-reel video camera, black and white. It was supposedly portable but the Portapack—the recorder and the camera—weighed at least forty pounds. Then there were the lights, and then there were the battery packs, but this was radical stuff—it meant you could go out and take pictures and record on video tape and that job began an education about the region that I had not gotten in school. There were no Appalachian studies at the time; most of what I had gotten in my training was that I had to lose my Appalachian identity—I couldn't keep it and get a job.

In the meantime, through Broadside, I also got involved with the Highlander Center, which is modeled after the Danish Folk Schools. It's based on the idea that people who have experience can teach those who need to know. At the time I first went, Highlander was involved with the Civil Rights Movement and it was the first I knew of blacks and whites sitting down to have a real equal conversation. Highlander was an absolute revolution in my thinking and my understanding about what was going on in this region.

And then, into the back room of Broadside Television here in Johnson City, there came to be a small theater company called the Road Company (it's a different group from Roadside Theater at Appalshop in Kentucky) and I had loved theater from the time I knew the name of it, and I wanted to write, so I begged and groveled and actually ended up writing for them. I think we did five shows over the course of several years which I wrote with an ensemble of several actors, and this started another whole education: theater didn't have to be about something way off in the distance: it could be about something that matters to you. You could grow your own theater. I also learned that I really could write during that period of time. One of the plays that I did with the Road Company, *Horsepower: An Electric Fable*, was a done with a Tennessee Humanities grant. It was about land use which sounds dull, until you begin to talk about how it's changing around here. And changing, it was! Remember the ARC [Appalachian Regional Commission] and the War on Poverty business? "How is it changing around here?" is a land use question that can get personal; "How is the change affecting you?" We got some incredible response, and I made a series of dialogues and monologues out of it and that was the beginning of the book *Stories I Ain't Told Nobody Yet*.

So I was working off and on for the Road Company over a period of years, and got a few "real" jobs over that course of time to fill in the gaps. My resume was so speckled with projects I had done between Broadside and the Road Company that I finally wrote a resume that was a lie that said I had been married for ten years and had no work experience at all ... and got a job with that one. The trip about that resume is that I had to live a lie while I had that job [laughter].

By the time I came back from New York City, Appalachia was becoming fashionable. Academics started opening Appalachian studies programs—that kind of thing, and all those new roads were beginning to change the culture. People were no longer so isolated. By the time I was writing those dialogues and monologues, Appalachia had become truly the new rage and having an Appalachian address got you work. So I began performing those pieces in *Stories* and did a lot in this country and several other places in the world. That was when I began something of a reputation as a storyteller, except it was as an odd storyteller, first because I was doing stuff I've written with the papers in front of me, and second because they were not exactly stories, and third, they came from people I met, not me. I was a conduit as a performer, which is an idea I'm still interested in. I ended up being invited to play at some really wonderful places. Alexandro Portelli invited me to the Appalachian studies program at the University of Rome in Rome, Italy. I played a month at the Perseverance Theater in Juneau, Alaska, and any single artist [who] gets as far as Juneau, the Aleutian Arts Council flies them out along the Aleutian Archipelago. That was a most amazing trip. So I did some wonderful things with those pieces—I even played in New York City. Those things took me a lot of places.

In the meantime, one of the "real" jobs I had had—when the arts weren't paying anything and I had to get a job to pay the rent—was in the food stamp office, and there were such stories that came through there ... I ended up writing out of it. I had to. I didn't like the job, it was brutal, so something had to come of it. So I wrote another book, a collection of short stories that are not exactly stories from the food stamp office, but their genesis was the food stamp office. The title is that book is *The Last Waltz Across Texas and Other Stories*, so then I had the collection of monologues and a collection of short stories out. But somewhere about this time I began to drop out of the literary picture.

My mother had early onset Alzheimer's and I realized very quickly that if I didn't help, it was going to kill my father, too. I set out to help. Duty is big stuff in my life. It was his decision about how long we kept her, but my mother lived sixteen years with Alzheimer's and we took care of her the first eight of those years. We finally put her in an assisted living home. By that time, I had truly run out of resources—out of money and out of the picture in a whole bunch of things I wanted to be in the picture for, so I wrangled some little gigs and left on a two-week trip and when I came back, he had put her into assisted living. If I had known he would do that, I would have left much earlier. Or maybe I had to leave for him to be able to do it. All during that caregiving time, I had been keeping notes because the experience was so hard and so astonishing. So with my mother finally in a home, I decided to work on those notes. I didn't know exactly what I wanted to do with them, but what I did do was a play called *Daytrips*. It's about duty and madness and if you think it's just the Alzheimer's victim who's mad, you're very wrong. Everybody's mad.

Over the course of the time of the caregiving, Grandmother came to need as much care as my mother did, so whoever had Marie for the day would take her in the car and go to Kingsport and spend the day with Grandmother, too. My father did the most of this—I was his backup.. We eventually got somebody to live with Grandmother, but that did not go very well. She thought I should do that job. When we finally got my mother into the assisted living community, Grandmother fell a few days later and had to go in a nursing home. So for the first time in eight years, my father and I were cut lose—we didn't have either of these people to deal with 24/7. So I went out and bought the horse. [Laughter] I always wanted one. And then I started working on the play. It was very hard because I was trying to be honest, and nobody wants to know how hard such a job might really be. So I wrote *Daytrips*. It began attracting some attention early on. It played the Harford Stage Company, off–Broadway in New York, and a lot in the Eastern U.S., and then it went west: the Los Angeles Theater Center did it. The literary department at that theater decided to submit it for the Kesselring Award for Best New American play.

I had been in Los Angeles for a month or so with the rehearsal and opening of the production—I took my old Volvo and drove west by myself, quite a trip. The play had opened successfully and gotten good reviews. When I began the trip back home—the play was still running—I got to Gray Mountain, Arizona, and found the only motel for hundreds of miles—and the only one before you head up the Hopi Mesas. They advertised telephones and air-conditioning. Turned out they had all those things in the room but there was no electricity in the room [laughter] and the telephone was disconnected. So, there's no air conditioning, no telephone, no television—just a bed. There was a phone booth out in the middle of the paved parking lot, and this was a motel that truckers used, so there was a bunch of trucks in the parking lot. Everybody had pulled a chair outside of their room because it was so hot; so there are all these truckers sitting around outside their rooms looking at the view which was magnificent, and this one lit up—it had electricity—a phone booth out in the middle of the parking lot!

My father wanted me to check in occasionally on my trip to make sure I was still alive, so I went out to the lit-up phone booth and called him. He said, "There's some woman in Los Angeles who was trying to get a-hold of you, and it doesn't matter what time you call back." I asked who she was, but he just knew she was with the theater. So I asked him if I said a bunch of names, would he recognize the one who called, and when I said "Lisa Mount," he said, "That's probably it...." So I called Lisa and she said that I should go to New York, that I had won the Kesselring. So I was leaping like a cricket in the lit phone booth, and one of the truckers finally came to check on me. "Lady, are you all right?" and I yelled "Yes, yes, yes!" [Laughter] So I went to New York, attended the festivities, and picked up a check for ten thousand dollars.

So *Daytrips* was out and flying around on its own and I was back here in Johnson City writing a bunch more plays that paid nothing, and whatever I could make pay a little, when I got a call from a woman named Joy Jinks from Colquitt, Georgia. She had read *Stories I Ain't Told Nobody Yet*. A man named Richard Geer, not the actor—I just wish—was working on his Ph.D.

in theater at Northwestern University, and he had talked Joy into using Colquitt as a model for a community performance endeavor that he wanted to direct. He was writing his dissertation from this, and they needed a playwright, and Joy thought maybe I was the one to do it. I drove to Colquitt, found it was a town of about a thousand, five hundred, and that it was in terrible shape economically, and farms were being bought up by agribusiness. The courthouse was on the square in town and every shop around it was boarded up except the city's offices. They wanted me to write a play, and they wanted me to do it right then, so I worked on Joy's screened-in porch—this was in August—since Richard was staying in the house and one artist in the house was enough already for Joy's husband. That was a rough time for me; I got jerked up by the collar and told to "be careful what you say about this place—you are not from here!" It was essentially a miserable experience, and I left before the show went on because I wanted out of there so badly. I had done graduate work in geography (yeah, I went back to school), and I drove out of town the wrong way. And I drove a hundred miles out of my way to avoid going back through.

As I was leaving town, Joy asked me to please come by her office to meet with her. When I got there, she asked if I would consider being the playwright again if the play was successful. I said, "Yes," because I didn't want to be rude, but that I had to be expensive to make it worth my time. I said ten thousand dollars for the next one, figuring I had just priced myself so far out of the range of possibility, that it just wouldn't happen. The next year, they called to say they had raised the money and they wanted a new play. It was not grant money; it was local money. People had liked what they had seen and thought that it might help save Colquitt. I felt like Spirit was speaking to me again, and I really had to say "Yes." So I did.

What that project has done—it is now 20 years old—is change Colquitt, that show and some very smart people. Now, every shop around the square is open. They do a show twice a year; they've got a film studio and a conference center, and some of the most amazing murals I've ever seen. They do storytelling and community plays. And Colquitt has a reputation as a place to come get involved, and live, instead of a place to try to get out of. Art did not change the economics, but it did change people's perception of their place, and that changed the economics. I'm very proud to have been a part of it. I wrote the first six plays for Colquitt—we did some really amazing things—and along about the fourth play, other communities started going to *Swamp Gravy* to see what was going on, and I started getting calls from other places to please come do the same thing there. Colquitt and I had something of a falling out after I kept asking for more stories to build another play. We were on a short deadline and I had to have something. When the stories didn't come, I took two older stories I had that I loved and I wrote them in a different format—they were longer treatments and they used fewer actors, so they were very different from what we had done and Colquitt said, "Oh, these are not us!" They did a play I had written from the past and hired a local playwright that I mentored to write the next show. She knew local stories. Good move. My long term relationship with Colquitt weathered the difficulty and I'm very glad....

So that's how I started doing the community plays, I've done a bunch of them, and soon, I want to quit writing them and teach what I know. If I want these things to be really ongoing, and I would like for them to be, I should be mentoring playwrights, and other (younger) people interested in carrying on. I'm doing some of that now. I'm working in Sautee Nacooche, in North Georgia, and I've got a co-writer there, a fine journalist, who will eventually take over the writing on that project. My desire is to do that everywhere I'm working on plays—to leave people with the capacity to move ahead with a project without being dependent on my participation. So I'm thinking a lot about how to give that agency.

I have written a story collecting manual for people who want to go into their communities and collect stories. The first thing I tell them to do is give up on the term oral history, because when people hear that, they clam up. Nobody knows history. Just say you are collecting stories, because everybody's got stories. I talk about asking open-ended questions like, "Tell me about where you come from." That triggers a narrative impulse in your brain and you have to make narrative to answer the question. If I can teach how to think about open-ended questions, then people can collect good stories. And the single most important thing for making good story plays is good stories to pull from. There are some wonderful tricks I also teach to the interview business and a good interviewer can learn to use them.... If a person looks up, he is accessing a visual memory; if he looks side to side, it's an auditory memory; and if he is looking down, it's a feeling—a kinesthetic memory. When potential interviewers have been through the workshop, they get better stories—a little bit of training about how to ask the questions makes a world of difference. And again, human beings are hardwired to make narrative and if you can trip the narrative impulse, you can get stories.

In 2000, I had been working for about 10 years with the community projects, and I came home from one of them, got in my bed, and got a brown recluse spider bite. The learning that came out of that became the basis for my next book, *Spider Speculations: A Physics and Biophysics of Storytelling*. It came to be an amazing journey, that spider bite, which led to a new way to think, a paradigm shift, about the change I was seeing in people's lives and communities with the story plays we did, and it led me to study quantum physics and chaos theory, and energy healing. Read the book.

I kept writing the plays, they were my bread and butter for a long time, my ecological niche as a writer, and in the meantime I was performing some of the individual stories I wrote in a performance called *Liars, Thieves and Other Sinners on the Bench*. I now have another book out by that title. It is made up of some of my favorite stories from the material I have written from [or] out of the thousands of stories that came to make plays with.

By this time, I've read more oral histories than I care to shake a stick at. I did one show for Lancaster, Pennsylvania, which had about a thousand, five-hundred pages of oral history with no stories. I got a lot of analysis in Lancaster; people would talk about how they felt and what happened out of it, but they wouldn't narrate the event so you—the reader of the oral history—don't know what happened. It is very hard to make a play from analysis. I ended up spending time there collecting stories I could use. I did a play for St. Mary's, Georgia. That oral history taker there had a favorite question: "Do you have a favorite Bible verse and can you say it?" [Laughter] Or, "Do you have a favorite hymn and would you sing some of it? Just hum some...." Turns out that project only gave me about a third of the oral histories they collected—and kept the best ones for "next time." I wrote a play anyway. My favorite community to write for was the Mennonites in Newport News, Virginia. They are brave and they have such a strong literary tradition themselves, that the notion of using a metaphor isn't the least bit scary. They wanted challenging pieces, and the real challenge to this writer was that everyone was musical, a choral singer, and they wanted to do a musical play. I worked with composer named Sally Rogers, and we did some truly moving things. I worked with them on and off for ten years.

And at this point I have done about thirty of these community plays. I have watched people's lives change through telling their stories and written my *Spider* book out of that. So that's how I've spent about twenty years. There are several important premises to the community work, most important is this: It is the process of art that changes people. Somebody can watch a piece of art and be moved by it, but if they get to participate in a process of art, it will open them up in a way that just watching somebody else's product will never do. So the bottom line is inclusive: who comes, is. And if people bring special skills, it is more fun if we try to use them. Everybody who wants to participate gets to. If everybody who comes wants speaking lines, then you double and triple cast the parts until everybody has one. Some folks just want to be involved because it is fun, but everybody who comes is part of it. In the Mennonite community, we have had as many as one hundred and forty people on the stage, I made a river of them—I'm surely the only playwright in this country writing for such large casts. In the Harlan, Kentucky, project, we had ninety people on the stage. We did the show twelve times in a two-hundred-seat house and sold out almost every time.

As a writer-playwright on these projects, I try to work with the stories that come in without having to search for others. This is why getting good stories is so very important: I write from what I get in any given situation. I will almost never use all of the stories—I select, and pick what I can make work together, what I can make a cogent piece out of.

Time after time, what happens in performance is amazing, it is closer sometimes to a religious experience than it is to traditional theater because you are taking the stories of a place and playing them back to that place with people who are invested in some fashion in those stories. Sometimes you get actors who can't act their way out of a wet paper bag, and sometimes that doesn't even matter because they are invested in the story at a different level— from the heart. They sometimes have to work through some stuff and see themselves in ways they never imagined, and most of these projects, when they are ongoing, draw more and more people each time we do one. People find them extraordinary and want to be a part of the ongoing endeavor. That's the process of art....

I have worked with a series of directors, including Richard Geer (and his partner Jules Corriere) and Lisa Mount, and a man named Gerald Stropnicky of the Bloomsburg Theatre Ensemble in Pennsylvania. Jerry says he has a recurring nightmare that he will spend the rest of this life making safe art for audiences who go home and feel good about it. This community business (says Jerry) is anything but safe art.

For instance: Robert Gipe (and his collaborators) got a grant from Rockefeller to address drug problems in Harlan County, Kentucky. There had been crooked doctors there who were serving their commitment from medical school to spend at least five years in a rural community that was "under doctored." Harlan. And they began selling Oxycontin prescriptions; they had lines outside their offices that were just there to collect the prescriptions, and people were re-selling the drugs. Harlan became the source of the Oxy problem in the east. It was a place where a lot of the drug was already being prescribed because coal mining is hurtful work. Then people with no pain at all—just the story of pain—started getting prescriptions. It was a huge problem before anybody realized what was going on. These guys were charging sixty dollars per office visit, writing a prescription to anybody who wanted it and making a boatload of money. They are now—I understand—both sitting in a jail in Kentucky. If you ask them why they did what they did, it is because they wanted the money. When they were closed down, people with legitimate prescriptions were attacked and robbed with astounding regularity because this drug is truly addictive. So this was the beginning of the drug problem there and some of the corrosive history. It's bad in other places, but it's terrible in Harlan.

Before we started writing the play *Higher Ground*, the guy who was running for sheriff on an anti-drug platform was killed right before the election. He won anyway, and then they held the runoff election and he almost won again on the write-in votes. So there was an underground of drug trafficking and drug culture in that place, and a frightened community that would vote anti-drug, but didn't want to say anything out loud; too likely to get shot. We were supposed to talk about the situation in the play. I was sitting over here in Johnson City, relatively safe, writing about this. Then the man running for sheriff got killed and people got scared. So when I turned the play in, everybody went "ah [expletive], we can't do this," and they re-wrote the play, and turned the second script in to director Jerry Stropnicky. He said, "This script is a dead chicken and I can't produce a dead chicken," and he started putting the play I wrote back together, increment by increment until we had essentially the script I had written. People were worried, but there were ninety who wanted to participate, and you can't very well kill ninety people. We had two bluegrass bands participating—we had incredible music. We did a play that talked about how the drug trouble came, and used the story of a man who died of his Oxy addiction over the course of it, and how he came to die. His wife told us the story. We have now done a second play in Harlan. We have many of the same problems, and some of us have considerably less hair than we did when we started. Not safe art, eh Jerry? Not the least bit easy, either.

I'm currently doing new stuff—a commission—it is another story for the Orchard at Altapass. I've done two previous stories for them that make up another of my books, *Teller Tales: Histories*. One of those stories was about the Overmountain Men and the Battle of Kings Mountain, a slice of Revolutionary War history. The second was about white–Cherokee relationships during that same time period. The two stories Colquitt rejected those years before served me well.... I used the same format in this material. The Orchard is my cousins' apple orchard on the Blue Ridge Parkway in North Carolina.

Do you know the 1800s story of Frankie Silver who was hung by the State of North Carolina for killing her husband? Sharon McCrumb wrote one of her ballad-novels of it. Well, twenty miles away on the Yellow Mountain Trail—it was Bright's Trace before it was the Yellow Mountain Trail— on land that's now the orchard, concurrent with the Frankie Silver business, lived a man named Charlie McKinney and his four wives—four to seven wives—nobody is sure exactly how many, and 48 children.

Now, Charlie McKinney is an interesting character. He started up there with a hundred and fifty acre land grant. By the time he died he had almost 1,500 acres and was a well-to-do man, a prosperous farmer in a place where there was not all that much prosperity. I mean, this is the crest of the Blue Ridge, along what's now the Blue Ridge Parkway. He and those women had forty-eight children and raised them every one. When Charlie McKinney died, he left his property to his wives and not to his sons, which was unheard of at that time, because women weren't allowed to own property. It tied that property up in court and the women lived on it until after they died, which means Charlie McKinney did manage to give it to them for the rest of their lives.

When you study what is available in the record and the stories, Charlie McKinney took in women. If he was a bounder, he was—at least—a responsible bounder; if he got them pregnant, he took care of them and the children. But it looks like more than that. It looks like the McKinneys (Charlie and his legal wife, Elizabeth) were taking in women who needed help. At least two of them had children by other marriages.... By the time there were 1500 acres to farm, they slaughtered fifty to seventy hogs a year up there—people ate well. He built each of the wives a separate home and she lived there with her children. None of them are fancy or big. He had a bear skin and the story is he laid it down at the door where he wanted to spend the night, but the woman had the right to move it. You know what the right to say "no" was in the early 1800s? A woman was a man's property then.

So the McKinney women had rights in a way that Frankie Silver just didn't.... Frankie Silver killed an abusive husband, and Frankie Silver hung for what should have been a misdemeanor crime. So I compared and contrasted those two stories. There's more even connection with the orchard—Frankie Silver may be buried there on what was Charlie McKinney's property. The legend is that her father dug three graves on the way home. She had become something of a cause célèbre and he was afraid somebody would try to dig up her bones. One of them was in what is now the orchard and family story says she's buried there. The piece is called *A Tale of Two Charlies* and you can see it at the Orchard.

The Orchard at Altapass: About fifteen years ago, my cousin Kit, who was a realtor in the Triangle area of North Carolina and had made some money, was moving up to Little Switzerland because her brother and his wife already lived there, and saw in the local paper that this orchard was for sale. As it happened, there were four phone calls from developers about the property on the man's answering machine, but the owner came home and picked up Kit's call first and sold it to her, because she promised to keep it out of the hands of developers. There are not many pieces of private property that directly adjoin the parkway. And so my cousins decided to see if they couldn't resurrect the old orchard. It was planted originally by the Clinchfield Railroad which comes through Altapass. The building of the Clinchfield is a story in itself, because going down the escarpment, the Loops on the Clinchfield start at the orchard and run thirteen miles and eighteen tunnels to go three miles down hill. The orchard land was the staging area for building the loops. There are some heritage apple trees up there. My cousins have worked at it for fifteen years. My brother is now working with them and I've been writing for them. The Orchard sits on what was the Yellow Mountain Trail that comes through the gorge on the Nolichucky River. The Overmountain Men came that way to the Battle of Kings Mountain, so I wrote that story. I got interested in white–Cherokee relations on this side of the mountain while writing it.

A Cherokee war chief, Dragging Canoe, literally turned this part of the country in the 1780s version of the Gaza strip. He did not hold with the Transylvania Purchase, and broke from his father and the elder chiefs. He waged a guerilla war and led a group that came to be called the Chickamaugas. His arch enemy was the Overmountain Men hero, John Sevier. We did that show at the Orchard, too, because John Sevier was charged with treason over the State of Franklin business and he was hauled to Marion, North Carolina to stand trial over the Yellow Mountain Trail. It was *the* road. These two history stories constitute another of my books, *Teller Tales: Histories*.

Angelyn DeBord

An early practitioner of "storytelling as theater," the storyteller, actress, playwright, visual artist and director Angelyn DeBord has performed and led workshops throughout America and in Europe. Her original plays have appeared on PBS and have been featured at the Carnegie Museum, Los Angeles Center for the Arts, the Kennedy Center, and the Spoleto Festival. Her performances share the sounds, textures and imagery of her own rich and complex heritage.

A founding member of Appalshop's Roadside Theater, her work reflects thirty years of commitment to encouraging young and old alike to honor their unique voices and heritage. Her theater workshops have led community participants to successfully perform on stages across America.

DeBord received a Rockefeller Humanities Fellowship in 2003 to pursue her interest in story theater. The results of this fellowship were published in the *Journal of Appalachian Studies*, Volume 9, Number 2. Among her playwright credits is the critically acclaimed *Praise House*. Written for the Urban Bush Women dance company of New York City, *Praise House* has toured all over America and was a featured play at the Spoleto Festival; it was also performed at the Kennedy Center and produced for PBS.

DeBord was born in the Smoky Mountains of North Carolina, and among her touring performances are *Lessons on Becoming a Woman*, based on Appalachian folktales, including ballads and original songs. *Homemade Tales* is an energetic, humorous, and often personal collection of folk stories, heavily laced with real life memories with a strong emphasis on Appalachian culture and dialect; *Stubborn Memories* is an original one-woman show that reflects the "growing up years" of a young woman in the Smoky Mountains in the 1960s.

DeBord's workshops *Creating Original Material* and *Telling Your Own Story* stimulate participants to explore their own memories and impressions.

Both workshops provide participants with the tools to create and perform their own original material based on their life experiences. Angelyn DeBord is married to Anthony Slone and lives on a farm on Clinch Mountain, near Snowflake, Virginia.

The Interview

I grew up in a holler in Swain County, North Carolina, called Toot Holler, and it was where my granny and pawpaw lived, and my aunts and uncles and all my cousins. My granny would stand on her porch and look up and down that holler and she'd say, "Now, Honey, you see that? That's my string of pearls," and she'd be talkin' about all of the houses of her children who lived in the holler.

**Angelyn DeBord
(courtesy Kentucky Arts Council)**

My granny was a Chambers. She was born on Chambers Creek and they'd been there six generations—they had deep roots in Chambers Creek, so when TVA [Tennessee Valley Authority] came in to build a dam and to flood the area to provide electricity—they had one building that served as the school house, community center and church, and the *suits* came in to tell them they were taking their land—I just can't imagine ... and these *suits* were there and everybody came to hear what they had to say, and my pawpaw, he would tell me, over and over, he'd say, "Your granny stood up there and she spoke agin it."

At that time, for a woman to stand up and speak out in public was a big deal, and I said, "Well, Pawpaw, did you say anything?" You see, he had married into the family—he had moved there from Balsam, some thirty miles away, and he was from "off." And he said, "Honey, I was like a barrel hoop. I was all around it, but not in it ... kept my mouth shut." It wasn't his family; he was married into it, but not of it. Of course, they ended up flooding it: Hazel Creek, Chambers Creek. It was that whole valley that was gone. Sometimes, later on, Daddy would take us out on a boat out on the Fontana Lake and we would literally ride the boat over the land that laid down deep,

deep below us ... the land where Granny had played as a child. Now flooded and gone.

My mama is now eighty-six years old and just this past weekend we were talkin' about Granny. What got us started talking about her is the snow still sticking to the ground, and I said, "It's so ugly, and I just wish it'd melt and go away!" And she said, "You know what your granny would have said? 'It's hangin' around waitin' on another un,'" and I said, "That's what I'm afraid of!"

When I was little, we were never allowed to use certain words like *devil*. When I started telling stories like "Jack and the Devil," I had to get over that. You couldn't say *devil*, you couldn't say *liar*, and you couldn't say *fool*. So instead of saying "you're lyin'," you had to say, "You're telling a story." It's interesting that I became a storyteller [laughter], oh, and we had a pump organ, but you couldn't bring a fiddle in the house, either, so I play a fiddle and tell stories ... I'm a backslider!

My granny told us stories about growin' up in the mountains and about her daddy—her daddy was her favorite. She told stories about clearing new ground with him. The timber was really big when she was a girl. She'd get on one end of a crosscut saw and help her daddy fell them huge trees. She said her daddy liked the way she did it, because she didn't "ride the saw."

Here's a poem I wrote. It goes out to all the grannies that ever were:

Poems of Ancient Grannies

Oh, ancient grannies
where are your poems?
Not written on the hallowed pages beside
the words of
Milton or Blake
Shelley or Byron
I do not find them written there.

Not penned down,
your words are lifted up,
written in the air
clear before my searching eyes

And even to my ear
the cadence of your poems is heard
in the rhythm
of the clear eyed man
he's been mothered well I think
I see his mother's poetry
written above his clear bright eyes

words sketched with a tender hand
across that smooth forehead

Ancient grannies
I know your words were sweet and strong
when I see your grandbabies
tilt their ear
at a whimsical phrase or a lilting song

Your poetry throbs in my blood
in the images of my dreams
in the cycles of my life
words strong with pictures
of what was and is and will be
written not on hallowed pages
but secretly written in my veins
secretly written there with your blood.

My granny does live on—it seems like every time we open our mouths we are saying something she said. She was so undemanding, but that's not really a good description of her. Modern words don't really fit her. She never, ever had an unkind word for anybody and she worked all the time. She was always 100 percent present with you, all the time; so dependable and steady, with such a good sense of humor, and sort of a little bit of a mean streak, sense of humor-wise. [Chuckle] She teased pretty hard sometimes....

If my granny was still alive today, she would be one-hundred-thirteen years old. She lived to ninety-eight, and I would still keep her; I don't care how old she would be—she should never have left—I still can't believe she's not with us.

I'm just entrenched in nothing but language and the sounds of the mountain. All of my family has been in North Carolina forever, and it's strange that I'm not there, too, but I can't afford to be. It costs too much and it's so developed now. It's so developed, and so many people. I'm sorry, but where I live now, in the mountains of Virginia is not developed at all.... Don't tell anyone, but land is still affordable here.

Appalachia and especially the Smoky Mountains where I grew up, it is just amazing. I can hear the water, and there are voices in the water. You know the women would go to the water for arthritis and get in it and submerge themselves. I wrote a whole story about that—that's what they'd do—it's an old Cherokee custom. And the Cherokee would take their babies and dip them in the water every day for two years for health—the Tuckasegee River–Oconaluftee River on the Cherokee boundary and the Little Tennessee—that's *cold* water there, and a big part of my childhood. They called it the Long Man. The river is so alive; the creeks and rivers just tell stories all the time. They have so much to say, and it's the same water that was there in the earliest times and this poem is about that river.

River Poem

The smoke floated low on the water
hanging there gathering in forms
like women with long grey hair
hovering with only tipsy toes touching the water

the trees lay bare and supine
graceful long limbed women
lazing in the gentle currents
their branches touching overhead
fingertips joined in prayer

up on the cliffs
the hawks squawked
and squealed
wheeled and dipped
furiously engaged
in battle with their
ancient enemy crow

and constant constant was the sound of the water on the shoals
a veiling sound
protecting our hearing
from the hard edged voices of
the world

Clingman's Dome is six thousand feet high, and Deep Creek is where the big waterfalls are; it's always a spiritual thing for me when I go there. Every time I go home I go to the water and I submerge some part of me and get a little baptizin'. The creeks, rivers and the waterfalls were just a bike ride from my house growin' up, and I head straight to them when I'm there. My mother, who didn't swim, would take us to the edge of the creek and sit there. She watched us play and learn to swim and she taught us "no fear," which I find phenomenal for somebody who didn't swim. She showed not a shred of fear for any of us in the water, and we all grew up to be water rats— we just loved it. She'd just sit there and never make us afraid—she just let us go. That's the way she was which I appreciate so much. She's still sharp as a tack, a lovely woman.

We were so raw; I had never seen a professional storyteller back then— there weren't any, but my daddy was *such* a storyteller, and he loved words so much. He had memorized huge, long poems in what they called 'noration. You'd 'norate at school standing by your desk everyday, and they'd recite all kinds of things—long, long poems like my daddy could do. His whole family was like that. They all loved language. They were from Whittier, North Carolina—that's between Cherokee and Bryson City, and I think they were Huguenots. They had a settlement on the bend of the Tuckasegee River and they were right there when the Trail of Tears happened. The story is that when the English came in and burned the Cherokee settlement down, the Huguenots helped them rebuild. I have Cherokee blood, and my last name is DeBord, which is a Huguenot name. The Huguenots were there probably back into the 1700s. We don't really know very much about our family history, but my family names are DeBord, Muse, Chambers and Boyd.

That holler where I grew up was at the foot of Clingman's Dome, so we had bears and wild hogs and panthers and all kinds of imagination things in the woods to play with. We had almost unlimited freedom and there was a gang of us, and we were creating all the time. We didn't have toys, like Walmart stuff; we might-a had one pack of marbles for the whole gang that we played marbles with, and we made up things, with the sifter and spoons that we scavenged from the kitchen.

There was a cave there, and we'd go up there and play. We built shelves into the walls and we saved candle nubs, and the boys would smuggle things up there like cigarettes and playing cards. I wrote a play about it called *Stubborn Memories* and it gives a visual of my early years. There was a barn there, and a cousin reminded me about it after he came to see *Stubborn Memories*, and he said I used to write and direct plays there, and that I was real bossy then. I don't remember that part, but we'd have performances up there and invite the elders to come see them. He also said I did a sacrificial funeral pyre for a frog. He said I built this whole thing inside of sticks and rocks, and I roasted that frog so we wouldn't have any more warts ever again on all of the earth. I don't remember that either, but it's what he said. Back then it was a world of creaking rocking chairs and wind, the sound of people's voices as they went about their business laughing, working—it was harmony, plus the wild, raucous sounds of the kids playing. We were wild. We got so much freedom! I've thought a lot about my childhood; people just left me alone, you know?

I had to go to school finally—we didn't have kindergarten, and I was this storytellin', livin' thing, and what do you think they said when I went to school? Sit down, shut up, smack on my hand, right? So I started settin' up behind my school books and drawing my stories. So the stories were still in there, and I was just drawing, drawing, drawing, you know; I was highly visual, but I pretty much gave up on the talkin' part of the storytelling world.

When I got out of high school, I went off to Appalachian State University and studied visual arts, because by this time that was what I longed for, the world of stories, and for me, that had become painting and drawing, not speaking stories out, but staying entrenched in the visual world. I finished my degree there and then I went to Europe and lived there for a year. That was the first time I'd ever seen real paintings ... Picasso, Matisse, Degas ... my head was spinning and I loved living in Europe. All the sights and sounds. I got jobs all over and worked while I was there. Independent as a hog on ice! What a wonderful gift to give myself and I did that. I will never ever forget that time. It was an amazing year; a totally wonderful, amazing year.

When I came back, I ended up at Appalshop in Whitesburg, Kentucky, as a documentary filmmaker in training. What was interesting about Appalshop was that when I moved there to Letcher County it was isolated, and like a Third World country. This man from Connecticut [Bill Richardson, the founder of Appalshop] had gotten a grant from the Office of Economic Opportunity to do some work there, and he was an architecture student from Yale. And when he went there, he got some of those high school kids involved in documentary filmmaking. They were going out and filming their grandparents butchering hogs, or cock fights, or makin' liquor—they were just filming what was going on in their families, so when the time came when they had finished high school, and it was time to go off to college—and they did—but instead of goin' to Hollywood to become filmmakers, their work by this time was so compelling that it was starting to get national notice, and they were getting awards, so they ended up staying there and creating Appalshop, which is the Appalachian Film Workshop. Our Appalachian kids were filming Appalachian people, so it was real organic. I ended up there because my cousin had ended up there, and my uncle had died and my cousin said, "You need to come up here." I got up there and got involved in the training program immediately. It started in 1969 and I was there in '73, so I was there right near the beginning—early on, but not the first wave.

I was working on some films and there was this wonderful guy named Don Baker there, and we got to be real good friends, and he said, "You know, I just love to hear you tell stories about your family." Now I was reluctant, but we started going out into the little schools in that county and telling them folktales ... stories we'd heard growing up and other tales. Now storytelling was not anything that was being done on a public level, like it is now—it was still homegrown, but anyway, we went to the schools and told some of the stories we grew up hearing to these little kids. I was terrified. You see, by this time I was behind an easel, behind a camera ... and my voice was ... I was a silent creature. I remember bein' in this little one-room schoolhouse in Kingdom Come, Kentucky. So, even in that little one-room school house I told stories in my mumbling, fumbling, terrified way, and this little girl came up to me—I was in my early twenties, and she said, "You sound just like my mommy," and I said, "Do I?" And she said, "Yeah. You don't reckon my mommy could get up in front of people and tell stories like that, do you?" And I said, "I bet she could!" So then I realized what I was doing there was important. It wasn't about me.

Later, I was one of the original members of the Roadside Theater. Still, it took me two years being on the frontline of performing, of storytelling ... we were down at a festival in St. Petersburg, Florida, and we were doing a show—I played an old mountain woman—it was *Pretty Polly*, and I was up there making my way through it ... mumbling, terrified and suddenly I felt a light, and something like a hole opened up in me ... and man, I knew then "This is the *call*! This is *alive*!" This hole opened up inside of me, and I heard a voice say, "Honey, it's through you, not from you." It's like at that moment my voice shifted and went *boom!* Of course, it ain't about me. I'll be long gone, but maybe the story will survive. I thought of all the people in my family who had not spoken out; people in my region had not told their stories ... if I can either encourage them to, or speak and tell their story where others can hear it? Yes ma'am, I need to get out of the way. I was just in the way. From then on, I just did it. Now, on a stage, tellin' stories, it's my favorite place on earth ... it's the most secure ... it is home—my place. From there I started writing mountain plays and tellin' mountain tales.

Since then, I've been in just about every state in the union, performing, and leading workshops in communities, even in London, England. Then, in the early '90s, I ended up writing a play for the Urban Bush Women, and that caught on like wildfire. I went with them to many different places, including the Spoleto Festival in Charleston. The play I wrote was called *Praise House*. What was so cool about that was that I got to be in the back of the theater as it was being "created," writing for the performers and handing the pages to the director for her to give to the actors. It was created on the spot—I had a loose script, a story, but then it became more and more specific as I got to know the actors, and understood their cadence and the language. I knew what I could do there and what I could create, so it was really a wonderful experience. It was a phenomenal experience and I was humbled. I sat there humbled by the opportunity and what was so cool was that all the while, I was telling a story about my growing up. It had an amazing, so very talented, African American cast, and a story about an African American visionary in the thirties who saw angels everywhere and in the final scene, the protagonist says, "Draw or die." And we better do that, right? We better draw or we will surely die ... maybe not our bodies but something else inside us will die. And drawing, well, you have to figure out what that means for you. What does it mean to you when the angels tell you, "Draw or die?"

Before I started this bout of going to college, again, I spent a lot of time writing, and a lot of what I use now came from those writings—I pull material from novels I've written, but haven't published yet, and I make my one-woman shows from them. There are still some yet to do.

Performing for me is like serving hors d'oeuvres to the crowd, making sure everybody can hear, and gets equal servings of whatever I'm offering. Material selection is the biggest thing for me—we have to have a diverse selection of stories because you never know where you may be telling stories next. You have to pick what you are going to tell 'em and sometimes I wait until I get there. Usually I do the best when I don't have anything planned—I just pick it up when I go in; I feel it. Sometimes when I plan, I'm never completely sure I've picked the right stories and the right story is very important: you can't just pick any old thing! That's one reason I like having specific one-woman shows where I can focus on content. I'm not making choices, I'm there to perform. I'm not just there for storytelling—it's like, this is what you're here for and the audience knows it. Then you can invest in just that and retain the focus.

In my shows, sometimes I tell some pretty heavy-duty things from my own family history, like my aunt who got very sick and had to leave her family. This story is told in my one-woman show called *Stubborn Memories*. This is all in the holler, and all of us were in close proximity, watching this and seeing the family's reaction and seeing who's gonna take care of the five kids she had ... she was married at fifteen. She went off for treatments and Granny absorbed the kids. Some of it I can't even think of without cryin', let alone share the stories. I'm pullin' on memories from the sixties, and late fifties. I was nine, maybe eleven years old, and some of the stories that I tell in this performance, stories that I have made up, I think, hit me harder than what I actually remember. I mean, something that I have created that I think would be good to put in this part ... and I present it as family history with freedom of interpretation. Memory is relevant anyway—there's no *one* way to remember anything, but most of it is factual. There is one scene that is so intimate, and as far as I know, I made it up, but I can hardly do this scene because it's so emotional to me. Every time I hit that segment [deep intake of breath] I have to prepare for it. To me, those are the best stories—those are the ones that take me so far into a place of fear, or terror and bring all of us back. We go there and we come back. I think that is what is missing in a lot of television and movies—catharsis—they don't really give you that. It is also a catharsis for me, and every time I do it, my whole psyche goes into the healing circle of the experience and back, so I know you can come back.

I've come to an understanding that for the past thirty years I have been doing ritual. Now that I work as a therapist and people come to me, what I do is I help them tell their stories. It's so important to remember the good stories, too. I know there's nothing like going through the actual telling of a story yourself. The actual speaking it [swooshing sound] and the coming back—even some of the scary mountain tales that I tell, that really go to some far places and then come back, are healing. There's something to it, especially since I've spent the last year, while I've been in graduate school, away from performance stories. Now I'm more aware of it. I've just, on purpose, taken this year as a sabbatical away from storytelling, and I can't wait to get back to it. It's part of me, and I can't live without it.

Storytelling is healing, and yet we live in a world that resists the healing that storytelling can provide. There's sometimes impatience with story, and with the storyteller. It's like that with the land, too, and a lot like strip mining. A mountain and a forest are very similar to stories. The mountains have so many hidden meanings and nuances. The mountains tell a wonderful story if anyone cares to listen. But, if greed steps in, the story is annihilated. No one remembers the story. They want coal, not secrets to living. The rape and pillage of mountain land in the name of strip-minin' or mountain top removal, it's always there, hidden in my mind and in my heart. I will never forget the very first time I laid eyes on a mountain that had been destroyed for the coal it contained. I don't think I can ever get over my outrage and the injustice of this horrible destruction.

The Kentucky Hills: A Bad Rap!

I think of the children,
they're young and they're willing,
to lift up their wings and to fly.

But their way it is tangled,
don't let them be mangled,
by the greed that we
pass down the line.

I lift mine eyes up now unto these hills
from whence always my help it has come.
I holler, "God help us.
Man's greed it has scalped us,
for a strange definition of wealth."

The mountains we love now,
God knows they're our home now,
they've helped, they've held us for years.
But the land of our mother is now seeking cover
as the bulldozers strip off her crown.

What God has created,
Man's greed's laid asunder.
You can't build a mountain back up.

> But our children have voices,
> let's raise them to use them,
> together we can save this land.
>
> Yes, together we can save this land.
> Say: together we can save this land.
> Pray: together we can save this land.

I have had so much prejudice against me because I am a "hillbilly" from the mountains—that kind of prejudice is alive and well today, believe me. People still mock us. Even on radio or television programs where there are all sorts of cutting-edge news and politically correct programs, people still will talk about ignorant hillbillies and good writers will use the word "hillbilly" in a derogatory way, too. It's still "okay" to talk about the ignorant "hillbilly," but it ain't okay with me! That's why I've kind of been an underground panther with Appalachian people, helping them find and use their voices to be stronger and more confident.

Poem about Voice

> I want to isolate my voice
> hide in the mountains where my voice will only echo upon itself
>
> The wind on the mountain gives my voice to me
> and the water on the rocks hitting splash
> and listen to the hawk squealing on the high air currents
> and the night birds
> and the morning birds
> and the high trees with their wind roar
>
> I listen to these every day
> and I hear the stillness too
> the sound a mountain makes when it moves
> I hear this
>
> and I have
> and I have
> in a world full of wanting
> I have.

It has gotten more and more difficult to find money for performance projects with the economy like it is now. There was money for the arts in the recent past, and there were a lot of programs that I could tap into. I'm a fundraiser—I've had to be. I write proposals ... and find angles and ways to bring things into communities for people who need it, but now there are more restrictions than ever.

I just worked with a community to create a play with some women who had never spoken in public before. There were seven of them and they did a performance about their growin' up years in a very isolated area of eastern Kentucky. The play was called *It's About Time*. The oldest member of the cast was sixty-five and the youngest was forty. It was just so strong and they were so beautiful, too, and they spoke to the audience the whole time, telling their own stories about their own lives, with their own beautiful voices. During our story circles, when we were still creating the material to later be used in the play, these women talked about menstruation rituals and they wanted to tell about them. I was amazed. They were sharing their stories and I said, "Would this be something you would like to put into the play?" and they said, "Yes!" Without any shyness they hit it. Talkin' about rags and rituals and women who helped 'em go through things.

In the play they tell a really amazin' story. This one woman, who is now 65, tells about sitting there at her desk in this little one room schoolhouse and looking out at the big schoolhouse windows at this little house across the creek. From the schoolhouse, you could get to the house over this little bridge. A woman named Aunt Sarah lived in that house. So, in the play, this woman is tellin' this story. She's talkin' about this woman called Aunt Sarah who has this little house across the creek and she's sittin' there watchin' the smoke come out of the chimney. She talked about watchin' Aunt Sarah in the spring time workin' in her garden and shaking her rugs, but what interested her most was she would see these girls go up and whisper to the teacher and then go out the door and over that little bridge to Aunt Sarah's house, and then they'd come back in a little bit, and she said, "That's what I always wanted to have happen." They said, "What she give us was rags," and then this woman's voice came in and said, "That's what girls had to wear back then—there wasn't any pads; they just wore rags they would have to wash out at night, you see," and they used that language telling about girls going across this bridge ... they'd leave this one-room school, goin' on their journey to becoming a woman.

What those girls were doing, is that Aunt Sarah was taking care of them, and giving them rags to wear. That's a ritual story—crossing the bridge and all, and the audience just loved it. You could hear a pin drop when they were telling these things. These women, who'd really never spoken out in front of other people before, told about all kinds of things like when the first cars came into the area; they talked about the Indian trails when the settlers first came in there, and the pack-peddler who got murdered while he was bending over to get water from the spring. He got murdered and how men took his body and took it from ridge to ridge to keep it away from the law when they were comin' and lookin' for them; how there was a door knob that somebody had picked up there at the spring that fell out of the peddler's pack.

They took it home and put it in their door and that knob would turn.... And they talked about how one of the grandpaws would wrap up in an old sheet and get down in the ditch and the kids would come by and he would scare them.

What an honor to get to hear these stories and help them tell 'em. Once I get through with this schooling, I've got to get back to it. I just have to find the way to package it all together with the healing arts and do what I do, because it is healing, by God! Whatever it takes, you know? Because it is real easy not to have a voice; I know, I've been there and I still have moments when it is terrifying to use my voice. I was called to use my voice—it wasn't my choice. I grew up with "Fools names and fools faces are always seen in public places." You just didn't put yourself out there. One of those seven women said in her story that she was told when she was little that if a car came, "run and hide." We were isolated then and it was appropriate for that time and place, but not now. There are too many important things we need to speak out about, I think.

My life's work has been one of helping people find and shape their own voice in their own manner without interfering, but keeping that place as true as I can, and I've seen people grow by leaps and bounds by being able to do that. At this point, I think of my life's work as survival! [Laughter] I have a garden and I'm in graduate school in professional counseling. I wish I could have been an old granny-woman, but I can't do that. These times just won't let that be! I mean, we live in a 120-year-old house and it is paid off, and we've got a lot of land and I don't need much, but I've always wanted a master's degree. A program opened in a college nearby ... well, I drive 35 miles to go there, so in December 2010, I'll get my master's in education in professional counseling. If anyone out there can figure out how to make the world of survival easier for those who are called to be storytellers, then, maybe they'll share it with us. If you need us, let us know. It is a hard and sometimes lonesome row to hoe. We can get to the end of one row and then, right away, start in on another 'un. It's a big ole garden, for sure, and there's always plenty of work to do. All we can do is hope we get more than one life to do all we dream of doing. All we can do is work hard and pray for a fruitful crop.

Elizabeth Ellis

Storyteller Elizabeth Ellis grew up in both Tennessee and Kentucky in a family of storytellers. She began her career as a children's librarian in Texas at the Dallas Public Library. She tells personal stories about growing up in Appalachia, as well as stories of heroic American women, Appalachian folktales, and the stories and legends of her adopted state, Texas.

Ellis has shared her stories at festivals and special events all over America for more than thirty years and was recognized as a "master storyteller" in 1997 by her peers at the National Storytelling Network with the Circle of Excellence Award. She is a favorite at the prestigious National Storytelling Festival and has been the teller-in-residence at the International Storytelling Center. In 1986 she was the recipient of the John Henry Faulk Award, presented by the Tejas Storytelling Association for a sustained and significant contribution to storytelling in Texas.

A respected teacher of storytellers, Ellis conducts weekend intensives, as well as workshops for teller growth, teacher training and parent education. She is a popular keynote speaker for conferences and conventions.

With Loren Niemi, she is the co-author of the award winning book *Inviting the Wolf In: Thinking About Difficult Stories*, published by August House. She has produced four CDs of her personal stories: *Mothers and Daughters, Meddling at Wal-Mart, Wading in the Jordan* and *One Size Fits Some*.

She is a mother and a grandmother, which she considers her most significant accomplishment.

The Interview

I guess I have to start with my parents' story. When my father went away to fight in World War II, he left his wife, and his son and his baby-baby daughter with his wife's mother and father, as many, many men did. When my mother discovered he was not coming home from the war, instead of staying with her mom and dad where we would have always been welcome, she packed us up bag and baggage and moved us from her parents' home in Kentucky to Tennessee to live in the house my father had been born in; to live next door to his brother and his sister, and across the street from his aunt and uncle, and in the middle of all his aunts, uncles and cousins in an effort to keep him alive for us—in an effort to see we grew up knowing as much about him as we humanly could.

When I tell people I grew up in Tennessee and in Kentucky, they think it means I lived in one place and then I moved to another place, and the truth is, I grew up in both of those places at the same time. Everyday that school was closed two days in a row, we went home, and home was always her mother and father's house. So I grew up in Tennessee, but I also grew up in Kentucky at the same time. My life was different ... in each place different, but similar in each place. Went to school here in Tennessee; better schools than we would have gotten in Kentucky in that very, very rural area—more opportunities to see things and have a bigger picture of the world than had I only grown up in Kentucky, but in Kentucky, among my mother's people, was the storytelling thread that ran through everything they did and a closeness with aunts and uncles and grandparents that didn't exist here in Tennessee, even though we lived in the middle of my father's people. I want to say that everything I know about my father I know because somebody took the time to tell me a story. I wouldn't really know anything about the man at all if weren't for that. There were stories about what he did and who he was, but the truth is I learned far more about that in Kentucky among the Kentucky people he went to live with than I learned right here among his own family. Most of the stories I heard about my father I heard from my grandparents—my mother's parents, her brothers and sisters—people who had been my

Elizabeth Ellis
(photograph by Charlie Mauk)

father's students, people who had been his friends. The picture I have of him is much more rich than I would have had as a child living here in Tennessee, even though I was brought up mostly among the Ellises. They're not talky people; never been talky people.

My mother's people, on the other hand, are a collection of traditional storytellers and raconteurs. My grandfather the Rev. I. H. Gabbard was a circuit riding preacher. More than fifty years, he rode through the mountains on horseback doing the marrying, the burying, and the preaching. Couldn't go home, couldn't go to a motel at night—too far to ride back home; he would go home with some family and spend the night. Before the days of television, he would hear their stories in this community, and ride on down the road to Lerose or Traveler's Rest or whatever; do it all over again—go home with a family from that church and tell what he heard from the night before in your front room to those folks; take those stories that he heard there and take them on down the road to the next church for more than half a century, spanning a time from the late 1890s all the way up to when I was a little girl in the 1950s. He never learned to drive. In his older years, people would come and get him in a car and take him places, but he, until very late in his life and when I was still a child, he was still on horseback going to specific churches to preach or to bury people. He was a repository for an enormous number of stories. I wish I could remember even a little corner of what my grandfather knew. Probably was somebody who should have been recorded by the Library of Congress because of that special set of circumstances, but of course when he was still living that thought never dawned on me—never in my lifetime thought about that until he had made this journey way over Jordan.

I think that one of the richest things about my life as a child is that each of my grandfather's parents came from a really strong storytelling strain. Gabbard is about as German as it gets. Michael Gabbard, my grandfather's father ... Michael Gabbard's people have been in the Appalachian Mountains since before the Revolution—that would be the *American Revolution* [said with a characteristic pause and tilt of the head] in case you have some other one on your mind [chuckle], but there was all that traditional story that we might think of today as the Appalachian mountain versions of Grimm's fairytales—mountain versions of a lot of those old stories that come from those Germanic heritages.

My grandfather's mother, Mary Ann Mangan, came from Ireland. My grandfather used to tell me she came from Ireland on a sailboat. [Laughter] When I was little I had this picture of something the size of a rowboat going across the ocean. I realize now that what he was trying to tell me was that she came on a sailing ship.... I didn't really get that when I was younger. And of course, with her she brought a huge—she was the most recent immigrant in our family—she came just before the Civil War and was my grandfather's mother, and knew a huge, huge strain of the Irish, Scottish, English kind of folk tales. After she had lived in the mountains for some time, she began to tell them more and more the way mountain people talk.

My aunt Ida—Ida Mae Moore—would have been her granddaughter Mary Ann Mangan's granddaughter. She was the finest storyteller that ever drew breath. She never told anywhere except on her own front porch or the upstairs bedroom at my grandmother's house and maybe sometimes to her elementary school class when she taught, but she was an amazing repository of story. I think sometimes men and women are drawn to tell different stories; men are much more drawn to tell tall tales, big folk tales, enormous whoppers, huntin' and fishin' stories—he fires the gun and ends up killin' the fourteen-point buck that catches the ducks, the fish ... [laughter] the bigger the better. I don't know that women are usually drawn to that kind of story.

Most women, it seems to me—most women who live in a more traditional way—are drawn to keep the old fairy tales alive and to tell romances, and to tell stories about things that happened in the community that men don't necessarily feel drawn to. Stories about family secrets and family curses; although men tell ghost stories and women tell ghost stories, they are often drawn to different kinds of ghost stories. Most ghost stories that I know that I've learned from women are not about revenge; they are about protecting people that you love, or unrequited love, or that boundary between the living and the dead, coming back to give a message or to protect somebody or help them, all of that kind of stuff.

Although my aunt Ida told stories and my grandpa told stories and they told some of the same stories, each of them also had really, really pockets full of tales that the other one didn't tell. "I don't know that story. You'll have to ask Aunt Ida; ask Ida, she'll tell you that." "Go ask Grandpa, I don't know that story, I never told that story." They just had different tales.

My uncles were storytellers—my mother's brothers—several of them were storytellers of the raconteur tradition. They didn't tell folk tales, or if they did you didn't know it was a folk tale; it was always starring the person telling the story, who was always the main character in that huntin' and fishin' yarn and "big windy" tradition, and all of that.

I'm really grateful that I had the chance to fall in love with story and with words long before I could walk. That's really true. I can't remember back far enough that I wasn't in love with story.

I've repeated some of the stories I heard, but not all of them, and certainly even in the repeating of them as a child, the significance of them—I'm still working on that—what all of that means. I sometimes wake up in the middle of the night and realize I've been dreaming about a story I heard as a little girl and oh, my goodness, look at that piece of that story and what it means in my life right this minute! All of those old stories have so many layers of meaning—like an onion—peel off a layer and another is underneath there; peel off that layer there's still another layer under that.

Mama named me Lydia Elizabeth in some hope that I would grow up to be a great lady; I was a terrible disappointment to her. I was named for both of my grandmas. My father's mother was Lydia, her mama was Elizabeth, so the logical thing, since my father's mother was dead ... the logical thing would have been to call me Lydia, but nobody ever did. I was always called Elizabeth, even though that grandmother was still very much alive. I never really quite understood that part, but there you go—life doesn't always make sense, does it?

Well, my grandma and grandpa lived on Meadow Creek which feeds into the South Fork of the Kentucky River, big ole two-story white frame farmhouse; outbuildings: barn, corn crib, wood shed, smokehouse—all of that. About an acre in vegetable garden; as big a tobacco base as they'd let you grow; most of the creek bottom planted in corn; probably 120 acres of woods. Depending on what time of the year it was, like tonight in August, there'd be beans to break, peas to shell, apples to peel. There'd be a lot of work to do at night, after supper, and people would sit on the front porch with a piece of folded newspaper in their lap and do what needed to be done to make sure that the food was ready for the winter. All of the bean breaking, cabbage shreddin' for kraut, would be done on the front porch with a folded newspaper on your lap to keep your clothes clean. And somebody would be holding forth with a story. It might get swapped around person to person, mouth to mouth, or it might be just as likely that one person would tell a story and when they finished somebody would say, "Oh, tell 'Jack and the Robbers,' or I love to hear you tell 'Like Meat Loves Salt'; tell 'Three Girls and the Journey Cakes,' tell 'The Stepchild Who Was Treated Mighty Bad.'"

Often, Aunt Ida, if she told one story, she might be asked to tell another. Everybody sittin' in that circle could tell, and many of them knew most everything that was being told, and certainly heard it being told many times before, but they wanted to hear her tell it or grandpa tell it, because they were the better tellers. They told with more expression; they made it feel more real.

My grandfather's voice as a storyteller was very different from the pulpit. My grandpa could powder a brick in the back row! [Laughter] It was a strange mixture of hard nasal with an Irish lilt laid over it from his mom. It would be hard to describe. Aunt Ida's voice was like a feather bed on a winter night—soft, soothing voice. Grandpa's voice was an unusual sounding voice, much more so than Aunt Ida's. It's hard to describe a person's voice;

he'd get into it, he'd make up stories and you could tell whether he was making them up or not, because his voice sounded different. I don't know how to describe that.

He was always using story as a way to discipline the children. We'd be on some big adventure going up to Cobb Mountain—we were always going up to the top of Cobb Mountain, which is a place that doesn't exist except on that front porch. And you always knew how he felt about what you had done that day by your position in the story as he made it up. If you had a good strong mount, a good looking horse—a pretty thing—a spirited animal, you knew he was proud of you and proud of your work. If you had been slacking off and not doing what you needed to do, you'd be ridin' some ole bedraggled mule on a ragged saddle with a broken girth that wouldn't even stay on the mule's back draggin' along behind ... it would make you want to cry that you had such a denigrated position in the story. I mean, it would literally break your heart, because it meant he was unhappy with you, and because it was just—in your imagination—it felt so real you could just see yourself not havin' what everybody else had, not bein' able to do what everybody else did. You'd just be upset. I remember crying many times, because I was the ragtag, ragamuffin. And if you had really made him mad, you'd be walking in the story. You didn't even have an animal to get where we were going. And that was just too much for words—I don't even know how to explain to you what it meant, mostly because you knew you had made him unhappy, because we loved him and we cared, all my cousins.

The "we" in that is all of my cousins. There was a lot of work to do and we were children. You know, we had our days when we didn't do squat and there were some people in the group who didn't want to do squat most of the time. Some people are more work-brittle than others. I wasn't really a person who would work at gettin' out of work, but I was a daydreamer, and sometimes that would annoy him a great deal. I would make mistakes about what I was supposed to do, because I wouldn't have paid enough attention to what he said when he told me what to do, or I was not thinking or concentrating on what I was supposed to do. He wasn't usually upset with me because I was tryin' to get out of work, but because I might have made a situation where things had to be done over. I am just being truthful.

I don't have a clue about the existence of Cobb Mountain; it existed before I was even born. You know how it is when you come into a family—it's been going on for years before you even get there. My mother said he did the same thing with his children when they were little, so this had been going on for a whole generation before I ever arrived on the scene. I was one of the younger grandchildren, so it had been going on for fifty years before I even got there. My Uncle Mike is still livin'; I could ask him about it. Cobb Mountain sounds like something that existed up in Kentucky.

My grandpa was always talkin' about somebody dyin' of "cornbread consumption." It was a terrible disease—you didn't want to catch it—it was highly contagious [laughter] just to try to put it in some perspective. People in the story, if you were sick or if you'd been really bad sick, and people were worried about whether you were going to live or not, you were usually either dying of either honkus of the ponkus or cornbread consumption! He was quite a character: he was a brilliant man and a very forward thinking man for his day and his age; a very, very forward thinking man—had been a Baptist—ordained Baptist minister. The settlement school movement came in to Kentucky and the settlement schools opened; all the old regular Baptists were hard against sending girls to school—wouldn't have it—wouldn't have anything to do with it. My grandpa preached so hard about sending the girls to school, they prayed him out of the church. I think, although I don't have information about it, I think for him that was a real "dark night of the soul," but after a time he became a Presbyterian and was ordained as a Presbyterian minister. One of the major attractions for him was that the Presbyterians supported educating the girls equally with the boys, which the old hard-shell Baptists wouldn't do. Didn't hold for it *a-tall*. Educate a girl you'll "rurn" her—"nobody'll never want to marry her"—all that old thinkin'. He served a couple of terms in the Kentucky State legislature—he wasn't some jake-leg preacher—he was well read and a very thoughtful man and a good preacher. I have some of his sermons from years back.

After my mama died three years back, at the home place in the upstairs closet in what they would have called a chiffrobe or a walk-in closet, I found, in a box, the journals that he had kept for every year that he had been in the ministry, going back into the 1800s. Some of it is very straightforward, some of it is really funny, and some of it would just absolutely break your heart.

My grandpa was a matchmaker, and I do mean a matchmaker! So some of the entries read something like, "April the twelfth, 1902, married Polly Ann Seavers to Thomas Witherspoon" and underneath it, "I told Elizabeth it would work,"—that was my grandma, "I told Elizabeth it would work!" [laughter] You're just dying to know what it was about these two people. In my mind I conjure up this picture of Thomas—I can invent a whole backstory: Thomas had been married before and his wife died and left him with little children, and he needed a wife, and she was somebody that was an older woman, that had never been married to anybody ... what was there about it that made him write that? I would love to know that, but those kinds of notations were often made at the end of writing down about a wedding; sometimes writing down about a baptism there'd be some notation like "I never thought I'd live to see this day," something of that nature.

And then you'd turn the page and go a little bit further and it says something like—this is from 1916, December 7, 1916: buried the Reynolds girls:

Amanda—age 14, Sarah—age 12, Martha—age 10, Edith—age 8, Polly—age 5, Lizbeth—age 1, and under that just one word: influenza. And at the end of that word, there's a big brown splotch and I can't help but think that it was a tear. I looked through the book, back in time and forward for weeks in time one direction, and for weeks in the other, trying to find any notation that might tell me if there were other children in the family; you know, did they have other children, or was that every child in their family that they lost? Now remember that people might die and be buried and not have the funeral till the preacher came to your community. They might not have died the same week, but they may have died within two or three days of one another in that influenza epidemic that swept through the United States—those people might have lost every child in their family at the same time. He made a record of everybody he ever baptized; I looked to see if he ever baptized any of those little girls and he had.

When you read through it you can see how carefully he wrote down what he did. I think all of that is just fascinating. Like if he wrote through a verse of scripture, I have to go and look it up, because I think it says something about that person and his relationship to them, you know.

He almost always wrote as much about the people as he could. Their mothers and fathers, their age, where they were born; if he knew any of that, he wrote it down. And he kept one of those books for every year that he was in the ministry, and he was ordained in 1898—those big ole tall gray ledger books with triangular corners ... he kept one of those for every year. There would be numbers at the bottom—he must have been getting some kind of stipend from the Presbytery for the mileage that he traveled because later, coming closer to our time, there was delineation. It would say "HB" and the next one would say "T." I finally figured out "HB" was horseback and "T" was the train. And when he'd go to preach at the coal camps, he would catch the train and ride to the coal plants to preach. I found a piece of paper folded up in the book where he had added up all the numbers. It was my little Rosetta Stone that I figured out what it was.

My mother was ... livin' proof that hyper-active children grow up to be hyper-active adults. She was never still a minute ... she was never still for the whittled end of a minute. If she couldn't move, she would sit and pleat her apron; *pop* it open and start over, pleatin' it all across the front ... *pop* it open—never ever still a minute. She was truly the most practical, pragmatic, down to earth person that I have ever encountered in my life, and I was a great cross for her to bear because I am neither practical, nor pragmatic, nor down to earth [laughter].

You know, sometimes the hardest thing in the whole world is trying to communicate with those you love. I think sometimes it's even more frustrating when what you do is communicate with people for a living and you still can't get the people you love to understand what the heck you're talking about, you know? You think if these people are strangers, and they get it, there must be something wrong with those I love, if they don't understand. But the truth is for people not to communicate is something both people contributed to.

My mother lived a very, very hard life. She never anticipated being left with two little tiny children to rear alone. If my father had lived, her life would have been radically different, economically, emotionally, physically, and she wanted more children. In Appalachia, in a rigorously male dominated world, there was no man to speak for her; no man to provide for her or for us.

A war doesn't stop when they sign the peace agreement; it lives on in the lives of the widows and the orphans for years to come—maybe for generations, the difference it makes for just one man to die in a war. My brother grew up without a father; I grew up without a father. We grew up with my mother scraping for us to get by instead of being well-provided for. My father was an educated man—he'd a-been bringin' home a paycheck that would have made her life radically different.

She was the best manager that any human being could be; for what we had, she could make it go a long, long way. She worked in the school cafeteria half a day and made three dollars a day—it was not an easy life. Back then food was cooked on the school premises, and there were five hundred people to feed at a time; she worked hard, throwing those big ole pans around that kitchen that were as big as the top of the table.

What time she had to be at work depended on what was being cooked that day in the cafeteria, because it wasn't cooked somewhere else and shipped in to be just handed out a window. When they were fixin' something and it had to be in the oven for several hours, she had to get up at daylight and get over there to get it done by the time lunch time started at 11 o'clock in the morning. She could lift pans that were probably fifty–sixty pounds; think about what a pan, a pot, big enough to make mashed potatoes for an elementary school cafeteria, how much that weighed.... If she had been living today, she would have been an athlete with all that's implied in that. She shot hoops in the driveway for years and years. I forget how old she was when she finally stopped going out to shoot hoops. She played ball back in the days when women played in nine pounds of wool—it's enough to make you faint just thinking about it [laughter]. The middy-blouse down to the wrist and up to neck, and navy-blue bloomers down to your knees, and black wool socks up to your knees that tucked inside your bloomers; big ole thick underwear under it!

My mother was tough, 'bout as tough as a hickory nut; she was a tough woman 'bout as big as a handful of beans. Her life turned out a lot different than she thought it would be, but she was a woman who believed in doing her duty and beyond. She could have raised us in Kentucky, but she was just as much in love with my father when *she* died as she was on the day *he* died. She was in her nineties when she died and there was never another man in her life; she was George Ellis's wife all her life, all her life. She lived that way.

My father's family was not as family oriented as my mother's family; they were not as close as my mother's family. There was more distance from them even though we lived in the middle of them. Their mother and father were dead, and that always makes a difference. Even though they lived in the same community, they had separate lives; they lived in their separate homes but it was more than that. One aunt lived in Erwin, Tennessee; the rest of them lived within spittin' distance of one another, but there was a distance. I think it makes a big difference when your mother and father are dead.

I don't think of myself as having gotten far away from my roots. I may have lived in Dallas for a long time, but Lord, nearly everybody that grows up in the mountains has to go somewhere else to make a livin', you know? We all live in economic exile someplace else and every one of us would come home if we could. So there's never been a year of my life that I haven't been in Appalachia two and three and four times a year. During the last five years of my mother's life, I have been making the trip from Dallas to Kentucky one week a month so my mama could die in her own bed. I made that drive till I wore out the roads coming back and forth, making sure Mama was all right and being taken well care of, and being there when she and her sisters needed me. And if I could turn back the clock, I would turn it back five years and start all over again in a heartbeat. Hardest thing I've ever done in my life, and I would give a million dollars to do it over again.

I have always lived in my own stories from the time I was little, and loved books and stories. Went to library school and became a librarian; went to work at Dallas Public when I was pregnant. Storytellin' was the part of my job I liked best; some days it was the only part I liked. As the years went by, it seems like it got a stronger and stronger hold on me. I was a children's librarian at Dallas Public library and I became absolutely convinced that adults wanted to hear stories as much or more than children, and that they had less chance to do that. I wanted to bring storytellin' to adults. A number of my friends were musicians; I would go to their gigs to hear them play and they would, from time to time, call me up on the stage to tell stories between their sets. So a lot of my early experiences tellin' to adults were for people who had come out for an evening to drink and listen to music. I was always struck by how much adults hungered for story. We live in a day when people have very little opportunity to exercise their imagination, so as dumb as this may sound, coming to telling stories as a way of making a life, was kind of like a gym. I like to think of it as a gym—so that people could come and work out. People could exercise their flabby imaginations. People could touch their imaginary toes, so that they could do the yoga of the imagination; so that they could do the tai chi of the imagination; so they could run in place. I know stories can help people do all of those things—all that imaginative kind of exercise. I wanted to assist in that process, giving people the opportunity to become more fully human.

I don't know a story that isn't a sacred story. From my point of view, there is no such story. I don't care what the story is about—it is sacred because it is story. The Creator spoke the world into existence; the power in the word spoke the world into existence. I can create a whole world made out of nothing but words and I can invite you to come in and live in it with me. That's the most sacred thing I know—it's the most sacred thing I've ever experienced. That we are allowed to create a world with words and we can come by choice together into that world; it can be very different from the rest of the world as we know it. That to me is sacred.

We can make a world of beauty; we can make a world of kindness, we can make a world of peace with our words. Every word we speak holds up a blueprint so people can decide what they want to make of their lives. So I don't really care much about what the story is about, on the surface. If it's about your uncle Frank pickin' his nose, if it's Johnny Moses talkin' about how butt holes were invented—I don't care what it's about. If it's that big ole fancy tall tale about killin' eight ducks and twelve turkeys all with one bullet, it's still sacred story because it gives us the chance to utilize that part of our brain which is most in line with the Divine.

But imagination itself, like every human quality, can be put to poor use. We do that every day—we call it worry. It is imagination put to poor use. "What if, what if, what if"—we run like squirrels in a cage. We run all those ideas of what if, what if, what if ... and often we attribute to other people things they don't have—negative thoughts and feelings that probably don't even exist in their hearts, using imagination in ways that doesn't represent the Divine. So even though I think that all stories are sacred, often the stories that I feel most strongly, that I feel most strongly that I want to tell, are stories that have in them something about holding up a blueprint for a way to live; something about being in relationship with one another; something about the kingdom of God is here—"the kingdom of God is among you"—how to live in relation to one another. When you call forth the good in other people, that good answers you—you hold up a picture of a deeper way of living life; a more sacred way of living life and maybe a risky way of living life.

Those words find people and slide down into their hearts. They have those images in there, and they take them home. Those images are in there the next day. Maybe they make little bitty change in their lives that result in their being people who live more peaceful lives, more loving lives. I said the other day that stories mean you don't have to make all the mistakes in the world yourself. That's important.

There's a whole piece of story that's about holdin' up a mirror. You know in our culture we give away so much. We take all our wisdom and put it out there and we call it an expert. We take all our beauty and we put it out there and we call it celebrity. We take all our holiness and we put it out there and we call it a guru. In story, there is a mirror that shows us who we really are. It shows us who we are at our "deep heart's core"—Yeats wrote that— I love it, "the deep heart's core." I often choose to tell about everyday experiences—common, ordinary, everyday experiences because I would like to hold up a mirror so people can see the holy in their everyday lives. I think one of the things a storyteller does is help us see the extraordinary in the every day; help us see the Divine at work in the everyday. Look at the story of what we think of as the nativity story. Two kinds of people find the baby Jesus— people who search for him diligently, and people who were just standing around at work one day. Who ever thought something sacred would happen when you are at work! There they are, dealin' with the Divine on the job. Here are these other guys—struggle, search, travel hundreds of miles, spend huge amounts of money, invest themselves in this journey and these other guys are just the equivalent of working at the gas station, dumbstruck by the appearance of the Divine in their lives. The sacred happens both ways. You can seek it, and seek it, or we can see it when it lights on the end of our nose.

I like to tell things that people call sacred story. They're usually experiences from my own life where I've had encounters that help me see the Divine more clearly. In the life of the homeless person, in a school kid, in a motorcycle gang, you know. In the voice of a friend who says what you need to hear in the moment of your greatest need. I think the Divine appears in our lives all the time, but we don't always recognize it as being what it is. So part of my work, I think, is about helping people be more aware of the Divine in their lives. It's showin' 'em the mirror.

I've been extremely lucky in that people have been very good to me. I have gotten amazing opportunities to go and tell to people. I would pretty much rather tell to people than eat when I'm hungry. So I've been really grateful people have been willing to listen.

I learned a great deal about being a storyteller from people who would call themselves musicians. Allen Damron. David Ruthstrom. People who are very, very influential in shaping the way I work an audience, the way I work a crowd. David was the first person to refer to me as a storyteller—to call me by name as a storyteller. He hadn't heard many stories as a child growing up, and he was in love with every story he ever heard. Often he would give me the opportunity to tell between his sets. He believed in me when I didn't believe in myself, and that's a great gift when someone gives it to you.

He could see very clearly how much adults wanted to hear story—so much so that he would make a space for me to tell in his evening concerts. I am indebted to him for helping me see that.

I had a lot of support from people early on who helped me financially, who helped me emotionally. I thank God for Connie Pottel. I don't know that I would ever have been able to continue what I have done without Connie's unfailing support. She has always been there for me, especially when my kids were young and I needed the help.

Other storytellers who have held out a hand—you know, walked along with me for a little way—those who didn't see this as a big competition. There's a line from the song, "This Is a Song for All the Good People" by Ken Hicks that I adapted to make it a song about storytelling: "We told in the kitchen, held no competition, knowin' that the other one was a good friend to have." I'm indebted to all of them. On one level, I'm indebted to every storyteller that gets up to tell. They are part of me and I am part of them—every person who chooses to tell. I'm grateful to those people who challenged me to be more than I thought I was capable of being.

I would certainly include Tim Tingle's name among those people. He calls out to me to be the best that I can be. He has seen abilities in me that I didn't see in myself. I am grateful for what I've learned about writing, for what I've learned about narrative—how to bait that hook so that you catch that wiggler, pull 'em in. What do you do if they can't see your face, see your eyes, see your gestures, can't hear the tone of your voice? What do you do in substitute for all of those things? For me, that is a great mystery. I've been grateful that he's been willing to teach me what he knows about that. I know only about a corner of what he knows, but I've been grateful that he's been willing to do some of it with me. I sure have learned a whole lot from the experience. I'm grateful for all the Texas storytellers—that whole community of people—and how they have supported me over the years, supported my work.

I had known Gayle Ross for many, many years, and we'd always been making a mythical trip back to the Appalachian Mountains. I applied for a continuing education grant from the library to attend the National Storytelling Festival and convinced Gayle that she would like to come with me. We came up here and did some exploring: followed the Trail of Tears back to the seven cities of the Cherokee; went up to Kentucky to see my mother, and then we came to the festival.

I don't think it would have ever occurred to either of us that there was such a thing as a professional storyteller until then, but here was an amazing group of people telling from the stage, and loads of people sitting in the chairs who called themselves storytellers, and that was the main focus of their lives.

So, on the trip back home, Gayle said, "We could do that," and about the time we got to the Mississippi River, we said, "I'll do it if you'll do it." We are such remarkably different people now ... it might be hard to feature, but I really don't think that either of us would ever have done it alone. We've changed a whole lot over the years. It was really good to have somebody to hold hands with when we jumped off the cliff. So we set out to be a duo and worked for five years straight in much the same way that the Folk Tellers [Barbara Freeman and Connie Reagan-Blake] were doing. Gayle married and then had children. It became harder and harder to travel and work together. We could easily have starved to death if we had stayed together, so we had to start telling on our own just to make a go of it. That was a hard transition to make, but it has been a good one in the long run. Each of us has developed as a storyteller and gone in very different directions than we would have had we continued to work together all the time.

The first thing I had to do was develop a fuller repertoire, because when Gayle and I were together, each of us had our own roles: she told deep and meaningful Native American Indian legends, and I was a teller of Appalachian humor. So, I needed to learn to tell all of those things that come from the heart, because I had always relied on her to do that part.

Back in the old days, there was not a huge storytelling community like there is today. Not very many places to tell, and if somebody had a festival, they might pay $250 for one storyteller and $300 for two people. You didn't have to be a Philadelphia lawyer to figure out that each person got $150. Of course, if they had been working by themselves they would have gotten $100 more bucks. It wasn't enough money ... I had children and Gayle had ... a horse and they all needed shoes! After Gayle married, and had her own family ... it was money, but it was also just the absolute logistics of it. I mean, we lived 300 miles apart, so for us to tell anything, one of us had to travel 300 miles. It was Elizabeth and Gayle and their entourage, because there were kids. There were babies, and there were baby-minders. It was like playin' the D-Day Invasion.

There's a long-standing tradition of Appalachian people migrating to Tejas, and always thinking of the Appalachians as home; everybody from Davy Crockett to Sam Houston, right on down the line—coming to Tejas and making a life for themselves. It had more economic opportunity, but they were always longing for home. The place you grew up defines who you are; the place is the bowl that holds everything—contains everything. It's external, but it's internal too. Your internal landscape is shaped by those mountains, by that sense of place. By the woods and the trees and the hollers: Andrew Holler and Elijah Rock over where the cliffs are—I can see all of that in my mind as plain as if I was walking in the woods right now. I can see where the gooseberry bushes are, and where this thing happened when

I was a child and down there's where Mama fell off of her horse when she was eleven years old and that's why her tooth's broken. Right here's where my mama and my daddy kissed for the first time, right on this spot. And right here's the last place she ever saw him, here in Kentucky; and this is the bed that I was born in—that sense of belonging to a place that a lot of modern people don't have. Not just that you belong to a place, but that internally, that place belongs to you—it's a circle—you belong to the place and the place belongs to you, because you're a part of it, because it's a part of your landscape, internally; it's a part of your thinking; a part of the way your heart beats.

Some of what's said about Appalachia is true, but not all of it. If your people came from western North Carolina a generation ago, what it would mean to me, is that you're a first generation immigrant—that's what my children are—first generation immigrants—from a different culture. It has significance to me, of course, to be from Appalachia—I mean, it's as simple as I'm not from any place else! I do think people from other regions of the country are different. This is a very distinct sub-culture. People in Appalachia are very in touch with their heritage, mostly; deeply involved in family; strongly marked by their religious beliefs; intensely patriotic; make real good friends and pretty bad enemies. The culture is as strong as the influence of Italy on Italian Americans, or the influence of Germany on German Americans: people may move away from Appalachia, but they don't move away from being Appalachian. I know of people who try to get above their raisin' and that happens all the time, but that set of core values usually doesn't change much no matter where you put the people down. Wherever they set down, they're gonna live by those values—wherever they end up, be it in Florida or Texas.

There used to be a time that mountain people headed north to find work. They used to say you could walk from Chicago to the head of the holler on the tops of the cars on Friday night, headed home. That old joke about the man that dies and goes to heaven and St. Peter says, I think you ought to take the tour and find out where everything is; and he sees the pearly gates and the golden streets and the harp factory, and whatever else there would be to see. He comes to this wall and he sees people chained to the wall and they're pullin' at the chains and screamin', crying, tearin' their hair, tryin' their best to get away—he feels so sorry for them and says, "Who are those people?" and St. Peter says "Oh, Lord, they're from Appalachia. If we turn 'em loose, they go home for the weekend!" [Laughter] It's just the way life is ... people go home. Appalachian people go home—Appalachia's home! I have cousins who have lived in the north and gone home every weekend for thirty years.

One friend I grew up with, she and her husband were in the boat business in Charleston, South Carolina, for years and years. She says to me, "Woke up the other mornin' and my husband was already out of bed, looking out the window. I thought—something's up, "What's the matter, baby?" And he says, "My heart can't take another hurricane season." She said, "Then let's retire." "All right," he says. I said to myself, they will be back here, living in the mountains by this time next year. Well it was October when we had that conversation. When the Christmas card arrived, it had a North Carolina postmark! They came home like homing pigeons when they were no longer feeling the pressure of making a living economically, Lord, people come home to the mountains. People go off and work an adult lifetime, and come home to the mountains to live because its home. Because it's in your blood; because it's a part of who you are; because you can't help it. I don't know what else to say, because you can't help it.

Last fall, the last of my elderly aunts passed away and with her demise I had to deal with a whole lot of stuff I hadn't had to deal with before 'cause there was still somebody there. We had to sell my grandma and grandpa's house—we had to sell the home place. I have grieved over that place as hard or harder, as I grieved over any of the actual people in my life dying. I'm serious. I have cried, and cried, and cried like a blubbering baby over the sale of that house and land. If it had been left up to me, I would never, ever, have sold it. I would never have departed from it. I'll probably grieve over it on one level for the rest of my life ... but to go there, to be there, to walk that land; to be able to pick up a clod of dirt, to gather black walnuts, to pick blackberries, to stick your feet in the creek, knowing it's land that belongs to you—belongs to your people—land that knows you in a way that city streets are never going to know you, no matter how long you are there. There's a special feeling that comes over you when you know that a place loves you. And there isn't really a way to replace that, 'cause no new place could become that container for you. [Tears and silence]

You could move to any place for a life that you would want to live, but that container, that new container, would never know you and love you the way the old container did—that old place did. The old place that knows you, that knows your people—that knows who you are. "You are not separate and apart from me;" your place cries out to you, that you are not ever separate and apart from it. You might live on the other side of the moon, but you belong to that place and that place belongs to you. I don't know that people who grow up in other places have as strong a sense of place as people who grow up in Appalachia do. If I live in Dallas a hundred years—no matter how happy I am, no matter how deeply my children put their roots down there—it is not my home. My home *is* Appalachia—my home is the mountains. My home is *those* trees and *that* dirt and *that* little running stream of water, *these* rocks, and these people—always these people [whispered]. People who, when you hear them talk, your heart resonates with the sound their mouths make ... that's the way it is.

John Thomas Fowler

John Thomas Fowler was born and grew up in Spartanburg, South Carolina, and has one son, Taylor. He is a project scholar and consultant for the South Carolina Humanities Council, and is currently working on a Folk Music in America traveling exhibit. The Smithsonian exhibit *New Harmonies: Celebrating American Roots Music* is planned to visit six sites in South Carolina in 2011 and 2012.

Fowler is a member of the South Carolina Community Scholars Institution and the founder of the Carolina Old Time Music Network. He has conducted a number of field studies and produced several documentaries for South Carolina Educational TV. A number of his field recording projects have been released nationally and several recordings are archived at museums and folklore websites. Fowler has produced an old-time music radio show for the past fifteen years called "This Old Porch" on Sunday afternoons on WNCW 88.7 FM.

A member of the South Carolina Storytelling Network, Fowler performs at festivals, colleges, schools, and libraries throughout the southeastern region and is an avid music collector. As a traditional musician, he has won a number of "roots" music awards. He plays a number of folk instruments, including the banjo, guitar, spoons, autoharp and washboard.

The Interview

Storytelling is part of me—a part of who I am. As I have worked in storytelling and music, I feel like I'm a piece of it, and the older I get, I wish I had focused more on some of the stuff I dilly-dallied with when I was younger, and more so. It's such a part of my life that I work, sometimes, seven days a week. Sometimes it feels like a lot of work and sometimes not at all, but it is a lifestyle with me. Every single day I work as a storyteller and an old-time musician, and a researcher and collector. I like to know where the things I do come from—the history and the background.

I work primarily solo, but I also work with some "pick-up bands," too—that's for dances and small performances. I'm not in an established band that travels. It'd be nice, but there's always a trade-off.

You grow up and you like certain things and I got an appreciation of traditional things from my family, especially my Grandmother Taylor. I didn't realize until much later just how Appalachian she was. You look back and you realize you were just used to it—it was just the way she was—she was not a materialistic person at all and everything she did was in the old-timey way from plucking chickens to her singing—she sang the Scots-Irish ballads.

My Grandmother Taylor was a no-nonsense type of woman who grew up in the part of Western North Carolina which is an area called Peachtree. There's two areas there that are called Peachtree, but hers was in the community there, and she had to work to survive. Her mama was also no-nonsense—we're talkin' about 1910–1915. It was a big thing when they got running water and she used to tell a story about it.

There was a black family that moved in and they [Fowler's family] had never seen an African American before. The little girl would come out to play and my granny said that one time her and her sisters sat her up under the pump and said, "We're go'ne baptize you." They pumped the water and it went all over her. It was a short story, and there wasn't any more to it, but it was her style of communicating.

Even if she was busy sweeping or taking care of the house—she listened very carefully. If you told her something once, she knew it. She would watch a dish cooking and if she was in another room and I said it ran over, she wouldn't say anything;

John Thomas Fowler
(photograph by Taylor Reid Fowler)

she would just get a rag and go clean it up. I was exposed to her mountain-type ways from an early age and she always heard what I had to say.

My grandmother always wore an apron and if anything happened, she'd always reach into that apron and pull out about anything like her sewing needle, thread, scissors or what have you. Mercurochrome—when I was about 7 or 8, I remember one time I stepped on a nail and she wrapped my foot—I never went to a doctor and maybe I had a tetanus shot or maybe I didn't, but she took a piece of fatback, soaked it in kerosene and slapped it on there where that hole was punctured, wrapped it up and I went to bed. I remember the next morning when I woke up, it was soaked. The poison from the nail had been pulled out by the fatback and I guess the kerosene was the antiseptic. She knew exactly what to do. I grew up and thought I'd remember that and do it if I ever needed it, but today they'd do all sorts of things and I might still get sick.

I was born and grew up in Spartanburg, South Carolina, and pretty much spent most of my school years in Boiling Springs, South Carolina, but when I was born I lived with her on the southern side of Spartanburg. She lived in a big huge house there. I'm not sure if my grandfather built that house or if he bought it and added on to it—I think he added on to it, and I have to tell you a short story about that:

My grandmother was born in the mountains and got married when she was a young lady, I want to say her first husband got a stomach ailment—it might have been cancer, and he died, and she was a young 25-year-old woman with a child living in the mountains. This is the area where Eric Rudolph disappeared, so if you've seen pictures of that, you know it's way out in the middle of nowhere. She didn't have any prospects of finding a husband, so she lived alone up there. Five, six, seven years went by and the man who became my grandfather lost his first wife. The story has it that he was originally looking for a housekeeper, and somehow he went up to visit some of his people in that part of the country. He met my grandmother and asked who she was. When he found out she was a widow, they courted—I don't think it was long, and they got married and she came to South Carolina in the late twenties. He was about seventy and she was about 35. He fathered two more children with her, and one of them was my mama and that's the reason I'm here today.

My mother was young when she got married, and the marriage didn't last, so we lived in my grandmother's house from the time I was about two to about six or seven years old. It seems like a lot longer time, but it was where my formative years took place. When Mama was at work, I was with Grandma, and the other kids were, too.

I look back and I realize that the reason I have more of a mountain drawl than most people around here is from her. She used to use words like "directly," I remember that, or "you-ins." She used that one a lot. She had a real high-type voice, like I said, and once she wanted to call you, you could hear her over the next holler or valley over. I think about that when I tell the story about our first telephone. You know how it is with storytellers—part of it is true and part of it's not true. You just have to figure out which one is not....

There's one thing about my grandmother's character that I want to tell: Living in her house and watching—when I was five or six, and my next brother was a year and a half younger than me, and my sister was about ten years old, my mother had just recently split up and got divorced, this would have been in the early '60s; it was an uncommon thing at that time. My father was stationed out in San Diego and just didn't come back home, so Mama would go to the Saturday night square dances and come home about 10 or 11 o'clock. She only did it occasionally and was coming back from one of those dances. The next morning when we got up, Mamaw told me my mother had had an accident. What happened, was when she was coming home an eighteen-wheeler blew one or two tires and came over into her lane and hit her head on and broke both her legs, both her arms and messed her up. She said the doctor even cried when she got up to walk because he didn't think that my mother at 23 or 24 years old would ever walk again.

It was winter-time here and the church paid for a hospital bed and my mama got to come home for Christmas. I remember her being in the back bedroom of that big ole house my grandmother lived in—it must have been close to a hundred years old—it was a huge house, and it was heated by a coal burning stove although I believe she had some gas in another part of the house. You had to open up all the doors to get real good and warm. My mother was in the bed and she still had the cast on.

Around that time it was late afternoon, I looked behind the coal burning stove and saw a pipe fall—it was drawin' and fire was rushin' out onto the wood floor. My grandmother was in the kitchen—remember I told you, "just tell her one time," and I went in there to tell her what I saw happen with the pipe.

I said, "Grandma, the pipe fell." She stopped what she was doing, and I remember walking behind her—she bent over and picked that pipe up and she put that pipe back together.... I remember seeing my mother in that bed in there; she wasn't goin' to let her burn up. That's what you call character—she had to do it right then.

When she got older and was close to death, she had fallen and was down, my aunt Fay was a good caregiver, but she was away on a business trip, and my grandmother came home about the same time she was gone. Aunt Fay was coming home and hit an embankment and got killed, and we got the word and everybody went to Grandmother's house, and she thought everybody was there to wait for Aunt Fay. Finally somebody said, "Well, we've got to tell her" and one of my cousins decided to go in and tell her. I went in to listen—I was in my early twenties then. Me and that cousin and one other person was in the room, and my grandmother—she never would walk again—they told her Fay was in a terrible accident, and that she died. This is one of her three children and she had never buried a child.

Everything got real quiet and my grandmother said these words: "When I was a little girl, I was about seven or eight years old there was this baby that died, and they made us girls fix that baby up. And they made a little homemade coffin and took the baby out there and all the mountain folk came around," and she said, "Law,' did everybody cry." And that's all she said.

That's always haunted me: did she not hear? And then I started thinking well, she has seen a lot of death and that baby might have been the first death she was connected with, and maybe that was the way she was feeling right then—"Law,' did everybody cry...."

Those two main stories about my grandmother left a big impression on me. You carry that kind of thing with you, and learn a lot about yourself and a lot about your family, and other things, too.

I've got Appalachian roots on both sides of my family. I didn't have as strong a connection to my other grandmother, Grandmother Fowler, because of the early split-up with my mother and father. She was from Old Fort, in Eastern Tennessee near Jonesborough. She came down to Spartanburg to the mill in Clifton in the early twenties. Her mama worked in the mill and the way she got a job at the mill was she went in as a "bat-filler" for about a week without pay—there was no interview. The second week the paymaster came along and gave her an envelope, but nothing was said. She looked inside and there was a dollar a day. She worked fifty years in a textile mill, which is twice what most people work today. She's 98 now. Her husband was Kelly Fowler. They got married in the thirties, but times were hard. He had one working shirt; and every day when he came home, she'd wash that shirt so he could wear it the next day.

Her Baptist preacher father was a big robust man. He went back to Old Fort for five years, and then he came back to town, and they said you could hear him all over the mill village when he preached. She told me a funny story about him:

> He was a big ole man and when he was preachin,' his shirt would come out of the back of his pants ever once in a while. He liked to get down from the pulpit and watch the choir sing and when he got down out of the pulpit that shirt tail came out and he reached around to grab a-hold of his shirt and grabbed a lady's skirt instead. She went to hittin' him and everybody went to hollerin'—I guess they thought somebody was saved. That was my great grandpa.

I didn't grow up around a lot of people telling stories, but I used to sit around and talk to my Grandmother Taylor, and she knew I was interested in old stories about our family and mountain things. When she passed away, I wished I had known then what I know now, and had the interviewing skills I have now, because I could have learned a lot more about her.

I learned a lot of the old mountain music and would sing mountain songs to her, and she would smile—she knew those songs even if she didn't always know the words. She was a woman who knew a lot about canning and dressmaking, and cooking and the folk-things like hanging your clothes out. You turn them inside out 'cause the stains will go to the middle. I learned later on that she sang Scottish ballads and songs, really after her death, from my mother. She was a Taylor but her maiden name was MacGregory.

If she did know the songs, she learned them from her mother because she had no other place to pick them up, I never heard her sing them. I'm diggin' after them because I believe in carryin' things on. That's what storytellin' is—it's passing it to the next generation.

Those memories make people emotional, too. Family type stories are not always fun. I would love to be able to tell some of them, but I can't work past the emotions—it's a powerful story. People would either appreciate it or wouldn't be able to handle it.

My process of how I tell stories is from my grandmother—I developed a sense for simple things—country things, whether it was from osmosis or just being around her. When I was young folk music was popular. Although she wasn't a big singer, I learned a few things from her like "Froggie Went a Courtin'" and "The Crawdad Song." I guess I got the appreciation of simple things from her. When I got a little older, and began to play the guitar some, my interest was country and folk music. And I learned it from her.

I liked old-time music in school, and out of school, and later learned to appreciate soulful narratives and ballads, if you will, and storytelling. I was already doing some narrative-type stuff before I knew anything about the resurgence of storytelling, but it wasn't to this avail. It was a different kind of thing; when I connected with storytelling, it was almost like an epiphany to see how it all connected together. I guess I've been doing that ever since—connecting it.

There's a neat thing about storytelling—you get to do about everything—you get to be the narrator, and all the characters and part of the scenery and you get to jump around, too—go back to first person, whatever the story wants. That's the magic of storytelling.

One of the earliest storytellers that I saw, that made me realize I could do that too, was Joseph Sobol [program director of the East Tennessee State University Storytelling Department]. I saw him when he was in a North Carolina residency about 25 years ago. I went after it [storytelling] because I realized it was what I had been looking for. A lot of storytellers see the magic and they say, "Well, I can make magic, too."

When I'm telling a story, even if I know the story well or I'm working on it, I don't know what's going to come out of my mouth next, but I know I'm putting it together in such a way that people are enjoying it. It happens sometimes that what I said I meant to be funny, but it wasn't funny. For some reason the next time I tell it, it is humorous, and that always gets me. There's people out there could tell you why, but what is amazing to me sometimes is I'm up there and honestly don't know where I'm going. I can't tell you what is going to come out of my mouth next. It's almost like I'm sittin' in the audience too, listening to myself. I've said things and it got funny, and I laughed, and the audience laughed, too. They enjoy the heck out of that—that you're gettin' tickled by what you're doing. That's what makes it real, I think.

Music and story are interwoven together just like they were in old times. They would play the jaws harp or harmonica, tell a story, sing a song, play the spoons or what have you. What we do a lot nowadays, that takes away from storytelling, is that we sometimes perform more than actually tell stories. In the old days it was episodic telling. I can tell a storyteller when he backs me into a corner and won't let me out. I think there were a lot more people like that in the old-timey days. In those days you were either valued by the money you had, or the stories you told.

I think in some ways that's what I'm doing when I don't know what's comin' out of my mouth—it's spontaneous. I live on the edge when I'm tellin'. Sometimes, when I get up in front of folks—and it happened today but you'd never know it—when I get up, look at the crowd, still, at that instant, I don't know what I'm going to do, or how I'm gonna start off. On some stories I do, one or two, and that always gets my motor runnin'. The ones I'm still workin' on—introductions and things are continually changing, you know.

I do storytelling residencies in the elementary schools, and sometimes middle and high schools. Occasionally I do some lectures at colleges, but at universities, it's more folk-music type, or folklore lectures. Storytelling's for the youth, but I do adult workshops, too. I like working with the young folks—you always learn something when you're working with them and watching them; it's great to see children come out of their shells with storytelling.

When I first started working with young children, I didn't realize the learning styles and all that, but I guess over the years you learn that. When I see a child who can't sit still, or one that's turning and talking, I know there's a learning problem there. There can be one child that is just focused in and the other child is bothering that child—that will bother me and I will stop and make a point about "you need to let that person stay with me," and usually that takes care of it. I'm a lot more patient now.

We all know adults who have to have things a certain way, and when we get adults who are more demanding about it—if they are random thinkers or can do several different things at one time—or if they can't, I spot it. There's research done on that and I'm glad for it. Some people know about cars and motors and know the make and model—that's intelligence; they didn't sit down and study that, it comes natural. The next person could tell you, "It was a white car. That's all I can remember." Some are good at sports or art—I can tell when I'm talking to people who are either left or right brained—some need detail and structure, other people are all over the place. Personally, I'm more attracted to people who are in the arts.

I like authenticity, everybody sittin' around havin' a good time—I would hate to be held to the strictest rules of time limits, but I try to be respectful of everybody's time. I hate it when I get long-winded, and I've done it before, but the art of the storyteller is that if you've got a story that is twenty minutes, you can also do it in seven minutes. That's the challenge—if you are a good storyteller, you can do it and they will be just as pleased, maybe not quite as pleased if you leave out the details, but they probably won't know.

It's like when you were in elementary school and everything was goin' along and all of a sudden there was a fire drill and you have to get out right then, or going into class and being told you have a fire drill in twenty minutes, or you are teaching a fifty-minute class and they tell you there's going to be a fire drill in twenty minutes—you know that's going to take out fifteen minutes, you'll leave out something.

I never have been big on commercial stuff—it's on the same line as liking folk music and politically left-type things. For instance, I was recycling 25 years ago and very much believe in socially correct things, and I was raised in an environment that you didn't use racial overtones—I was lucky for that. It came from my grandmother and my mother, and I'm grateful for all that.

Jonesborough is getting more commercial. It didn't start out that way and maybe it doesn't mean to be now—it used to be really laid back. Those gals—Connie Reagan-Blake and Barbara Freeman—meant to bring in some of our folks like Ray, and then Guinn Bowen came down and they were the locals. And some others figured they could make money on it and when they brought down Jerry Clower, it went that way. I'm not judging them on it, because if they hadn't done it, we wouldn't be out here today.

I do worry about storytelling being too flashy and overdone—commercial. We live in a packaged world and that's not what it's meant to be. That's what drew everybody to storytelling in the first place—it was not on TV, it was not anything that was in a shiny package that you could go buy. That's why they will sit in a room or a tent for hours and enjoy it—it's nothin' but jawin'.

I'd rather be outside for storytelling, but I think the inside works better because you don't have the distractions. Outside you can have anything happen, from a walnut falling and hitting the roof, or somebody walking by that's talking, or people are scattered, or the blacksmith decides to hammer.

What I do is a lifestyle—and it's never-ending, I tell you. My plans with storytelling are to tell more, present more and collect more stories. I also enjoy the music and play a number of musical instruments. I play probably ten or twelve if not a few more. Some of them would be the guitar, autoharp and of course the banjo, harmonica, jaw harp, and more. I incorporate those into my storytelling. I'm planning a biographical book which is a collection based on traditional music, so I can educate folks as well. I see myself as a collector, researcher and presenter of folklore if you will, in the music and also storytelling. I'm one of those people, I'd love to leave something behind in my work—I think we all would.

I worry that the music traditions and old stories will get lost, and I often worry about how many songs and stories that are lost already, because they died out. I heard somebody once say that the test of a good song or a good story, for that matter, is the test of time. And that's why you have the great Biblical stories and some of the tales that we know.

When I'm in a festival or listening to a storyteller, I think, "Oh, I can tell that one!" It's not that I'm going to steal it—I can find the resources for it or ask permission, but when I find a story that suits me, I go after it. Some of my sources are storytellers and books and then there are my own family's traditions that I make my own. People used to say that about music, too—they would say, "I made that song," instead of I wrote that song, which is the modern way. My best one is listening and conjuring up stories from what I hear.

In the past, mountain people didn't write or read too much, so they used different terminology. And even now, some of those words and phrases are still used in some places. For instance, I love the way Rosa Hicks, the wife of late storyteller Ray Hicks, phrases things; she reminds me of my grandmother and I hear her say things and I think, "Well, that's something my grandmother used to say." It's that simple mountain-type of talk that has a lot of wisdom to it and when I hear it, then I start understanding again—brings it back.

My grandmother is still a major character in my life, more so than I would let on to a lot of people, because my mother was so young at the time and she was still finding her way, as we say today. When she came back home, she didn't have a complete high school education, but worked her way through that, so in a lot of ways I was mothered by my grandmother, who took care of me.

She was the type of woman who, if she had to check your temperature, she would lay her head on yours, that kind of thing. She wasn't a real loving or gentle person, but it was there ... it was there. It's strange because some of our family who did not live with her saw her more as a hard person, but I never saw her that way because I was around her all the time. I remember one time—and it comes from that mountain heritage—some people hear me tell this story and think it was cruel, but one time I had a toothache. She told me, "Well, we'll put a string on it and pull it out." She tied the string around it and put it on the doorknob. About that time I started whining, "I don't want to do this," trying to back out. She made like she was going to take it off but instead she jerked it and pulled that tooth right out. As soon as she jerked it out, bam! There was my tooth, still on the string and I didn't cry at all! There was a quarter up under my pillow that night [laughter] and there was no more whining.

I've got a CD called *Fiddle Traditions* which is a collection of the last of the old-time fiddlers in Upstate South Carolina that I started collecting in 1995. I visited with eight of them, and recorded them playing, and then ended up with the South Carolina Historical Society as my fiscal agent. Then we met with a philanthropic group and explained what I had, and that I could put it into the archives and no one would ever hear it, but we wanted those musicians to benefit from it while they were alive and we wanted everybody to hear it and they gave me all the money I needed plus an extra $5,000 and I didn't even have to match it. They saw the value of sharing folklore instead of archiving it. I sell the CDs, give them away and send them to museums around the state, and that's a mark I want to make—I do it because I love it—preservation.

One project was to collect the stories at a textile mill, but they were hard to collect. My grandfather told me that when he was a little boy—I don't think he was living on the Mill Village at the time; that would be my grandfather Kelly Fowler, who came from a hard existence and adapted well—he could make money when no one else could. You could drop him in the dessert somewhere and he'd come home with money in his pocket. He and his neighbors had chickens on the Mill Hill, and he snipped one of the toes off of his chickens, and that marked his chickens with his brand. He caught rabbits and took them to the restaurants and sold them in the 1920s. Times were tough and he was a sharecropper before he went to the mill, but they lived close to it. He used to take his little wagon and go to the ice house, and they had scrap ice—the ice that came off a chunk in a big chip, so they couldn't take it around to people. They actually threw it out and let it melt, so he would buy that scrap ice for pennies, load it onto his wagon and then go back through the mill village and sell chunks of ice to the neighbors. They'd buy a little chunk to put in their ice tea or extra to put in the icebox or whatever, and I can often see him comin' through and that ice meltin' on a hot day, and drippin', and him tryin' to get it all sold, but he'd make his money back and a little bit more. When he got home his mama was pleased because he had just enough ice for him and her to have a big ole glass of iced tea together, and he's made a little more money. It's a family story that I've set down on paper, but I've never told it.

I'm working with a visual artist to produce a show at the museum in Pickens, which has an accompanying CD that will have different types of music from South Carolina that will represent the Upstate all the way down, so it has string band, blues and Piedmont blues and gospel and Native American and a few other types of music. I've sought these people out and worked with them to record the music—jazz, too. The show is going to travel around South Carolina for about five years in exhibit form and the CD will travel with it.

I just want to give everybody 110 percent, and I see myself as a good performer and I enjoy doing it; I hope that I'm making a little bit of difference with what I do, and I hope I'm adding a little bit to this thing we call storytelling. I've got my health and a supportive family, and I've got my son Taylor. It's not easy—income ebbs and flows all the time, but when people ask what I do for a living there's too much—what I do for a living is at the root level and sometimes it's just too much to try to say it all, so I like to hang out with folks who are like me—musicians and storytelling, artsy-type people who think alike. We are very competitive, but we think alike.

I see myself as a storyteller, a musician, a writer, a collector and researcher, and that's what I think of myself as, but it all depends on what day it is. You are never off—you have to stir the pot every day. If you have a day you are not working, get in there and work it. I have several irons in the pot all the time.

What I am really doing is preserving who I am as a person. I am Southern and Appalachian because of those roots. I don't want to lose it, that's my identity.

Linda Goss

Linda Goss is one of the pioneers of the modern storytelling movement which began in the early 1970s. She is a co-founder, with Mother Mary Carter Smith, of the "In the Tradition" National Black Storytelling Festival and Conference, which began in 1982. In 1984 she co-founded the National Association of Black Storytellers, known as NABS, also with Mother Mary Carter.

Born in Alcoa, Tennessee, she grew up where she could see her beloved Smoky Mountains every day. Goss earned her undergraduate degree in drama from Howard University in Washington, D.C., and a master's degree in education from Antioch University. She is a member of Zeta Phi Beta sorority.

Her professional career as a storyteller began while she was in school at Howard, and since that time she has won many awards for her work, including the 2003 Oracle Lifetime Achievement Award from the National Storytelling Network, and the Benjamin A. Botkin Scholar Lecturer Award from the American Folk Life Center at the Library of Congress.

Goss is the "Official Storyteller" for the city of Philadelphia, Pennsylvania, and is also a co-founder of Keepers of the Culture, an affiliate of NABS, and a founding member of Patchwork, a Delaware Valley storytelling guild. She has been the storyteller-in-residence at the Rosenbach Museum and Library in Philadelphia since 2001. She has collected hundreds of tales and legends and a timeline of African American literature.

In 2005 Goss received the Fellowship in Folk and Traditional Arts award from the Pennsylvania Council on the Arts, and received the 2006 Leeway Foundation Transformation Award for Women Artists; she is also listed as a folk artist with the Philadelphia Folklore Project and is an artist-in-residence through the Philadelphia Arts in Education Partnerships.

Goss is the author and co-editor of six books, including *The Baby Leopard* and *Talk That Talk*, which features an introduction by Henry Louis Gates and is widely used as a source book for other storytellers; *The Frog Who*

Wanted to Be a Singer; and *Jump Up and Say* with an introduction by Ossie Davis; *It's Kwanzaa Time*; and *Sayin' Somethin.'* In addition, two of her recordings are part of the Smithsonian Folkways archival series—*It's Storytelling Time*, and *Afro-American Tales and Games*.

She has been a featured teller at the National Storytelling Festival in Jonesborough, Tennessee, numerous times and continues as a speaker with the Commonwealth Speaker's Bureau sponsored by the Pennsylvania Humanities Council. Goss has also been featured in a number of national publications and has been highlighted on the *Today Show*.

Goss is married to playwright Clay Goss and they have three children, Aisha, Uhuru and Jamaal.

The Interview

I was born in Alcoa, Tennessee. Alcoa stands for the Aluminum Company of America, and we say we are from the foothills of the Great Smoky Mountains. Even when I went to Charles M. Hall School, we would always say we were from the foothills and that area of Blount County. Charles M. Hall was the one who developed a cheaper way to process aluminum.

I was born on Bell Street. Blount County's hospital started in 1947, but Mama didn't like hospitals, and most of the black people were born at home anyway, so I was born in the house on Bell Street in a black segregated community. The streets were named after inventors, so the first street was Franklin, then Bell, then Edison and on through Stevenson and Volt.

I lived in Alcoa all of my youth until I got married. I went to college at Howard University in Washington, D.C., and I got married in D.C. Once I got married, I no longer lived in Tennessee, but when Mama got sick back in 1996, I more or less would go back and forth, and sometimes I was more in Tennessee than I was in Philadelphia. I did it for six years, back and forth, and sometimes I would drive back and forth from Philadelphia to Tennessee four times in a month. Luckily I had a great lady there, Betty Mahone, who took care of Mama. She took care of many people in the community, and I wrote a poem in her honor.

Mama was a teacher in Alcoa and taught just about everybody there in the town. She taught most of Betty's children and grandchildren, so Betty took care of her while I wasn't there. The time I would drive up, Betty would pull out, because she would be so tired from taking care of Mama, as well as her grandchildren and all of her church activities, which included being the church cook and singing in the choir and more. I would do it all over again if I needed to: our parents take care of us and the time comes when we need to take care of them. We have to take care of them because of the sacrifices they have made for us. Mama and Daddy did everything they could to help me, raise me and do everything for me; they really tried to do their best by me.

Mama had a series of strokes, so sometimes it was difficult for her, but she could recall some things like songs. Before she was ill, she was quite the storyteller, and she would tell stories. In fact, she was a public speaker in Blount County and she spoke to the white churches and the black churches and to schools, and she was always a speaker at Women's Day events. As a matter of fact, my speaking skills, I would say, came from her. Really, the way I talk comes from her, because she would have me practice and pronounce the words correctly. She would write out her speeches—she was very organized in her speeches, and she would always practice, and so I get a lot of that from her. She was so encouraging and so proud; she would go through the town telling everybody I was her daughter; even when she went to the bank, she would say, "This is my daughter the storyteller."

Some time ago, I came back to Tennessee to do some workshops and storytelling in Pigeon Forge, and my mother was still able to travel at that time. I had been invited to do a writer's workshop for the children, and my mother came to hear me. In the evening I held a storytelling program for the parents. The kids were excited and told their parents about it, and the auditorium was packed that night. I couldn't see the audience at first, but I knew it was a room full of people. In those days I made a big entrance, and I came in ringing the bells and making my grand entrance. When they introduced me, out of the corner of my eye I saw the audience, and I saw they were shocked—they didn't know I was black! I had to do some quick thinking and I turned around and said "It's always good to be back home in these mountains. I am one of you—I am 'GRITS,'

Linda Goss
(courtesy Philadelphia Folklore Project)

a girl raised in the South; I was born in Blount County!" Before I knew it they did the call and response with me, and they were clapping. I really had to think fast to turn that thing around. I was so used to performing up north for school kids I had forgotten the parents might not realize that I was black, and I hadn't thought about it either. They thought of me as a Northerner because I live and work in Philadelphia. That is the power of storytelling—and why you make the connection, and why it is important.

Daddy loved jazz and he loved Billy Eckstine. He also loved organ music and listening to music, and he was a singer. I remember—I must have been about four years old and I loved nursery rhymes—and I remember singing this little nursery rhyme in the hallway for Mama and Daddy. I was singing, "Hey, Diddle Diddle, the cat and the fiddle, the cow jumped over the moon" [singing it in a simple, melodic way] and they both clapped and said, "Oh, Linda, that was beautiful!" However, Daddy said, "But you know, Linda, you could put some rhythm in that. You know, snap your fingers and put a little somethin' in it," and he was kind of scattin', walkin' around the house imitatin' Billy Eckstine. When he said that, I thought about it, and just like in the spur of the moment I sang the song again, and I remember singin' it this way [singing the song in a jazzed up way] and when I did it that way, they jumped up, Mama and Daddy, and they really applauded.

So I always say I got my style from Mama, because she was a very formal type of person, and very poised and very graceful, whereas I got my rhythm from Daddy—I got my soul from Daddy and really it was through him that I developed a love for jazz and blues and a love for black music. Mama loved gospel and spiritual music, and she loved country and western music. Every morning when I would get up to go to school, I would be woken up by Tennessee Ernie Ford, Hank Snow, Eddie Arnold, Hank Williams or Tex Ritter on the radio at 5:30 in the morning, so I knew all about country and western music. She was crazy about Mahalia Jackson, Wings Over Jordan, Mighty Clouds of Joy, and some of the local choirs and quartets. Each one of the local black churches had great choirs, and we would go to hear them on Sunday afternoons, because we had the talent right there in our own churches. She loved the white gospel quartets, too—she loved the Blackwood Brothers and the Chuck Wagon Gang, and so I was influenced by all kinds of music. I am a child of the radio and I listened to stories on the radio when I was growing up.

The reason I mention that is because when I tell a story, I hear music when I tell the story, and I like to tell stories to music. Where I grew up in East Tennessee, and even if you go there now, when people talk there is like a melody in their voices, and even the way they walk—there is a rhythm there, so I've always been influenced and aware of the rhythms and the styles, and even the sounds of nature, growing up in East Tennessee. Also, too, the love of storytelling, in terms of story, that came from Granddaddy Murphy. Mama and Daddy were both great storytellers, and I remember the stories they told me, but it was through Granddaddy Murphy that I developed a love for storytelling. He and I didn't always get along because he was born in the late 1800s, and he came from the generation that believed children should be seen and not heard, and he was very, very strict. When you were in his presence, you knew to say, "Yes ma'am" or "No sir." If you didn't, he was liable to spank you, so I was very quiet around him.

What happened is that he was visiting a friend's house, and I happened to be there—someone was babysitting me—and he came in. I didn't say anything to him, and he didn't say anything to me, and the people I was staying with started laughing and teasing saying, "Your own grandchild don't even know you?" He was very sensitive and he felt that I had embarrassed him, and by the time I got home, Mama and Daddy knew about it and were very upset and angry with me, and again, I couldn't have been more than four or five years old, and they left it to me to solve this problem between Granddaddy Murphy and me.

And so the next time I went to see him I was really nervous. He thought I hadn't showed proper respect to him, because I didn't speak to him, but in reality, he didn't speak to me either. I came and stood at the edge of the walkway to his house and I was kind of quiet. He came out, and in those days I had pigtails, and so he asked me what was I doing. I said, "Nothing, Granddaddy," and he said, "When I was little, I had pigtails and I wore dresses made out of potato sacks," and he laughed. That was funny to me so I laughed, too. Whenever he would laugh, he would go [mimicking her Granddaddy Murphy with a deep, hefty laugh] and his teeth had these gold crowns on them. He was a very tall man; granddaddy was about six-five and he was a very imposing person. He rarely smiled, and he was known for being stern, and he was known for packing a gun. Granddaddy Murphy's hands were so large, and he could do all kinds of things with them like twist them and do tricks with them, and he later told me he had healing hands.

So, it was through storytelling that Granddaddy Murphy and I really became friends. Every time my brother Barry and I would go up to visit him he would tell a story, and he would tell us stories about growing up in Alabama and he would tell us about his granddaddy growing up as a slave—it was just very interesting. I have to admit that many times I was half paying attention because my brother and I wanted to watch television, but Granddaddy would tell us, "Turn that TV off because I've got a story to tell you." When he first got the TV, it was tuned to CBS, and he never changed the channel. In his mind, if you changed the channel it would break the television. Naturally we were not allowed to touch the television unless he said so, so most of the time at his house, I don't remember seeing too much TV, but he would tell us stories and he would start off by asking you a question or by saying the word "say"....

Mama would tell us stories, too, but she would read stories to me because she really wanted to promote reading. I loved Peter Rabbit, and Mama read to me from her own Beatrix Potter books. I learned later in life how much she loved Peter Rabbit, too. She told me all kinds of stories from the Bible, and Daddy loved to tell me funny stories, but each of them, in terms of their storytelling, had their own style. Mama might tell you a story that might start at the end, or Granddaddy Murphy might tell you a story that started at the middle, depending on what the purpose of the story was.

Daddy liked hero stories and he also liked to read books by Hemingway and John Steinbeck, so it was through him that I learned to appreciate the great American novels, and later the African American writers James Baldwin, Richard Wright and Zora Neale Hurston. Mama was widely read, too, but she truly loved Christian literature and went to the Christian Book Nook every week; she loved Longfellow, and Ralph Waldo Emerson was her favorite poet, but when I was young, I loved Henry David Thoreau and Walt Whitman.

I could read at a very early age and I used to go around with my little red wagon and it was full of books like *Buh Rabbit* and *Li'l Red Riding Hood*, and *Three Li'l Bears*, and they knew how to tell those stories to me so they came to life for me, so when I started to school, I would always turn to the folktales when we got to literary books each year.

I was six years older than my brother Barry, so I was like an only child there for a long time and was kind of in my own dream world, my own make-believe world. I loved the folktales and fairytales and the fables, and to me, Buh Rabbit was real.

Growing up in East Tennessee, you would see rabbits and foxes and all of these little critters everywhere you went, and I did a lot of walking by the Pistol Creek on the railroad track and saw a lot of them there. In those days we didn't have trails, we created our own. Daddy would tell me how he swam in that little creek when he was a boy, and how he had to be careful about water moccasins, and how he had stepped on one when he was at the golf course, so snakes were part of life especially in the summertime. People had gardens then and there was a lot of tall bamboo canes and across the street was this huge cornfield, because people grew their own crops. We would go through the seasons with the fruit trees, and our neighbor had a grapevine, and there were hickory nut trees. We weren't supposed to be doing this, but we were sneaking through the yards eating the fruit from the trees.... Now, everything is manicured and cleaned up—it's not like it used to be. In the early days our houses were not underpinned and my house was on four stacks of bricks. Later, they started putting cement around them, but it was always things crawling around there.

East Tennessee is on hills and I was always climbing. I was a tomboy and I loved climbing on the rocks and making up all these stories. I remember when I was a cowboy, and the reason I say *cowboy* was that I didn't want to be a cowgirl. I wanted to be a cowboy. I remember Mama bought me this cowgirl outfit for Christmas, but it wasn't what I wanted. It had a skirt, it had a pink holster and it had fancy boots, but I wanted the pants and I wanted to be like Roy Rogers and Gene Autry. So that was a whole big blow-up between me and Mama over the cowgirl-cowboy type of thing.

Mama tried to resolve the situation by taking me down to her sister's. There was one house between our house and my aunt Maggie, but I didn't call her "Aunt" back then because since Mama raised them, too, they seemed like my sisters. So, she took me down to Maggie's and Maggie was trying to convince me to try it on and trying to tell me how cute I looked, saying, "Oh, you'll look so cute in it," but all of a sudden I screamed at the top of my lungs, "I want to be a cowboy!" and I remember Maggie saying, "Oh, she is such a sassy, unruly child! Bill (Mama's nickname was Bill and Daddy's nickname was Junior), you should spank her behind."

I was the type of a child that would always come at a problem with a question on my tongue, always fighting for my opinion. Like I said, back in the fifties, that was kind of unheard of. No one had heard of feminism or women's rights, or children's rights, or individual's rights or even the Civil Rights Movement or activism, but I was always asking questions.

Mama encouraged me to ask questions and she encouraged me to be myself. Even though she wanted me to be a Christian, and I am a Christian, she wanted me to think for myself and so she would always tell me to think for myself, so when I would, sometimes there would be a conflict. At the same time, she always valued my opinions.

Mama was born into a family of fourteen children and eleven survived, so she came from a large family and she would tell me stories about her family. Because it was such a large family, they would make up games and stories and so she taught me a lot of play party games, too. I grew up in a segregated community, and we were aware of the spirituals and of our stories, but we were not aware of how important they were at the time. Langston Hughes and Paul Lawrence Dunbar and James Weldon Johnson were so familiar to us they were like family, and Mama could recite them, and there were people in the community who could recite them in the church, so the church, the school and our home life were very important. We sang spirituals and recited black poetry in all of those places, and the community was like one big family.

I remember when a group came to our house and they were from the NAACP, and they came there to talk to Mama and Daddy because they had chosen me, as well as some other students, to be the first to integrate Alcoa

High School in Spring Brook. I remember Mama and Daddy didn't say anything, but again, me being the kind of person who speaks up, I told them what my decision was myself. I said "I'm going to stay at my school, because Hall School is *my* school." It's where Mama was and where I had been all of my life, even though I was aware it was important to desegregate. I thought at the time of all we had to give up, and I didn't want Mama to lose her job—I was afraid she wasn't going to have a job.

Even now, when I think of Hall School, I think of our school song which was written by Mary Cross, who taught at the school way before my time. This song was set to the tune of "Carry Me Back to Old Virginny":

> In the foothills of the Smokies in a little vale
> stands a school I love so dearly and I always will
> Though the years may separate us from these dear old walls
> we will keep the love light burning dear old Charles M. Hall

I always tell people I was born in the civil rights era and into the Civil Rights Movement. When I went to college I was highly influenced by the Black Arts Movement, and the Black Power Movement and I've always considered myself an activist. I've always used storytelling to promote justice and human rights.

I remember when I first started telling stories in public, it was on the campus of Howard University while I was still a student, and I would say that "I'm tellin' old stories for new times," because during the sixties you were influenced by people like Angela Davis and Malcolm X. Many political leaders came to the Howard campus and the D.C. area and I saw Martin Luther King, Adam Clayton Powell and Stokely Carmichael during the ten years I was there. In those days it was hard to distinguish between the artists and the entertainers and political leaders who came to the D.C. area, from Nina Simone to Aretha Franklin, and James Brown saying "Say it Loud—I'm Black and I'm Proud"—so once I went to Howard I developed a great pride after doing research on my African heritage, and I became very proud of my southern roots.

That whole era greatly influenced me, because I remember I really wasn't even aware of what death was until 1955 and I was only eight years old, and my birthday was in August, and August was also the month in which Emmett Till was murdered in Mississippi, and it affected my whole community. Mama was crying, my aunts were crying; Daddy was very upset and Mama was saying, "How could they do that to a child?" At that moment, I realized death was real and that it was a character and that some day, I was going to die.

In December of 1955 Rosa Parks refused to give up her seat. Years later I had the opportunity of meeting her and hearing her story, and she said the reason she had the courage to do that was because of Emmitt Till and what was happening to the children there. The children were being hurt and they were speaking out and she had no choice, but to do what she did for the children. She had been influenced by them, and I was greatly influenced by the civil rights movement because I was a part of it. I also remember when I was seventeen Mr. Wilfred Warren asked me, and several others from my class, to go around to each house in our community—to every house on every street, to more or less interview them and give them a survey, to get them to vote. That was such an eye-opener for me.

I was interviewed by StoryCorps recently and I talked about that experience. I remember one woman I interviewed, and she was in her nineties and she was so old she was ancient, and her hair was just beautiful and white and her face was filled with wrinkles, and she told me she had never voted in her life and that she did not intend to vote, that she didn't see any point in it. She was from further down South where she had been treated so cruelly and she didn't think it was going to matter. Some people told me that they had been afraid to register; some people said how when they had been down in Alabama they were forced to count things to register, charged fees, and threatened. This is something people in East Tennessee don't like to talk about—and that is that the KKK was, and still is, very prevalent in Tennessee.

Those stories were eye-openers for me although I didn't know what to call it at the time, but I later realized that oral history is very valuable. People's stories are very valuable—these stories you're never going to see in a history book. Also, I was raised in the St. Paul A.M.E. church which was founded by Richard Allen. Richard Allen was a political activist and he and Absalom Jones left the Episcopal Church because they didn't want them to sit downstairs at church—they wanted them to sit upstairs in the balcony and he refused to do that.

As a young child I knew about him, because we were taught in Sunday school about him and what all he did, and once I went to Philadelphia, I learned how he helped people through the yellow fever epidemic. He was quite a person: he wrote about his own life, and he published a collection of hymns; he started the Free African Society with Absalom Jones, and he was a Mason. He and his wives from both of his marriages did amazing things, so again; I was surrounded by all of that in my community.

In my church, the mother of the church when I was a child was Mother Bradford. That's what they all called her—Mother Bradford and she was a tall lady, and she wore long dresses and long skirts to the floor—this was something out of another age and no one else in town dressed like that but her. She wore bonnets on her head and a shawl, and what was interesting about it is that she once had been a slave, and she was the only person that I knew who had actually been a slave—that's how old she was. I never really heard her speak, but she would sit on the front pew of the church (that's how much she was honored), but I remember Mama saying she heard her say, "Slavery was *awful!*" and that's how Mama said it. When you looked in her face, you could tell, yes, it was a truly horrible thing.

All of that influenced me, because I later realized that Granddaddy Murphy told me the Buh Rabbit stories differently than the way Joel Chandler Harris had written them and the character of Uncle Remus that he created. I'm not knocking that—Jackie Torrence told stories about Buh Rabbit and a lot of people do, but Granddaddy Murphy was not an "Uncle Remus"— he had nothing to do with Uncle Remus. His stories, the way he would tell the Buh Rabbit stories were similar to the stories you hear out of Africa, that Buh Rabbit was a trickster. The stories had political overtones and Buh Rabbit used his wit—his common sense—to get in and out of all kinds of situations, and Granddaddy Murphy would always say, "I want you get as much 'book sense' as you can, but don't you ever forget your 'common sense,'" and that was the whole thing about the animal folk tales and stories, it was about surviving and being aware of nature.

A lot of times, in my stories, I talk about food, because food and storytelling go hand in hand in terms of where I'm from. I remember Granddaddy Murphy telling me a story about a Li'l Rabbit. My brother was called Li'l Rabbit, and true to form, he was always in and out of something. Granddaddy Murphy would always say how Li'l Rabbit couldn't wait, wouldn't listen to his Mama and he went blackberry pickin' in the evenin' when his Mama said, "We go blackberry pickin' in the morning."

> He couldn't wait, because he wanted those blackberries, and so he goes blackberry pickin', and naturally he was eating more than he was pickin', and so he sits down to eat the blackberries, and sits on a log, and that log starts movin' and lo and behold he's sittin' on a *snake!* This snake was going to eat him up, but luckily there's a skunk nearby and the skunk saves Li'l Rabbit, but in saving Li'l Rabbit, the skunk naturally had to chase the snake away so he had to spray, and it got on Li'l Rabbit, too. When Li'l Rabbit gets home, he is really stinkin' and they had to put him in the outhouse where he had to stay until the smell leaves him. Needless to say, he don't go blackberry pickin' and he don't get no blackberry pie, none of that stuff!

When I was a child we would go blackberry pickin', and there are still blackberries around the train tracks in Alcoa. True, I was like a little rabbit because by the time we finished, my bag would be empty because I would have eaten all of my blackberries. My face and my hands would be just full of blackberry juice—all red and everything, you know. I'm sharing that to say that the people in my community make some of the best blackberry pie you ever tasted—a cobbler actually—you ever had in your life. One story of mine, which is a true story, was published in *Talk That Talk*, and it is about Mama and her peach cobbler pie. [Her re-telling of the story follows:]

> Daddy loved Mama's peach cobblers. By her being a school teacher, and him working at the plant, he would get home an hour earlier than she would. She would get home and she was tired, but people didn't realize that being a teacher was tiring work. Even her sisters teased her saying, "You don't do nothing but teach," and about how I'm workin' in somebody's house, blah, blah blah washing and ironing.... Bill shouldn't be tired. But she was tired, and she still had to grade papers.
>
> During the week, she would use canned goods, and packaged foods and some of her sisters would tease her, because they were so-called "cookin." They were peelin' potatoes, stuff like that. On Saturdays and Sundays, she would cook bigger meals. And so Daddy got tired of her cooking out of a can and opening up jars, so he brought some fresh peaches home and he said "Bill, I want some fresh peach cobbler pie and I want fresh peaches; I don't want no canned." So she said, "Okay." So she went ahead and made a peach cobbler pie and we loved it. We ate every bit of it.
>
> Later that night, we were in the living room and my brother, Li'l Rabbit, had gone in the kitchen and he had found the sack of peaches that Daddy had brought in. She had hid them under the sink and he had found them and he was rolling them in the living room like baseballs. Mama saw these peaches come rolling across the floor and her being the Christian that she was, she thought God was punishing her, but she stepped up and confessed, "I cannot tell a lie, Junior, I didn't use those peaches; I used a can of peaches and I used Jiffy Pie Crust Mix—I didn't even make a pie crust."

When I tell that story, I put the recipe that she used in the story. I was in Pennsylvania, in Chester County and I was doing a residency there with seventh-graders, and I was there a whole week. They surprised me and made peach cobbler pie using that recipe, I believe it was for the whole seventh grade, and it was good, so I later made up a li'l ole song to go along with the peach cobbler story. That's a true story, and I share stories like that in my workshops to show people their stories are very valuable, and how that's a family tale and a part of family folklore, and how those stories need to be told just like the animal story, "The Frog Who Wanted to Be a Singer," that Granddaddy Murphy used to tell me. That's a story that I later started telling in my own way.

Most African American animal folktales come from Africa even though the environment in America changed them. For example, in Africa you had monkeys and lions and elephants. When my ancestors came to this country they brought their animal folktales with them. The stories took on new meanings and new themes because of the experiences and pain the people experienced in America. The stories became African American folktales in style, language, rhythm and storyline.

My story "The Frog Who Wanted to Be a Singer" is definitely rhythm and blues—he wants to be a singer but nobody wants to hear him sing, "Rib-it, rib-it, rib-it," so he keeps on practicing and once he just bellows out his tune, it was something new and different, and the animals started snappin' their fingers, movin' their feet and dancin'. They had never done that before, but they realized the frog had given them something new.

When Granddaddy Murphy told me that story, I would think of people I liked, like Louis Armstrong, and I imitated the frog like he would when I told it, and I added a boogie-woogie element to it, and scatting. That song really talks about the greatness of black music, and a lot of my stories incorporate music, rhythms, and chants because I kind of grew up with that. As I grew older, I realized African stories have singing and ritual behind them—my whole definition of what I do is a combination of narrative song, call and response, dance, and costume—a little bit of a lot of things.

We have a tendency in America to separate and classify everything, but I really don't. I've been criticized for it—some people would say, "Linda, you're not telling the story, you're singing," but I remember that during the time of the enslavement of our ancestors, many of our stories were told in song, and they were coded—and if you read the words of those spirituals, you will see there's a story being told about what our people went through in the 1700s and 1800s, for example: "Sometimes I feel like a motherless child, a long ways from home," "Get on board little children, there's room for plenty a'more," "Wade in the Water—God's goin' to trouble the water." Our spirituals are coded!

Sometimes when I tell a story I incorporate many African American storytelling techniques—including spoken word and rapping. I don't like all rap music, but some raps are good. Back in the sixties I saw *The Last Poets*, who laid the foundation of contemporary spoken word and rap. It was pretty heavy, but you can trace it right back to Africa because it is talking to the rhythm of the drum. The drum is the heartbeat of the people, and black storytelling is filled with rhythm and narrative.

There are some storytellers and scholars who have studied my culture and who feel they know more about my culture and my stories than I do, and I've always maintained, and this is my mantra: I define who I am and how I create my work.

The blues tell the story and I come out of the blues. One of my favorite singers is Son House because he tells a story in every song he sings, and even though Billie Holiday is known as a great singer, she was also a great storyteller. And no one can sing a story like Aretha Franklin can, and Bob Marley. And many of our black preachers are storytellers, as are many of our comedians—Richard Pryor, Bill Cosby, Red Foxx—those are storytellers, Dick Gregory—he's a storyteller and an activist. Sure, he's doing comedy, sure it's funny but that's part of all storytelling.

I have been criticized all of my life as a storyteller, from the time I started out to this day, about my particular style. But luckily, early on, I met people like Brother Blue, and Brother Blue freed me. He was so unique in terms of his style, and he was such a beautiful human being, and he was so encouraging. He actually listened to you and he listened to the story. I remember he told me, "You are the living bell," because I ring bells. I've always rung bells and it just came naturally to me, as with so many things I do that I can't explain. Carl Jung would say that's the collective unconsciousness. A lot of things I do, I realized later, can be traced back to Africa. I began ringing bells back in the seventies when I was performing at the Smithsonian at the Festival of American Folklife, and I had these great crowds and when I wanted their attention I started ringing bells. I bought these bells that came from India in Silver Spring, Maryland, and I just started ringing the bells and they just became part of me. When I told Granddaddy Murphy that I was ringing bells, he got this beautiful expression on his face and he said, "You are doing what I used to do. I used to do that for the people on the farm, and the roosters would go cocka-doodle-do and wake up Shep the dog," and Shep would come by and lick his hand and then he would wake up and blow that bugle and that would wake up everybody else, yes, that meant it was time to get up and go to work—it was time to wake up the people. I now use that phrase in many of my workshops, saying that I am waking up the people.

I ring the bells at the beginning of my storytelling, at the beginning of my workshops and especially at the festival sponsored by the National Association of Black Storytellers—I'm known for ringing my bells. If I don't pull 'em out, they will say, "Where are your bells?" Now that we have lost some ... several of our older members have made transition—like when Mama Mary passed—my bells are usually draped in ribbons of many different colors, but they were in white for a whole year in her honor. I've had them dressed in many different colors to represent certain people, like red, which was Mama's favorite color and is my favorite color, too. And now that the executive director of NABS, Linda Brown, and then Brother Blue passed away, they are draped in blue and they will be for a while.

For me, storytelling is telling a story in your own way. You do it your own way—do your own thing, but tell your story whether it's mime, dancing, narrative or visual arts, whatever. In Africa, the women wear jewelry that tells a story; the hairstyle tells a story about whether she is married or has twins, you name it. In Africa, there are many, many ways to tell a story and that's why I like to use storytelling as a frame for all kinds of arts. Brother Blue was a one-man show incorporating the riffs, chants, scatting and doing his thing, and I kind of do that, too.

Because I work in the city, I do things that relate to people who live in the city. A lot of the children there are into rap music. I don't try to compete with the rappers, but I have children who grew up listening to rap music, so I rap, too. It came natural. I am inspired by the people I am around. I was working in the inner city in the first day of my residency at a public school. When I arrived, I saw police cars, ambulances and the fire engines and TV cameras and the yellow tape—everything was roped off and I couldn't even park near the school. I had to park a couple of blocks away and had to walk up. When I got to the office, I was told that across the street an elderly lady was found murdered, cruelly beaten to death. When school was dismissed, the children would be leaving by the back entrance and the school officials told me I didn't have to stay, but as a storyteller, I had to stay. I had to come in there and tell stories to those children. This was a school where many of the students had behavior problems, but all storytelling isn't easy. Some of those kids had such behavior problems that they couldn't listen, but I really wanted to reach these children—I wanted them to see their potential, so I created a rap called "The Caterpillar's Blues." I didn't realize it at the time, but Brother Blue influenced me in this, because his whole thing was the butterfly. In the story I say:

> You are story; You are Poem;
> You are a Shining Star;
> You are Unique; You are One of a Kind;
> Be Proud of Who You Are
> Life is not always Pleasant
> Many Things will make you cry
> But You've Got to Hold On
> Because within Your Soul
> Lives a Butterfly

They started doing it with me and it was unbelievable, and it became part of my repertoire. Even in that story, I used the mountains—I use them in a lot of my stuff—I'm always referring to the mountains or the river. I can't escape them and I don't want to escape them. Even though I've lived in an urban environment for most of my adult life, I can conjure up Tennessee, my Great Smoky Mountains and the Tennessee River any time I want to, and there are parts of Pennsylvania that are just gorgeous and are also a part of that same mountain range.

I consider myself a black Appalachian. If you want to say Afri-lachian, I don't have a problem with it. That's the thing about being in America, especially being a black American: we frequently come up with different names to identify ourselves by. For so many years the government, or the powers that be, were determining who and what we were and were calling us a particular name....

In the sixties there were fabulous programs and gatherings at Howard

University, and I remember seeing all these great writers—you name it, I saw them—Toni Morrison and Claude Brown—it was a Mecca of people coming through there. Mohammed Ali and Sidney Poitier—it was a place for writers, poets, singers and dancers, Andre Watts, Andrew Young, and the Alvin Ailey Dance Theater, which featured the incomparable Judith Jamison. The conferences they had then were unbelievable; to see these great people and to hear their words was wonderful, and I really wanted to start something like that, only I wanted to focus on black storytelling, because even at these conferences, emphasis was on the writers, on novels and on poetry. There was no storytelling.

My husband, Clay Goss, was the playwright-in-residence at the Institute for the Arts and Humanities at Howard University. Stephen Henderson was the director of the Institute. He was a great scholar who wrote the book *Understanding the New Black Poetry*, which is considered a classic. The institute sponsored programs on black culture and one day, Dr. Henderson said to Clay, "We need some storytelling. Where are the storytellers?" Clay told him, "Well, Linda tells stories there at the house," so he told him to bring me in to do a storytelling program and I was ready for it, because I had been telling stories for years on campus to my friends, and I used it for my senior final, and I was telling stories to our children, so when they said they needed a storyteller, I said, "Here I am!" And that's how I began as a professional storyteller back in the seventies.

I am the co-founder of the National Association of Black Storytellers with Mama Mary Carter Smith, and together, we are the founders of "In the Tradition..." National Black Storytelling Festival and Conference. That's the whole title now. It used to be called "In the Tradition..." National Festival of Black Storytelling, but it changed and in 1996 we added "conference" to it. The festival was founded in 1982. Mama Mary and I met in 1975 in Washington, D.C., on the grounds of the Smithsonian Festival of American Folklife, and since we were both telling stories there, we talked about organizing a festival at that time.

In 1983, we were both featured at the National Storytelling Festival in Jonesborough, Tennessee. I remember at the time that only three other African American storytellers had been featured—Jackie Torrence, Harriett Bias Allen and Brother Blue. We knew there were thousands out there and millions of stories, so it wasn't anything against Jonesborough, and I want to make that clear, but I am saying we have to preserve and cultivate our heritage—our stories.

The stories of our grandparents, mothers, fathers, aunts and uncles are important—I forgot to mention Uncle Buster, who was a storyteller in Mama's family; he was a character—so we decided to start up our own festival. Mama Mary said, "You know, my sorority, Zeta Pi Beta sorority in

Baltimore, Maryland, might be able to help us," because we didn't have any money at the time. So she went back to Baltimore and they got a grant from the Maryland Humanities Council, and in 1983 the first festival was held in Baltimore at Morgan State University. There were almost a thousand people in the auditorium, and we formed this huge love circle composed of storytellers and story listeners from as far away as Alaska.

The next year we took the festival to Philadelphia and I became a Zeta, and they helped me get a grant from the Philadelphia Humanities Council. It was there in Philadelphia at the African American Museum which was our base, that the storytellers as well as the community said that we needed to organize, and so the festival came first, and out of that came the Association of Black Storytellers which then became the National Association of Black Storytellers. We are still here, *praise the Lawd*, and we just had our twenty-seventh festival in Little Rock, Arkansas, and our twenty-eighth festival will be held in Minneapolis, Minnesota, in 2010, and will be hosted by one of our thirteen affiliates, Black Storytellers Alliance in Minneapolis, and the theme is the "Stories, the Breath of Life."

One of the things that makes our festival different is that from the very beginning, we traveled and went to different places around the country such as Baltimore, Philadelphia, Washington, D.C., Chicago, Berea in Kentucky, Oakland, California, Brooklyn, New Orleans twice, and Horry County and Georgetown County in South Carolina because we wanted to bring out storytellers everywhere we went, and to bring the people out.

The mountains have had a profound influence on me. I love the Smoky Mountains—just thinking about them or hearing the words makes me emotional. I love the Tennessee River and the Smoky Mountains—I grew up with them, seeing that mist in the early morning ... and I use that symbolism in a lot in my stories. I've even made a song about the mountains, and I used this symbol in a story entitled "Tale of Falling Leaves," which I adapted from a story written by one of my students at the Folk Art Cultural Treasures Charter School in Philadelphia and her name is Chhi Chhi Heng. This story provided the link between the different artistic mediums in an exhibition that I curated called *Totems* in Philadelphia. This is an example of how I use storytelling in many ways. *Totems* was an exhibition of breast shields, masks, dolls, quilts, narrative coats, artistic boxes, and found objects. It represented the symbols we use to protect ourselves in the face of danger. The featured artists were Martina Johnson-Allen, Kooki Davis and Gretchen Shannon—I incorporated their work into my performance of the "Tale of Falling Leaves," which was accompanied by percussionist Papa Ed Stokes.

"Tale of Falling Leaves" was a storytelling performance and was theatrical storytelling with a lot of audience participation. The story was created and performed as a fairytale and had four parts: Call of the Drum;

Libation; Creation of the Magic Forest, and the Tale of Falling Leaves. The themes showed the vulnerability and sensitivity of the male character. I purposely told that story in a way that forced people to listen to me as though they were listening to the radio. Usually, in fairytales, it is the female who is vulnerable and the knight in shining armor comes to save the princess. In this story, it is the princess who comes to save the prince, who is not really a prince. In this story I talk about the mountains and the foothills. The audience doesn't know I'm talking about Tennessee, but the man in the story is from the foothills and the young lady is from way on top of the mountain, so it is all about the mountains and the foothills and the autumn leaves falling—to me, that's a beautiful time in Tennessee, so all of that is in the story. The foothills are a very important part of the story, because that is where he is from, and that's where she has to go—down to the bottom of the foothills to rescue to him.

So yes, I am very attached to the Smoky Mountains and to the Tennessee River. Even when I do the "Creation of the Magic Forest," the audience helps me create the story. I will say, "I am the apple tree; I am the mountain, I am the river, I am the Smoky Mountains." There is also this thing I do where Papa Ed accompanies me on the harmonica and I use it to go back to my Southern heritage, and I start going back down to Tennessee, and I will say what I am, from that place at that moment—those are all things I knew as a child.

Growing up in Alcoa, you were surrounded by railroad tracks. Everywhere you go there's a railroad track. And then I talk about the tracks and I talk about the whistle late at night when that train was coming around the bend and Papa Ed plays that harmonica to make that train sound, and so I try to put the whole style and flavor of Alcoa, Tennessee, into my storytelling. I always let people know that I am from East Tennessee, because Tennessee is long and has middle and then the west. The further west you go the flatter it gets, so that's why I love East Tennessee—I love those hills and those mountains.

I talk about how I drive I-81 South onto I-40 West and down the Alcoa Highway, 129, and onto Hall Road which is the main road that comes through my town—you know, about how when you go back home you don't need no money, you don't need no bags. That's all in a poem I wrote about home.

All of nature is sacred, but my mountains are peaceful and sacred. I've seen the Rockies too, but everybody has their favorites but the Smokies are mine. I just love driving through there, walking through there. I've never spent the night out there, because I'm afraid of bears, but where I lived you could see the mountains all around you and it would only take fifteen minutes to get up there in them.

I have a story-poem called "There Is a Place," and it used to be in the Martin Luther King Center. It's a poem where I talk about Tennessee:

> There is a place where I can go
> When I am tired and feeling low
> It's called Alcoa, in Tennessee
> Where Mom and Dad will wait for me
> Don't have to write, don't have to phone
> All I have to do is go on back home,
> Down to Alcoa in Tennessee
> Where Mom and Dad are waiting for me
>
> Tennessee ~ mountain green,
> Morning dew
> Dad is smilin'
> Mom's cookin' beef stew
> Tennessee ~ mountain green,
> Morning dew
> How I love ya, yes I do

Stories make us human and give us a reason to live—we must have human contact and touch and it is through story that it comes. As Brother Blue would say, our hearts are real, our feelings are real. We are spirit and we are soul, and it is through our stories and storytelling that we are able to connect with another human being, even if we can't always understand each other's language. What has been great for me as a storyteller is that I have met people from all over the globe, people of different languages and different religions—Hindu, Buddhist, Black Hebrew, Jewish, Bahá'í, Jehovah's Witnesses, agnostic and atheist, witches, humanists, Methodists, Baptists, Catholics, Pentecostals or Muslim—people from all walks of life, and I met them through my storytelling. If I hadn't become a storyteller, I would never have met these people. We are one big human race and with our stories we should continue to develop a tolerance for each other's beliefs and opinions.

Rosa Hicks

The great-granddaughter of the Beech Mountain storytelling tradition founder, Council [also called Counce] Harmon, Rosa Hicks is a storyteller and singer of ballads in her own right. She never told stories on the stage while her famous storytelling husband Ray was living, saying she didn't have time because he had so much to say, but she frequently performed the "New River Train" song on stage with him.

Rosa Hicks was born at home in the town of Matnu, near Valle Crucis in Western North Carolina. She was just seventeen years old when she married Ray and moved to Beech Mountain. There, in a marriage that lasted 55 years until Ray's death, they raised their children in the two-story farm house built by Ray's grandfather, and where she continues to live with her youngest son, Ted.

She was at Ray's side most of the twenty-seven years he performed at the National Storytelling Festival in Jonesborough, and when he received the Heritage Fellowship Award from the National Endowment for the Arts in Washington, D.C., in 1983, she was there. Ray Hicks was also awarded the Brown-Hudson Folklore Award of the North Carolina Folklore Society, and the North Carolina Folk Heritage Award from the North Carolina Arts Council.

She was with him, if sometimes in the background, when he was featured in *The New Yorker* and countless other magazines, including *National Geographic* and *The Smithsonian*. He was also featured in the PBS series *The Story of English*.

Now Rosa tells her own story in a deeply moving personal narrative about how she met Ray and what it was like to live with the great Beech Mountain storyteller all those years, and her longing for him when he was gone.

The Interview

When folks started coming up here, it wasn't that bad for me, no, not really, not for me. They came to see Ray, so after they got settled, I took up my own work. They didn't call, they just showed up and we had to be ready for them. I used to joke with those folks saying you need to hear my stories—he's just pulling your leg! But no, really, Ray entertained and he had so much to talk about, and the boys always know more than the girls anyway.

The kids were bashful growing up, especially Kathy. She would run and hide when anybody came. She said, "What are them old things a-comin' for?" I said they are coming to hear Daddy.

Then I said, "Okay kids, remember how when you were growin' up, Mama would say, get you'ns something to eat? Well, get you'ns food out now; you'ns get your food and go on outside;" and then I called the men and the women in. I said [to the children], "You help carry the wood in, get the water and grow the vegetables," so I said, "You'ns goin' to eat first!" So I think they liked that pretty good. Let them eat first.

When I was still at home, the men ate first. Mama always made a fruit cake—put applesauce on it, and Mama made one every weekend when the apples were in season. And we had a friend who came over every weekend on Saturday. Well, they hollered "dinner's ready," so me and her go in and got a piece of that cake, and one had cinnamon candy beads on it, and one didn't. And they got the one with the candy on it. I said, "You are supposed to get the one without the candy on it"—it made me so mad [exasperated laugh] Kids can do the awfullest things and say the awfullest things!

After I was married, I'd be alone; Grandma Hicks would be around sometimes, but I'd get that lowed down feeling, homesick or something and I'd be sick for where I wanted to be at. I couldn't think about being over at home and I didn't want to be in another place, so I decided this was where I wanted to be, and I started working at it. I don't want to be anywhere else but here in these mountains.

You get sorry for yourself and want to be in this place or that one—I always did want to be in Florida, and wished I could see South Carolina where I couldn't see snow and that cold wind a-blowin'. I did want to go, when I was growing up, to the ocean and pick up sea shells. That was my dream as a girl. So I did get to go after Ray passed away. Jean [Rosa and Ray's daughter] went with me, so this woman we knew, somehow she got to know about I wanted to go to the ocean. I said, "No use now, I'm too old, everybody's done picked the seashells up and I won't find none," keeping myself from wanting to go. "Well," she said, "When the time is right, you go'n' go see the ocean," and I thought, well whatever.

I went with my friend; they bought galax for Christmas, and her son had bought a big ole place down through there, and she brought one of her kids here to meet me and see the place. And she said; "Now Rosa, you need a timeline," and I said, "No, the time ain't right yet; not yet."

So after Ray died, my friends, the Bernards, said, "Now Rosa, I'll take you to the ocean. I'll take you there." So we finally got ready to go early in September. At least we didn't get in a hurricane—nothin' like that, and the ocean was pretty, but there was too much of it. And all that water—too much of it! I got homesick. All you could hear was that roar, roar, roar and see them old birds flyin'.

When we got down there, she had some cookies and some Kool-Aid, and she spread out a little towel and put her stuff on it, and the birds were getting it and that was kind of funny to watch, but still it was good to get back home. She had a place where there were these oaks and they had moss on them. And it's so quiet, and we'd drive around to these places and I would hear Ray playin' his harp. I didn't want to move away from it, but she was driving. And then we'd come to another little place where there was one of those big old Spanish oaks and I'd hear Ray playing his harp or a tape or something. It must have been him [an emotional catch in her voice]. I hear things here—I don't know what they are. I saw him from in here [the kitchen] one time, out of that window—in his hat—he didn't lift it up.

I don't know where to start at about me and Ray, it's been so long; [chuckling] let's see if I can get it in my mind. [Gentle laughter]

I know back, Papa always rented to this man to grow the cabbage, and so that year he'd keep on planning what he was going to do the next year, cabbages ... and I thought, "That's silly, wait till the next year and then do your plannin'." So I said,

Rosa Hicks
(photograph by Valerie J. Menard)

"I won't be here," and Daddy said, "Why?" and I had to say something fast so I said, "I'll get married, I'll just get married." And then, I didn't give much thought about it—I had to say something to save face, so I guess I was a little *saysy* about it. [Laughter]

We knew Ray by this time, and he'd come by to see how we were doing, whatever. One day, Papa went over to visit at the house of one of the girls Ray went with, and her daddy and mama was there. Ray walked in and Papa wasn't sitting in there yet, and they said, "Ray, I thought you'd be married by now." He said "Nobody won't have me." Then Papa said, "I've got some girls." [Laughter] Well, Papa come in that evening and said, "We've got you a boyfriend." My sister Mae went all to pieces. "Papa, you think we can't pick out our own boyfriend?" I said, "What's his name?" "His name's Ray, Ray Hicks. I told him I had some girls for him."

That week, on Saturday, he come, but some way we was missing each other, so he come to Cool Spring Church (it was a plank one, but now it's a block building) so I seen he kinda wanted to go with me or something.

It went on till a little bit before Christmas, maybe November, but I don't know how Ray felt about us girls or what, and my sister's son and that other girl in there is their daughter—my oldest sister's kids, I think Floyd—him and Ray were pretty close friends—they were some kin. And Ray and Floyd would sometimes tell stories and listen and some way or another he came down and we were courting like through the week.

We was coming home on the truck from church, and there was a boy on this side and a boy on this side. And Mae said, "Oh, here's a sweet boy." I said, "No, over here's the prettiest one, Mae," so we went on carrying on with a bunch of junk like that. Well, one night, us girls wasn't on the truck, and so they thought Mama, Papa and maybe Aunt Terri was in the back of the truck, and they thought it was us girls in the truck. Somebody said Ray got his foot hung and he couldn't get it out. Said after he did that, he got back out since there wasn't no girls on it. We had all jumped off. [Breathless chuckle] When they come in, they said, "Great goodness, somebody might kill themselves—they's some of them on the truck and they jumped off and might have got killed." See, nobody knew to stop the truck.

I didn't know who it was. I went with them, and after they come in that evening, that's when they got to telling us about this guy getting his foot hung. They thought it was Ray, but it was really his friend jumped off, not Ray.

Then I think that Sunday we were going to have songs—go other places to sing—the Clark kids were. Of course you could go with the others. The night before that, I kept looking.... Somebody said Ray wanted to go with me. It scared me, you know. I went for him, but I was too bashful—so at the time, I looked out of the window to see if Ray was out there, and I looked everywhere.

I didn't go up to the singing place because I was hoarse—that's what happened! I went outside and it was cold and I took a chill. Ray came up and said he thought I might get up on the wind [laughter] and I said, "You know I did." My goodness, I could sound so *saysy*! We went on up the road and those girls on either side of me, and he went with me and I looked around and I didn't know his arms was so long, and he had a hold on me [laughter], I was bashful more than anything and I said, "You git your big hand off of me!" "OK," and he did and I said, "Lord ah mercy!"

I got home and I couldn't sleep. I said he orta slapped me for saying such as that to him and I said, "God, if you will forgive me this time and let me go back, I'll make it up." He told me later-wards, he said, "I just about did slap you, I was so pissed off." [Laughter] He said, "Well, she didn't know better." And I said, "He didn't want no girlfriend, it was the wine."

The next Sunday morning, when I saw him with that wine, we'd gone on the truck up to the church house. He got up on it, but he wouldn't look me in the eye. When we got down here to the church, someone else was going to get down off the truck, and we got on with them cause the one we was on wasn't going down where they were having the singing.

So we got down here at the other place and we got off. I don't know where Ray went to at the time. But he didn't give up—later that evening, here he came, looking for me. Then we missed each other. The girls always sat down on the bridge courting in the rain, so I asked the girls, and they said they thought he was supposed to be at the church.

And he come back around the next Saturday and we still missed each other, but he kind of knew a little bit how to get home. Grandmaw and Grandpaw's house was just a little bitty thing and nobody living in it, and we had about three preachers in our family on Paw Paw's side—I said we ought to have been pretty good girls. So my sister Dorsie had her baby with her, and we went into the little ole house and then to the church, and Dorsie, she seen a glimpse of Ray, but I didn't see him. She had seen Ray and she said "Rosie, it's getting too hot in here, let's go on outside." So we stepped out holding the baby, and lo and behold, here he was, he was a-sittin down, squatting outside the door. Well we walked across the porch and we just got set down, and I held the baby awhile, and then Ray got up and went over to the other side of the porch so he could see me. And Dorsie teased me, and said something to him, like, "You ought to get up here and get these boys off Rosa, or something."

Well, see, I thought he come with another girl. That's what I heard, and we went back down to our cousin's house and stayed down there talking, but we were walking in front of Ray, the woman and the two girls. We didn't quite make it to the house—we were waiting to see which way he was going and wasn't going; he was back there talking to that ole woman. And I said, "They told me he went with that girl!" It made me mad.

He said he didn't quite get to the house, and called her name, and said, "Are you going to go with me or not?" She said, "Go back over there and get some of them other purty girls I seen over there."

Well, my youngest sister was looking in the window, and the other one was a carrying on at the church, and so Ray finally found me and I keep a-kindly challenging him a little bit, but he talked and told stories and talked about Grandpaw Harmon. He knew a lot about his grandpaw when he was a-livin' and all that.

One Sunday I decided enough is enough. No, first, I got my sister to put a valentine in his pocket for me. I said that if I do it, he'll notice me, but you do it easy—I told her to put it in kind of easy. I put "To Shorty from Blacky," 'cause he was so tall. [Laughter] I don't know if I told him about it or not, I just don't remember. Anyway, I got her to put it in for me. And now his sister, Nell, when I couldn't see him cause he didn't come in the church, I said "Is Ray a'comin' tonight?" She said, "Yeah," he was going to come.

So I went outside, but I still couldn't see him nowhere. He had his wine and was enjoying the wine. After that, Papa wouldn't shut the door—it didn't make no difference how cold it was 'cause of where he was a-settin. Grandpaw, I mean PawPaw, had to keep the door open so he could see him. Said "He's crossin' the bar fence! I see Ray a-comin,'" 'cause he was so tall. [Laughter]

On Sunday, I said, "Girls, let's sit on the couch and give enough room for Ray to sit down," and they said okay. He started to set down, and the girls jumped up and made room, and he just set on down by me. I just scooted over and we started talking. We were going over to the church on Sunday, and Ray went with us, of course.

And one time he saw my sister, and thought it was me and started up the hill, and I said, "What's Ray doing up there?" I thought maybe there was some reason he saw up there. He laughed and said, "Rosie, I saw her up there and thought it was you!" Grandpaw, he slept in another room, and I went into the kitchen and he said, "Rosa, if you don't go in there and go with him, I'm gone kick your butt!" [Laughter] He was going to speed it up in a way ... went through a lot of crooked roads and ups and downs but in three months, we were married!

Yeah, I think Papa missed Ray more than he did me. Mama always teased me. She was putting in some galax and I went in [the house] to get supper. I was thinking off, probably about Ray or somethin'.... By the time I looked at my bread when it was cooking I said, "Oh, my gosh, I didn't put salt and sodie in it!" And Mama said, "She's in love, bad in love!" [Laughter] I hollered at Mama and said I forgot to put salt and sodie in the bread. Oh, my mama was a sayin', "When you forget to put the salt, when you forget to put that, you need to see the doctor!"

Ted Hicks

Ray and Rosa Hicks' son Ted is a tradition bearer. A life-long resident of Beech Mountain, he is a direct descendent of Council Harmon, who is credited with being the root of many generations of Appalachian storytellers; he has continued telling the stories he heard growing up on the mountain, but he tells them in his own voice, and that voice is rich with the old English sounds seldom heard today.

Ted is the youngest son of Rosa and Ray Hicks. According to Hicks, he "always knew the stories," having heard them from birth, so it was only natural, when the time was right, to take up the storyteller's staff and do what he does best—tell stories.

Until recently, Ted Hicks stayed home and looked after the farm when his mother and father went down to Jonesborough, Tennessee, for the annual National Storytelling Festival, but in 2008, Connie Reagan-Blake, nationally known storyteller and family friend, convinced him to go down to Jonesborough for the festival; he hasn't stopped performing since. While he was there, he held court much as father had before him, telling stories in the courtyard of the International Storytelling Center, and selling walking sticks to those who wanted to carry a piece of Beech Mountain back home.

The Interview

Mountains have got ins and outs, ups and downs, coves, hollers and ridges and we've got all of them. We've got forty-eight acres of land up here on Beech Mountain. We stay warm in the winter—we've got the wood heater; got a little bit of wood. We cut most of it from right here. I've never been out much.... Get out, I want back; get homesick, get back quick as I can. I've not been that far, but I always wanted back. They say people look for greener pastures; I never did want to *see* a greener pasture. I never did get married; still looking.

I been a-tellin stories for years, stories and jokes. I knew the stories for a long time and I always did like a good joke. You ought to put yourself in it. Don't tell about somebody else—tell it about yourself. People like that. See, in "Jack's Hunting Trip," you always say "Me and Jack's huntin' trip;" I went hunting with Jack [chuckle].

They say preachers like fried chicken ... like old preacher Dry Fry when he used to come by here. They say he was eating so fast he choked to death— I guess on a leg bone, or was it a thigh bone?

This one here started when I was sort of small, goin' to school, I was goin' to catch me a mess of fish. I cast about for a trout and something hit my pole. I pulled back and it was a big catfish. I was fishin' for trout but if I didn't get anything else, a catfish would have to do. I kept castin', must have been two hours. I looked around and my catfish was still a'breathin', just layin' there. I shoved him back down in the water, got him wigglin' pretty good. Then I went around to the house and got a big washin' tub, put water in it and put my catfish in it. Every day in the summer, I'd take that catfish out a little longer; got where he didn't need to be in the water, get up like this and come along behind me like a little dog, yupy, yupy, yupy yup. Didn't I have a good time that summer! Kinda got worried with school startin'. When school started the next morning, I said, "Oh, oh, if I take my catfish with me to school I'll get into trouble. I'd better tie him like a dog," so I put a leash on him and tied him to the corner of the house and took off to school. I hadn't gone maybe half a mile when I heard him behind me going yupy, yupy, yupy yup.

I said, 'Well gosh, I ain't got time to run back to the house and re-tie him; I'll be late for school.' I headed off to school with that ole catfish right behind me going yupy, yupy, yupy yup. Right when I got to school, I had to cross over a little bridge that crossed over a stream. As I crossed the bridge I noticed a board had fell out and was gone, you know. I walked on to the other end of the bridge waitin' for my catfish to come across. Never did come across, so I can't go to school, got to find out what happened to my catfish. I crossed the bridge and got to where that board had fell out and I looked down into the stream and I saw where my catfish had fell into the water. You know what happened? He lay there and drowned. [Laughter] And that was my Walkin' Catfish.

The first time I told stories in public was at the nursing home in Boone. Then they [nationally known storyteller and family friend Connie Reagan-Blake and her husband] had called me about going to the Storytelling Festival in Jonesborough [2008] and I told them to call me on Saturday morning, and, "I will tell you one way or the other." So this was the year I went to the festival and told there for the first time.

When I went down to Jonesborough, I didn't know I was going to be taking Doc McConnell's place. I didn't know that until I got there. Folks stopped by and we told stories—that was storytellin'!

It felt good to do it—it was just my second time tellin' in public, I guess.

I told "The Lucky Jack," "Barbara Freeman's Wicked John," and I told "The Mule Egg" story, and I told "Hardy Hard Head," I believe. That's the first time I've been to Jonesborough, but I just decided to go see what it looked like. See, before, when Mama went, I always stayed here and held the fort—that's what I called it, and minded the farm. I always stayed. Jimmy Neil [Jimmy Neil Smith, founder of the National Storytelling Festival and the International Storytelling Center in Jonesborough, Tennessee], always wanted me to come I guess, but I couldn't go.

Chase [Richard Chase] come through here about 1938 and wrote the *Jack Tales* book, and then he got the *Grandfather Tales* probably in the forties; he saved the stories—grandpa tales—see that book got it out in public, kept it goin'. There's eighteen of 'em in that book.

Counce Harmon had the stories and they came through him. He was my great-great-grandfather—great-great-great, I think. Daddy's dad told stories, too. See they come and collected the songs along—Marshall Ward's daddy's songs. His daddy took care of Counce when he got old. When he got to college he told them, "They got the songs, but they's stories in the mountains," and here they come to get them in "them thar mountains," and heard people sayin' things like, why be you here? Instead of why are you here? There's a lot of words like that—kivers for covers; sayser for saucer—bring me a sayser, not saucer. Dad would always say, "bedad." Let's see, I had it figured out one time: "Bedad"—I'd be on my way, or pardon me, I'll be on my way, like if I can't help you, well, bedad, I'll be on my way. Like pardon me or I'm leaving, won't bother you no more.... On my great grandpa's side they used speech like that. Taters, they'd say. "Thank you Mr. Hicks," and he'd say, "Not a tosser"—means "Don't thank me." There are a lot of words like that.

I always heard the stories—I knew them from the time I was knee high. Somebody would come and say to my dad, "Tell us a Jack tale," and here he'd go. Everybody that would come, he'd tell 'em a tale. If he had two or three listening, and another one came by, he'd say, "Come on in" and keep a-goin with his tale. Maybe he'd say, "Hey, how are you doin'; what's your name? Just come on in and join in."

When the magazines started there were people here all the time; at first seems like it was worse when we didn't have company. We got used to it. When we had company, we got out of work. [Laughter] Hot days, we were *wantin'* to see somebody come in. We always had to keep a hoe in the ground to keep ahead of the weeds, and we looked for any chance to stop. Most of the time he [Ray] might be talkin' in the field, restin', and he'd just keep goin' and forget about it—what you were doin'—just listenin' to him tell them stories. When Daddy got in the magazines and stuff, and it came out in *The New Yorker*, I don't know how many people came up here. There might be two groups here and three more a-comin. Said they had to see it. It was in *Reader's Digest*, all those big magazines.

When they first started coming I didn't want to see nobody. Kids will be kids; boys will be boys and girls will be girls. They were bashful. They would run and hide. They'd be ashamed to eat, you know. But if they asked you to eat and you did not, then it was too late. They did not ask you again.

Like I said, we were always tickled to see them after a while. When I got in the hospital, I got more used to people and started telling stories. I was always, like Mama said, bashful. I'd jump out of the way when I see'd 'em coming. I'd jump in the briar patch! I didn't want to see nobody. I acted like a wild animal [whistled] gone, just like the wind. [Chuckle] I'm fifty-four now; I grew out of it. [Laughter]

Ted Hicks
(photograph by Valerie J. Menard)

One time when Daddy was in the hospital, he started tellin' stories to the other folks that were in there, and him sick. Said there was a man there got it in his mind there was a cat in his stomach. Went to the doctors and they decided to put him off to sleep and take a picture of his stomach. They give him morphine—they did that back then. He came back to, and there was a big black cat sittin' in front of him. They said, "We got the rascal," and he said, "What? The one that was in my stomach was a gray one!" [Laughter] They didn't ask him what was the color of it!

Said there was another man, guess he came back from the war, and he decided to go get him some disability. Three doctors put him in a room and then they got to talking. One of them said maybe they should take his arm and the other one said take both of them. The third one said maybe legs ... when they went back in the room, he was gone!" [Laughter]

Dot Jackson

Dot Jackson is the award-winning author of the Appalachian novel *Refuge* (Novello Press, 2006). She was an investigative reporter for many years, and her career brought her into contact with numerous Appalachian storytellers; her stories about them are legendary in the newspaper world.

She was born in Miami, Florida, on the rim of the Everglades to parents exiled from the Keowee River Valley in the hills of Pickens County, South Carolina, due in part to the sad state of the economy in the mountains and the availability of work in South Florida, and partly to "some pretty fierce disagreements between family members over my folks' courtship and runaway marriage."

In Miami, her family was part of a clan of "Blue-Ridgers" who gathered on the porch at night to stare at what is now priceless beach property, to disparage the bugs, land-crabs and pervasive heat, and to listen to the sound of the mountains in their talk. It was their way of remembering home, always the "hills and clear waters; the homefolks, and the stories."

She attended the University of Miami on a music scholarship, married and had three children. When she moved to Charlotte, North Carolina, she took a job with the *Charlotte Observer* and began her career as an investigative reporter.

Jackson's time with the newspapers was not without disagreement, but she acknowledges it was the papers that sent her into places she needed most to go, to be with the people "I needed most to cherish—to the fight over the New River, beside people who did not get dammed out of their homes. And into the struggles of the people of Tellico, Tennessee, who did. And in time, it was the papers that helped me, with jobs, to come home."

During her years as a reporter, she and the teams she worked with were nominated for two Pulitzer Awards, one for their reporting on the Catawba River when she was with the *Charlotte Observer*, and the other, when she was with the *Greenville News*, which resulted in a good portion of Pickens County being named a Superfund Site designated for toxic waste cleanup.

In 1980, she was awarded the coveted National Conservation Award by Trout Unlimited for her reporting on the Tellico Dam. Jackson received the Alicia Patterson Foundation Fellowship in 1991; the Appalachian Studies Association Weathertord Award in 2006; the silver medal from the Independent Publishers Association in 2007, and the Appalachian Writers Association Award for Fiction in 2007.

She has long been a freelance book editor; she is the author of numerous published stories and articles, and she co-authored, with Mike Hembree, the self-published and regionally highly popular *Keowee: The Story of the Keowee River Valley in Upstate South Carolina*.

When Jackson was in her fifties she came back to live in Pickens, "knowing everything the old ones would tell me," to find peace among the bones of her ancestors, and that place "unfolded like a map of memories before her."

She and a group of friends purchased an old farmhouse, circa 1813, at the foot of Table Rock Mountain above Pickens, and named it the Birchwood Center for Arts and Folk-life. Among their working partners are the nearby state parks, the region's universities, area museums and most recently the Smithsonian Institution. They are in the process of restoring the old house in an effort to further serve the arts and traditions of the community, and Jackson is its ambassador, telling stories in the community and making sure the children of the region never forget their roots.

"It's worth a lot to be here, and see it bloom," she said.

The Interview

The Boggses of Pickens County in upstate South Carolina are ubiquitous; practically everybody is in some way connected to them. Everybody in Pickens County whose people have been there as long as my family—everybody is connected. It has been an isolated place, plus our ancestors didn't like to see their land carried away by outland marriages, so they kind of liked for us to marry one another so that we would hold on to our land. The Boggses have been in Pickens County since the 1780s.

My great-great-grandfather, Aaron Boggs, was married twice and had nineteen children, and his father had a jillion children and you can see how they spread all over creation. There are a lot of Boggses in Pickens County. And of course the girls have different names now—there's a lot of Boggs blood in Pickens County.

My daddy worked for the Tennessee Valley Authority for a while when I was little. Because of that, we lived a lot better than many people because they paid everybody $100 a week. Outside of that you'd get about $25 a week. So my daddy made money while he was doing this, and we thought it was great because everybody lived so hard during the depression. As I got older and I saw ... I think what opened my eyes was the last job that Daddy had for them, which was to go in and start building housing for the men that were coming in to build the Fontana Dam.

He took us over there to the dam site and they were tearing down or moving out all the houses that were in the Fontana basin. He took us to ride down this dirt road that went down by the Little Tennessee River a long way past where they were getting ready to build the dam. There were houses there that were all boarded up, here again to keep the people from moving back into them, and they had paid the people something like $38 an acre for their land and said, "You can go down and buy something nice for what we are paying you and get a good paying job in town"—this was in 1941.

They actually built the dam in 1942, and they had to bring all these men in there—like two or three thousand workers, and they brought their families with them, and there was absolutely no place to live. One of the old legends is that when they brought in a 72-inch culvert pipe, that it would be occupied within seconds of the time it fell off the truck and hit the ground. The families would move into each end of it and sleep in there and keep their food dry. My daddy was building cabins for some of the men who were going to work there. He took us to ride on this road and it made a profound impression on me and my thought was, "Where have the people gone, where have the people gone?" We left there when they sent him back down to Homestead, Florida, to build a blimp base in the beginning of 1942. I didn't see that part of the country for many years after they built Fontana.

Daddy was working for the TVA when we lived in Hothouse Township, North Carolina, right off U.S. 64 west of Murphy and near Ducktown, Tennessee, when I was a little girl. We lived in all kinds of weird places and twenty-seven years after we lived there I went back to Murphy to cover a murder trial—a notorious murder case, and when the court wasn't in session, I went out to see what the Hothouse Township looked like. I drove the 18 miles out there and of course the roads were changed—everything was changed, radically, so I drove up to the top of Franklin mountain which separates Tennessee and North Carolina; from one side you look down on Ducktown and from the other side, you look down on Cherokee County, North Carolina.

I rode up to the top trying to find the place where we used to live. When I came back there was a woman standing on the side of the road waiting for somebody. I pulled over, rolled the window down and said, "Hester?" She looked at me and said, "They Lord have mercy!" Then she said, "Let me in this car." She thought I was Mama. The most interesting thing I noticed about

Hester and me, was that Hester's language had been changed a lot by television, where mine was more like Hothouse in times past than Hester's. She'd never been out of there, and she had not made the concerted effort to maintain that identity, whereas I had made it my entire life mission to maintain that effort. So we rode around—she was probably in her seventies—she realized it couldn't be Mama; it had to be me. We went down to the house where my brother had courted a young woman, and we went in to see those people and I just cried the whole time. I couldn't exchange a single word with them—I just cried. I know they thought I was crazy as a loon. Anyway, it was a happy, happy situation as a child. I was telling Linda [her cousin, Linda Bowie] that I was eight or nine years old then. It couldn't be beat.

**Dot Jackson
(photograph by Cindy Morris,
courtesy Novello Festival Press)**

For the most of my growing up time in my dreams, that was home, that was where I lived, in my mind, until I was a grown woman. Seven months—I went to school there one term and probably got about more education there, where there were grades four through eight in one room, than I ever got anywhere else. I remember more about everything there. That was the story of the ugly duckling right there—I had been the ugly duckling my entire life—this "hillbilly" child that other children imitated. I remember that one of them that I eventually married said, "She's got bugs in her har." When I got back to Hothouse, I found there were a lot just like me and I liked them; I loved them.

Incidentally, it's curious how much of our verbalization is genetic. One of the cousins gave me a typescript of a letter that my great-grandfather wrote to my great grandmother before they were married. He was in the Civil War. I read that and I thought, good Lord have mercy, that's right out of my mouth. I could have written that exactly word for word as he wrote it. I think it's genetic.

This [Appalachian dialect] is the most descriptive language I know—well I don't know very many languages—[laughter]—I know Miami Beach. I heard my father speaking the Appalachian dialect—this is his language and I am so blessed you know, that it was. It will die out if we don't use it and I was aware of it as a small child. My daddy followed the money trail all the way down to Miami, Florida, when he and my mama had to leave Pickens—the family disapproved of their marriage and there was a shooting ... anyway, here we lived down there in that polyglot society: our next door neighbors were Greek and Polish and fought in both languages all the time, and our air raid warden was a member of the German American Bund and acted like one of the most classic Nazis I've ever seen in my life. We bought the piece of land from a Danish woman who came back and visited us, and English was her third or fourth language. There was a woman behind us whose family escaped the Bolsheviks but not until they had killed her parents because they were high society in Russia—Jews—and made her drink their blood. These were our neighbors, but the thing was, if we accepted the polyglot culture and began speaking the polyglot speech, eventually we would have none of our own. So even as a child I was very conscious of "Let's not lose what's ours," you know. Nothing beats hearing these [Appalachian] people speak in their own language.

And we also had what I think of now as the "Blue Ridge ghetto"—everybody from the Carolinas, north Georgia and Virginia would come sit on our front porch at night down in Miami. They were down there looking for jobs—that's what everybody was down there for—we weren't down there because we loved it. God no! I didn't love it then and I don't love it now, but that's where my daddy found the money was and so he was gonna have to be there for the duration; as it turned out, he died there, which he hated more than anything. I remember him standin' on the front porch, looking off in the distance and saying, "Oh, I can see too far!"

My mother was a great talker and very well educated. She was a professional artist—she painted and taught school. She was the one who did most of the talking—my father said absolutely nothing—and she loved to tell stories she remembered from back home. Bird Montgomery, my aunt who lived with us part of the time, was one of the great storytellers of all time. She was also my cousin Ben Robertson's caretaker, because his mother died when he was a small child. This [storytelling] is a very internal thing in our family.

My cousin Ben was the great writer in our family. His ability to get to the essence of an issue very quickly was a phenomenon. Talk about a storyteller; that was one. Steven Vincent Benet wrote, after *Red Hills* was published, that it was the most beautiful book about the South ever written. His storytelling—he could tell a complete story and you not realize a story was being told to you—in one or two sentences; so wonderful was he at capturing the essence of knowing exactly what should be said ... he's really the only teacher I have ever had, really and truly. I've had some wonderful editors, but he's really the only storytelling teacher I've ever had.

The book *Refuge* was an act of compulsion—totally an act of compulsion; an obsession outside of my own will. Something spoke through me—I had to write it, and I had to change it, because my mother said, "If you tell this, I'll kill you. This must never pass your lips. It's a terrible disgrace—it's a scandal that would ruin us." 'Course, it's a hundred years ago—right now, it's a hundred years ago, but she would have come back from the dead to kill me if it had been obvious that I used this story, so I had to disguise everything in the book. A couple of years went by when I was trying to write it, and I had gone to work for the *Charlotte Observer*. I started it while I was working at Belks, long before I went to the *Observer*, but I didn't know what to do, didn't know where to go with it, or how to make these people so nobody would know who they were.

I think this happens to just about everybody who writes a work of compulsion. I was sittin' down there in that basement one night hammerin' away at this old skeleton of a typewriter and suddenly [voice dropped and she spoke quietly with emotional intensity] it was very spooky—that whole place was spooky—it was like someone came and stood beside me and said, "Get out of my way. Let me do this because I know what happened there. You don't." And Mary Sen [Mary Seneca is the heroine of *Refuge*] lived with me for the next fifteen years and Mary Sen was my best friend, and my dearest companion. I love Mary Sen just about above all people, which is just so weird. And I'd say, "You can't do this, you just can't do this," and she'd do it anyway and I'd sit there and type it. It took fully fifteen years to write. I never had any idea anybody on earth would publish *Refuge* until Frye Gaillard called and asked, "What did you ever do with that manuscript?" And that's how it came to be published.

Well, this is the way it was: I didn't care anything about writing fiction—I never wanted to do it—the facts are way too interesting, but my mother came up with all of these stories about things the family had done. My mother was never interested in anything much outside of her family, but she kept a lot of stuff about them to herself. As she got older, her tongue got looser and she would tell things that she regarded as not fit to tell before. And it was in the early sixties she hit upon this story that she thought I should know about. It was about this first cousin of hers, or two of her first cousins and something they did—I was very much a fan of this cousin of hers; I loved her very much. She was very beautiful, a high-society lady and butter wouldn't melt in her mouth. She was also one of Mama's very favorite relatives and she said, "You need to know what she did back when she was young." "What did she do?" I asked. "Well, she ran off with this cousin of hers."

One of their uncles had been dispatched away from the family because he was a bad egg very early in life, and he had gone off down to Alabama and found Aunt Liza down there. She was quite pretty, but apparently not very bright—they talk about how Aunt Liza used to sit on the front porch in her blue taffeta dress with her skirt pulled up to show her legs ... and read her book upside down [Laughter]—you know her exactly!

What had happened was this uncle had been dispatched down there and had been kept away from the rest of the family ... but he became extremely prosperous. And nobody knew by what means he had prospered until quite some time later. Anyway, he and Aunt Liza had two sons and at the time of this incident—at the time the boys were eighteen or nineteen, and he decided that news of this prosperity just had to be known back among his relatives. They had not been terribly kind to him back in his youth, and sent him away. He wanted to show what all he had done, so he brought his wife and these two boys up here for the first time.

That uncle's sister had this beautiful young daughter, who was seventeen, and she and one of these boys laid eyes on one another for the first time—*just locked*. Before anybody knew anything, they were gone, and they stayed gone for quite some time. The girl's daddy set out to find them and brought them back and then he dispatched his brother-in-law and family of fiends back to Alabama.

'Course, there was a question about whether she was pregnant from this, because she was most certainly, in their vision, *rurnt*, and that certainly they had *done it* by the time they got her back. And so, anyway, he locked her up in the house. Not very long after the brother-in-law and his family got back to Mobile, the boys were killed boarding a yacht in an act of piracy. And quite possibly this was how the whole family fortune was made—I don't know—I'm just supposing. Apparently, they were inveterate pirates, and they were shot and killed by the owner of the boat. It's real family history as recorded by my mother. Here was this girl at home, *rurnt* and the boy dead. After so long a time of living this maiden lady existence at her parents' home, she met this man from over in Greenville who was at least twice her age, well-fixed, and able to take care of her beautifully.

Well, this man just fell head over heels for her and prevailed on her father to let him marry her. So, the father said, "Well, yeah! I've got these damaged goods here, let him have her." And so they made a big splash in society. He died fairly early in this marriage, because he was so much older, so she was a very well-fixed widow for a long time and a very prominent woman.

On her ninety-second Christmas, I went to see my aunt on Christmas day. She was sittin' up in bed—beautiful, with all of her jewelry on and her hair done, and her face painted, and vanity was her middle name. The nurse was sitting nearby. She had no idea that I had heard the tale I just told about how they lived this life when I went to see her, and she didn't know I had already written *Refuge* by that time. She said, "I have something I need to talk with you about." I thought to myself, "Oh Lord, is it coming, you know? Is she finally going to spill this tale to me?" And she said, "I'm having these dreams. I can't talk about them to anyone else." And she said, "Well, I dream it repeatedly." So I said, "What are you dreamin'?" And she said, "I don't like to wake up from this dream. It's so strange, and I don't know what it means: I'm dreaming that I'm running on this beach and I'm very young. I'm barefooted, and it's just this feeling that I'm the happiest that I've been anywhere." And I said, "Where are you?" She answered and said, "Well, this is what's so strange—I believe I'm on Mobile Bay, but I've never been there." And I said finally, "Do you think you could be down there with your uncle and aunt and their children?" Her face looked just like the sun had risen and she said, "I think that may be it."

Six days later her nurse called and said she didn't wake up that morning, and I knew what happened—it just about killed me—that boy came and got her from whatever limbo he had been in for seventy-something years. He was visitin' her in preparation for taking her with him to wherever he was. Well, whatever happens in my own book you know—yeah, waiting for her [the cousin Ben Aaron, waiting in the nether-world for Mary Seneca] watching over her all those years, and this is what happened there with my cousin when she died.

I met Ray Hicks, the storyteller, but I knew his first cousin Stanley real well and spent a lot of time with him over the years. The Harmons I knew well, and visited them as often as I could. Richard Chase of course, visited with them quite a lot. They were all totally individual—each one all his own.

Stanley Hicks was a perfectly natural person; just a good ole mountain boy who killed a hoop snake and hung it on his fence one day. All of his neighbors came by to admire the hoop [with emphasis on a hard "h"] snake, you know. They are real but they are not a snake, as one of my environmental friends reminded me [drawing her face down and looking very educated], they are the eastern grass lizard: "If you will notice, they have eyelids and vestigial legs under the skin. It is not a true snake." Well, it looks like a snake to me and the one I did see up close—Ambrose Dennis had beat its head off with a shovel when he perceived it was comin' after him. It didn't have no eyelids—it didn't have a head no more. It was coiled up in a jar! It was mottled by the time I saw it and it was about 18 inches to two feet long and it had a spike—a calcified tail or horn at the end of the tail. What makes people think they make a hoop is that when they get excited, they kick that tail over their head and it makes a circle and these little vestigial legs are going about 90 mph. Anyway, Stanley had caught one in his field and he had hung it on his fence and everybody came by and looked at it. He told me about it.

It was real exciting to everybody around there that Stanley had caught this snake, because you know, you are not supposed to escape with your life if you encounter a hoop snake. If you do, *hit'll hoop up and hit you with that stinger and you done dead.* And if you get behind a tree, to get away from it, *hit'll kill the tree first and then hit'll get you dead as a doornail. Ain't no end to the "pizen" in that tail—it can roll faster than anything that can run.* The reason we never see 'um is they are nocturnal. They eat night bugs and small children who are out when they shouldn't be....

When I visited Stanley, we sat around and talked and he made things out of wood, and told "Hicks tales." They had a spiel that was all theirs. I never did know Ray like I knew Stanley. I'll tell you another one that's overlooked this day and age, and he's Willard Watson. He was both the real thing and a professional mountain man. He was a first cousin to Doc, and they lived in a little knot on Wild Cat, off Deep Gap Road. Willard made toys—wooden toys and sold them at fairs and music shows—some for adults and some for children.... He was marvelous and he had a vocabulary that was unique to him. He's the one who referred to that ole dust coffee [instant] and called his wife the ole dough-beater. He played to the crowd, but his wife Orie was an exquisite quilt maker. The two of them together were kind of a treasure.

I met a lot of them [storytellers and folk musicians] at Union Grove; they tended to show up there and I gravitated to them and I loved them. Certain people, when I run into them, like Betty Smith—God, how I love that woman, she's just so real and so gifted—she's a ballad singer, you know—a good person and would never do anybody dirt for anything in the world. She's written a good book about Jane Hicks Gentry, the singer, that she learned a lot of stuff from. A lot of her songs that she sings came out of Madison County. She's a friend of Sheila Kay Adams—she's a friend of just about everybody. And Charlotte Ross—she's in Boone now, teaching at the university and still telling all those stories—she knows them all by heart—as far as I know they are still not written down, and she made only that one recording and we talked her into that. We all know each other by heart.

I met Richard Chase at one of those gatherings, too. He was always the star. He was always the one who knew the most of everything, and if you encountered Richard Chase, you were there to learn from him—you know the type. He was this very, very angular hyperactive guy, thin, with his beret pitched over—always with his beret and a beard—just his whole demeanor was cultivated, but he had made a profound study for many years of folkways: dances, songs and stories. He told me he had learned his Jack Tales from the Harmons, which were the fountain of Jack tales, and that he had stayed with them at one point. The next time I went to see them—the old lady was in her nineties then—she made me a pine needle basket one time, and I still have it ... anyway, I asked the old lady, "I understand you know Richard Chase and he learned some Jack Tales from you." She answered, "Yes, I certainly did know him." And then I said, "He said he stayed with you at one point," and she answered, "Yes, he did—twenty-one years!" [Laughter] He was irascible and impatient in his old age, but he was a gifted man and it was sad he didn't have any place to be old in. Those people up there don't take kindly to people who act superior and he always had that, but what he wrote was accurate.

The ballad writer John Jacob Niles was from Kentucky, very well educated and out of an educated family. He was musical. Anyway, somehow he got in with Doris Ulmann who was the great photographer of that age who was to that age what Annie Liebovitz is now, but she was society, the photographer of photographers and society. He was in his twenties and she was in her forties or early fifties when she met him and hired him to drive her big automobile and take her back into the mountains. And he would take her into these very difficult places to get to, drivin' in creek beds and stuff, drive her as far as he could, scout out the territory and find out where a good photographic subject was for her, and then he would take her in there. And she was fragile—she had TB [tuberculosis]; he said her way of getting access to these people or getting them to open up to her, she was strictly Manhattan—she looked like a princess and wore long chiffon dresses and lots of jewelry and always had her hair done gorgeously. She wore beautiful shoes and he would carry her to keep her from getting messed up on the road and she was very frail.

He would drive the car as far as he could, and then he would carry the photographic equipment to the site, and then carry her up to whatever holler that there was. He was a wiry, stringy person, but I imagine very strong. The women of the households would be so charmed by her looks they would do just anything. He said that often they would come up very shyly and ask if they could touch the dress she had on. I guess back then they used glass photo plates or whatever it took, tripods and stuff. Those mountain people had the patience of Job with her while she took their pictures and never expected to see them. I bet a nickel she sent 'em pictures. I don't know that, but they were extraordinary and looked like you could look right into their souls—no posing, just them in their old clothes—whatever they had. He and Doris did this and there was a romance of sorts between them. They stayed over at John C. Campbell Folk School. Anyway, while she was taking their pictures, he was collecting their songs and then he would record them in his notebook.

Now, what John Jacob Niles did that I didn't like, and some scholars did not like, is that he would take their songs and then he would re-write them to suit himself, largely to suit his own vocal equipment. He had this [pitching her voice high and mimicking Jacobs] high falsetto voice that sounded like wind through a pipe; it was intriguing, mesmerizing. He could shut people up when he got started. But, he would take some of these songs—I remember he and I had quite a discussion one time: what you hear these days as "Black Is the Color of My True Love's Hair," being a folk song—if it's a John Jacob Niles version, no it ain't. He took the tune and completely re-wrote it, and what you hear these days as "Black Is the Color" is John Jacob Niles' version, because it is very melodically beautiful and suited to his style of singing. I said, "What made you change that tune?" he answered, "Because it was ugly. It didn't suit me." Well, no, it didn't suit his vocal style; therefore, any number of these folk songs he recorded in his books is not the way it was sung to him. He used the lyrics—he mainly wanted the poetry. He was one of the most fascinating old men I have ever known in my life—I absolutely adored the ground he walked on. He was very scholarly and very mystical. He and Thomas Merton were very close friends.

Here's a classic John Jacob Niles story: He did a presentation at Winthrop back in the seventies, and I went down there and made arrangements to see him. I spent the day with him and his wife, a beautiful Russian woman about thirty years his junior. He had a dulcimer that he played (wang, wang, wang), and then he would sing a bit here and there, and I was thinking, "Good God in heaven. This is a heavenly situation with this wonderful soul who knows everything I want to know, and he'll be dead soon." Then he turned around, looked at me and said, "That's all right. I will be dead soon, but I'm leaving a record of everything. Everything I left is recorded. (Wang, wang, wang.) It's all notated."

I had to grow into this kind of music and didn't know the true value of this stuff until I was old. I was very interested in what he was doing and how he was changing things. He was one of those people you connected with on a very deep level. You don't do that with just everybody.

When I was working in Charlotte and then in Greenville, I'd roam all over those mountains. One day, I drove down to Pickens County, South Carolina, and onto Hickory Holler Road; when I saw the old house, Birchwood, I fell in love with it. That place has been dear to me ever since—really all of my adult life. I was determined, I guess, to get back.

Now, I am trailer trash at this moment—oh man, am I ever trailer trash! [Laughter] Well, it's perfect: I have a little trailer parked next to the big house; it's only 12 feet wide and I can't fall down very far cause it's all jammed up with books and boxes and papers and all kinds of stuff, so I'm very safe in there you know. Well, do you know about the black bear that used to live underneath my bedroom?

Well, this is what it was. One evenin' in the fall of the year I took a chicken pie to a lady who was sick. I guess the smell of it was still in the car when I got home, right at dark. It was nice weather and I left the car window down about halfway and went inside, not thinking.

You know, a bear loves the smell of chicken just about better than anything in the world. So, way in the wee small hours, I heard this racket, out at the car, this scratching and huffing and clatter. This was a car that it would be hard to steal—you couldn't ever get it to crank till the sun had shined on it an hour or so. So I just left things alone and went back to sleep.

By the first light of the morning, I got up and looked out and there was the *quarest* sight. Everything—or nearly—that had been in that car was stacked in the yard as neat as could be, in little piles; papers, books, jackets, the camera bag unzipped—as it always was, with the camera and lenses ready to take a picture.

And there was the car. It was mud and big footprints all over; just a tiny place torn in the upholstery of the front seat, where he must have clung on as he went in and out of that impossibly tiny window hole, carrying stuff out. And, he had uncovered a bag of birdseed in the back seat, and had opened it. The whole car was upholstered in bear hair and grease, slobber and birdseed. I laughed out loud.

He had done run off, and dropped his favorite things as he went—a little red pocketbook that had lipstick and stuff in it, and a pair of new underpants, still in the plastic wrap, that had been under the front seat. The reason I know these were his favorites, is later.

Anyway, I had a prescription I needed bad, waiting for the drugstore to open, and I thought, well, I will just go to town in the mess and clean the car up when I get home. I gathered up all the stuff and got in that car, and Lord—stink is not the word. It just reeked, going down the road. When I got to town and got out of the car, I looked like Bigfoot with all that ol' black stiff hair and seed stuck all over my shirt and britches. And smelled worse. People stood aside—and stared.

I got my pills though and came home, and made a quick trip into the house to take a dose, and I was not in here 30 seconds till WHOP! That booger was back on the car. By the time I got out there, he had broke the windshield, and had his panties and his pocketbook a-runnin' for dear life.

Now, I hollered and raved at him. A broke windshield is NOT funny, and when your wallet is broke, too—and your pocketbook is headed for the woods. (He DID drop his play-pretties, but there was spit all over everything.) So, some neighbors with a bunch of dogs came and got the car and took it to their house, because he would have been back in it, in an instant. And I called the wildlife [service].

Now, I had had prior experience with the wildlife. I had gone with him and several others to haul a bear off to the backwoods, one time, and I had made the mistake of writing a funny story about how one poor guy in this bunch had been assigned to stand on the ground and open the cage, while the rest of 'em (including *this* guy) hopped up like fleas to the roof of a pickup cab when that bear come out of there a slobbering and growling. And this wildlife [officer] remembered that, when he come out, he set up one of those big long cylinder traps and baited it with several cans of sardines.

He says, "When you hear that trap spring, you better come out here and make *sure* there's a bear in it before you call me. And you better call me before six in the morning, 'cause I have to be out in the field by seven. And if there's a bear in here you ain't going to want it to spend all day in this trap, 'cause it will be mighty mad when it comes out." So, I promised to call him when I knew it was trapped.

Three days went by. Coons or something small ate the sardines, and the trap didn't spring. Then way in the night, on the third night, it went FLAMMMM! And the whole world shook. I called a cousin and said, "That bear trap is sprung and I wanted you to know I have got to go out there and make sure it is in the trap 'afore I call the wildlife."

And he said, "Well, I would sure take care if I was you. That bear may be just part ways in that trap. Or he may not be in it at all, but just a-waiting for you to come out and see."

I thought about this. Finally, about 4 o'clock, I got up and got my flashlight, and my walker, and put on my bedrooms and hobbled out into the night. That trap was way down in the woods; black as ink down there. I had seen the thing, of course, it was a little small bear, probably weighed a little over a hundred pounds. Its mama had run off with her boyfriend and left it, and it was lonesome, you know. I called to it and said everything was all right and not to be scared. Then I shined the light in that trap, and saw *nothing*. I commenced to talk to it then, but I couldn't see a thing. I felt so bad; I knew it was hunkered down in there, scared to death.

"Don't you worry, Granny's Baby," I said. "We are going to take you to ride to some real pretty woods where nobody will bother you." It never offered to answer, a-tall.

Finally, when I shined the light, I saw the shadow of two ears, against the back of the trap. That was all. So I stood there a while, and talked to it, and sung to it a little bit, and when I begun to cry I figured it was time to go in the house, and call the wildlife.

"Are you *sure* it's in there?" he said. Well, he come on out, just at daylight, and he didn't look a-tall, just hooked that trailer with the trap on it to his pickup and started to leave.

I said, "You ain't a-goin' to take it all by yourself? Don't you want me to go?" He was still smarting of course from being made fun of. "NO I DON'T!" he said. "You said it's just a little old bear. I can take care of this!" So off he goes, and I am hollering goodbye to Granny's Baby. A couple of hours later, I get a call from a reporter at the newspaper. "I hear you have had some bear trouble out there," she said.

"How did you hear that?" I said. And she said, well, if she was me, she would stay out of the range of the wildlife. Said she had called him about bear problems and he had told her he had just hauled one off from here. Said I had promised it was "just a little feller." But when he opened that cage, way out in the boonies, "That bear just kep' a comin' and kep' a comin'" It was a big ol' bear, probably woulda weighed in at four hundred pound.

Right after I talked to her, a lady across the ridge called me and said, "Guess who's over here in our yard right now! *Your little bear*! And he's the *cutest* thing."

I love these mountains. I dream about them all the time. I think it's about the land—and the people are incidental—that's bad, but it's the facts of life. I don't know if I'm hearing things in the yard, but I dream about them, and they're just there with everybody and we're all living together you know. I've done got my tomb rock with my name on it ... I ain't leavin'!

Charlotte Ross

Charlotte T. Ross is an oral tradition storyteller, free-lance folklorist and a teacher. She has collected over 3,000 stories from the mountains of Appalachia, spending a lifetime taking notes on regional stories and legends. She then researched and crafted them into original stories filled with real people and places.

Known as the "Legend Lady," Ross is a ninth generation Appalachian from the mountains of North Georgia. She is an adjunct professor in the Communications Department at Appalachian State University in Boone, North Carolina, where she teaches English, folklore and storytelling, Appalachian studies and speech.

Other accomplishments include serving as the director of the Appalachian Regional Collection at Appalachian State University; assistant director of the Center of Excellence in Appalachian Studies at East Tennessee State University; president of the Council on Appalachian Women; chairperson of the Appalachian Studies Conference, and program associate and acting director of the North Carolina Humanities Council.

Ross specializes in Appalachian culture and is in demand as a lecturer presenting programs and workshops on Appalachian storytelling, history, folklore, vernacular architecture, material culture, Appalachian literature and Appalachian speech and dialect. Her historical play, which is based on her own family's five generations of stories, *From My Grandmother's Grandmother Unto Me*, has been aired by PBS. She has been interviewed on NPR's *All Things Considered*, and the BBC in Glasgow, Scotland.

Ross has performed at numerous festivals, conferences and universities, including the American Folklore Society, the Smithsonian Institution Folklife Festival, Opryland, the Ulster Folklife Festival in Ireland, and the New University at Ulster in Ireland, the Kellogg Institutes, Harvard University, and the National Institutes of Health.

The Interview

As a kid I was always telling stories. But when I started teaching, storytelling was the way I illustrated things and it was the natural thing to do. You can make a point more deeply and more memorably with stories; besides, I'm a ninth-generation Appalachian mountaineer, and consequently my style is narrative and anecdotal. I can't give you directions to the post office downtown without telling you a story—it's just the way my mind is organized, and I've thought a lot about that. Claude Lévi-Strauss [French anthropologist and ethnologist, 1908–2009] said the region in which you are born gives a certain kind of shape to the way your mind will work, and that there are geographic and cultural differences in the way we approach and process information, and I think he's right, and I think our way down here is storytelling.

There are very few of us left who relate everything—story, history, song, architecture to the landscape—even my husband couldn't do it. He was my high school teacher and I married him because he could tell a story and he had orange hair ... anyway my husband gradually became interested in Appalachia, which is strange because originally he wasn't, even though he was born in Appalachia, but we worked very well together. He could get lost in the mountains; it's really hard to lose me. What I'm doing is watching the shape of the mountains and the valleys and figuring where the roads branch out, but I was taught to see it that way and it became instinctive. You get an identity—we are a very place-bound society. I love Boone, I love North Georgia, I know East Tennessee and that little corner of western North Carolina where some of my people come from, but we just don't do well outside of mountains.

I am a card-carrying member of the Cherokee—it's in my handbag right now and it is through the Texas remnant, although my people are from North Georgia and were from right around here—the old Cherokee nation, and a lot of the stories I tell are pretty much place-related from around this area. There are, I think, many, many people with Cherokee blood—you knew you had it—it wasn't exactly a family secret; nobody talked much about it, but I was always very curious. A couple of things happened in my life that caused my grandmother to break her silence about our Cherokee heritage.

You know, landscapes can trigger memories—I want to go back to North Georgia and build a house on the bluff where I grew up—here's the creek [drawing imaginary lines on the table] and here's the bluff; I want to build a house there that looks down on the creek. Beyond the creek, over here, are our fields and there is nothing else until you get to great wall of the Blue Ridge. I can see my three favorite mountains from there, and you can look up and down about forty miles and see the line of the Blue Ridge—it's a pretty place, and you'll see why it's important in a minute.

When I was nine, we were building the ranch house that I grew up in. It was October, we would not move into that house until maybe April, and the dog Shep and I left—the dog was smarter than the girl—and we just started walking, going up. Mother and Daddy were building the house up on a little knoll [continuing to diagram on the table], it went down through a dell where the little branch ran—it was a tiny little hill, and up the hill there was the big road and here was the old farmhouse—what we called the Big House, which had been built and finished in about 1867, in that field. And the dog and I started walking, and it's less than half a mile—you know your land, like every farm child everywhere knows this—you just can't get lost on your own land. And the music started; it was such an odd and lilting sound and I didn't know what the instrument was—I sort of guessed it was some sort of instrument like pipes, but I couldn't have said.

I did not hear that music again for thirty years until I went to a private celebration in Cherokee, and I heard the pipes again. And when I heard it I thought, ahh! It was like something you'd hear in movies that were for children when we were kids, and I wanted to see where it was going.

The dog got scared and pushed—she was a shepherd—and Shep pushed back and tried to stop me, but I was going to try to follow that sound and the sound went everywhere. We got off the driveway and went into the woods and I was following the sound. And it seemed like it was just elusive and just ahead of me, and sometimes I thought I saw a flash of movement—I never actually saw anything, and that is significant as it turns out. I felt this music, and what was so powerful was that it pulled me on, and it was flutes—it was pipes, and I could not stop. I could not stop following it and the dog was upset and she was pushing me back, and that was not like her, and suddenly, I didn't know where I was. I had been in pine trees that Daddy planted and suddenly I wasn't in pine trees anymore—I was in hardwoods and there was some pine, but there were no telephone poles, no electric poles; there were no driveways, there were no roads, there was no sound of the train in the distance, or a car a hundred yards away going up and down what was a fairly busy back road.

So I said I'll go up the hill where the big house would be, and there was no house—there were only the open fields. And here's the curious thing—I never, ever got scared. The dog was smarter than the girl and the dog was scared. The reason I didn't get scared is because I could look up and see my mountains—I could see Grassy Mountain, and I turned around back towards the new house we were building and I could see Little Mountain up above.

I had been taught from my earliest childhood by my great-grandfather to name the mountains. Every morning after breakfast, he and I would go outside and he would take his cane and he would point to a mountain, and he would name that mountain for me in English and in Cherokee, and he would tell me any story or facts that he knew about that mountain, and such things as the names of the creeks and which rivers fed into which creeks, and the names of the people that drew the land lottery lots in 1832, and the names of the families that lived up there. He would tell me any Cherokee stories that he knew—anything that was place-related and geographical, so all my life, from the first weeks of my life, I had learned to look at the landscape and to identify them all, so I think that's what it was that kept me from panicking.

Four hours went by; it felt like minutes to me. My grandmother—she would have truly hated the word psychic, but she truly was, had been panicking. She was up at the big house and she sent word, "Where is that young'un?" and Mother and Daddy sent word back from the new house where they were workin' and then they sent out a search party. I think they had close to twenty people searching.

One of the reasons she had been so quick, besides the fact that she was intuitive, was that something had happened to her mother almost ninety years before, when her mother was a little girl—it's like there's a time warp. The Cherokee had always said there was a time warp on that land, and for the second time, someone had gone missing in plain sight. Of course, I didn't know I was missing. I was just hearing this wonderful music, and I know now it must have been flutes and pipes—reed instruments of some sort. I just followed them—it was like a dance—and I was following them and I thought it was only for a few minutes, and they had had time to get a search party goin' to find where I was.

Finally, my grandmother was praying; she and I were closely connected in our minds—my grandmother was the most magical person—and she was calling me, [whispering] "Charlotte, come back" and I'm standing up on that place where I want to build my house, and I am looking down, and for the first time I see something that is evidence of being manmade—human—I saw corn. Now, before, all of our fields had been gone and all signs of modern life had been gone, but I did see corn on the other side of the creek. It wasn't our kind of corn—it was different—it was Indian corn. And I was standing there and a feeling of Mama calling me came, and I turned around and thought I would go back to where the big house ought to be. Course I had just been there. I started back and had gone about twenty yards and all of a sudden I brushed against one of the men in the search party, and he screamed and jumped back, and I screamed and jumped back, and he started saying, "Where are you, where are you?" and I said, "Well, I'm right here," and he said, "Where did you come from?"

And there was this big harangue about it, and everybody's getting me back to the big house, and my grandmother is pulling me into her arms and she's just almost weeping, and they're asking me all these questions like where were you and why did you cause all this commotion? And I'm saying, "Mama, I never left here, Mama I could see the mountains, but there weren't any houses and there weren't any roads and there was nothing planted; there were no people, there were no animals, there were no chickens—there was nothing." So that's when my grandmother told me this story—to get back to that Cherokee Indian thing—a story of her first husband's family.

All she had ever told me about them before was that my grandfather Lester Woody was not a bad man nor unkind to her in any way, but he drank and he would not stop and she left him. And she would not go beyond that statement or say anything about it. My mother didn't remember him—her father. But that day, because I was so upset by this and everybody was so upset with me—they thought I had been hiding someplace just for meanness or something—she told me about a little girl, whose name you might have met in your research.

She said there was a little girl from my grandfather's family—an ancestress of his—who had been born just below the sacred city of Chota, it's over here, just below the Little Tennessee—it's all under water now—and that she had been born into the Wolf Clan. And that when she was born, her grandmother "took her to water" which is a spiritual practice, to bathe her, and when she was wrapping the child back up—swaddling her—she looked across the river, the Little Tennessee, and saw two wolves perched on the other side, just looking across at the grandmother and the new baby. And the grandmother took this as a blessing, because the child was born in the Wolf Clan and it was a matrilineal society, and so she thought it was a blessing. They named the child Wild Rose.

She was a bit of a tomboy and in fact, she was hard to deal with; she wanted to go and play with the boys. She had a cousin she admired and she wanted to follow him, and he was maybe six or seven years older—her senior—of course he didn't want anything to do with her. When he got to a certain age, he and his friends were being initiated into hunting and they were to go on their first long hunt. She got into her head as a five year old that she would follow them. She followed the boys and they came to the river and used logs to float and push their way across. When she got to the river, she saw that she could not follow them and she thought she would wait for them. She went over to a log and covered herself with leaves because it was getting cool. At some point, the boys came back, but she was asleep under the leaves and they did not see her. They went back to the village which was just below Chota. Just about a mile away from it there was another little village and when they got there, everybody was looking for Wild Rose. And they said to the boys, "Did she follow you?" and they said no, but they joined the search party.

Anyway, the little girl woke up on the bank of the river and it was dark and she was cold. And she had enough sense not to get up and try to wander about in the dark. And she said, "I'll wait for morning." And she was scared and she pulled the leaves back over her and slept up against that log. When she woke the sun was just beginning to come up and there were two people bending over her, and she would always say for the rest of her life that the people were shining—that they were luminous and that they sparkled. They were very small people, and not that much bigger than she herself was and she was just a little girl, but they were grown people. And the woman laughed and said, "little one, are you hungry?" And she realized that she was very hungry and the woman said, "I will make a fire and make the bread. You go with my husband to the river and he will show you how to catch a fish."

**Charlotte Ross
(photograph by Marjorie Shaefer)**

The man took her to the river and they walked along a series of stones, and he put her to stand on one of the stones so the water could not push her over, and she would be safe. And he gave her his weir—fish basket—and he showed her a trick, and he said, "Now here is what you want to do—you have to stand very still in the water and dip this down, and I will go under the water and I will tickle the fish and I will drive them to you and when they come to you, you are to pull this weir, flip it up against your tummy, and the fish will tickle but you must hold it very tight or the fish will get away." And he made her practice the motions, pulling it against her and she would do that, and then he went under the water and was gone the longest time, and she began to be afraid that the man had drowned and that the man was not going to come back, and then all of a sudden POP! there came a fish, and she held her basket against her stomach and the man came up out of the water laughing, and took the basket and the fish and picked the little girl up and carried them all up the bank.

The woman cooked that fish and they talked and they played and she was having the best time ... and then they looked up at the sky and the man and the woman said, "We will take you back now to your people." And she thought that made perfect sense as a little girl. And they began to walk back towards the village, and as they did, as they got closer, she began to recognize certain features—a low tree high on a rocky hill; the shape of a rock and she was talking with the man and the woman and then she saw a rock, and she knew where she was, and she ran up to that rock and looked down into the valley where her village was and she saw people out there searching, and somebody looked up and saw her and yelled, "There is Wild Rose!"

And the people started to come towards her and she turned back toward the man and woman but they were gone, and so the people came and gathered around her and somebody called for her mother. And the mother came and the grandmother came but not before the others got there ... and they started to question her [speaking in a slow, measured tone] and she was just ... a ... girl, and she did not know to be careful how she answered. And they said to her, "Where were you?" and her cousin and his friends—they had been blamed and they were angry with her, because it was pretty obvious she had tried to follow them—and they said, "You did not try to follow us! You are only a girl—you cannot hunt." And she said, "Well, no, but I can fish." She was holding that fish basket—she was holding that beautiful fish basket of such intricate work—just the finest work that anybody had ever seen, and they gathered around her and they said, "Where did you get that?" And she said, "From the man and the woman," and she turned back and looked again but they were not there. And the people began to ask her questions about the man and the woman and she said, "The woman, she cooked and told me stories, and the man, he went under the water and tickled the fish and they came into my basket and I flipped it and held it against my tummy," and they got very quiet. They looked at her and they said, "Did he take you to his magic home under the water?" And she says, "No, he just went under and tickled the fish and they jumped in the basket."

By that time, her mother and grandmother came walking up and they tried to get her to stop from answering this line of questions, because the people around her were drawing back in fear, and they were beginning to whisper and they were beginning to say, "She saw them. She saw the Nunnehi, the little people." Her mother said, "Oh no, it was only a man and a woman who stopped to help a lost child. I shall find them and thank them some day." But the others were not deluded and from that day, she was no longer called Wild Rose. She was called Nunceahi—"She who has seen the little people, the Nunnehi."

That was the story my grandmother told me. She told me just two other things about that woman, and I fell in love with that legend forever, because she said that when the little girl grew up, she married when she was about fifteen and they had a baby, and that there was a great war in North Georgia between the Creeks and the Cherokee. The Creeks had always had superior power and the Cherokee had always lost, but at this battle, that did not happen. The women and their children were on a hill and they could see the men go into battle and Nunceahi saw her husband her young husband—fall in battle, and the Cherokee line began to break and men ran in retreat, but she was running, the magic girl who had seen the little people. She was running for her husband's body and she picked up his staff and ran charging towards the Creeks. When the Cherokee men who were leaving the battlefield saw that, they turned and went back to the battle and they won the battle of Talawa. They were inspired by this magic girl who just ran in and picked up a spear and started charging. It was a great victory for the Cherokee, and the last time they had major trouble with the Creeks. After that, she was called, not Sacred Mother—there are two chiefs in the Cherokee tribe, one is for peace and one is for war—and she was called Beloved Woman. But anyway, later she married a white trader, and Nunceahi became Nancy, and she was Nancy Ward and she's my eleven, twelve times grandmother.

I would never have known this story if I had not had that experience that day of hearing the Nunnehi. Now, she saw them and interacted with them—that's why she was treated as such a magic, sacred person among the tribe, because very few people among the Cherokee ever saw them. You might go generations without anyone ever seeing them—a lot of people heard them, but she saw them. My grandmother told me that to calm me down, and I knew where Nancy Ward's grave was—just about twenty miles away, so I made it one of my favorite places as soon as I was old enough to drive. That place still triggers me. If I live long enough and sell this place, that's where I'm going—North Georgia. It's hotter there in the hills and I will miss the cool of Boone.

I love my mountains and I miss the old ways, so I guess there's some nostalgia involved when I think about the stories from the North Georgia farm where I grew up.

I look a bit like my grandmother's people, and I look like my father— I got my Indian cheekbones from him—but I was not close to him. When daddy went overseas to the war, Mother and I went back home to the farm to live with the old folks, and I was my great-granddaddy's girl, and I loved that. I spent five and a half years with that old man—my magical great-grandfather.

I'm the before-the-war child. My brothers and sisters didn't know our great-grandfather, but I did, and they will look at me (Mike is six years younger, Pat is like seven and a half years younger and Nancy is eight and one half years, or as she likes to say—nearer nine—years younger than I) and they will look at me and say, "We didn't grow up in the same world did we, and yet we're siblings." It's because I was born at the very last moment that you could be born into that older world of Appalachia, and it has affected me all of my life.

I just loved my great-granddaddy. He was the one that taught me to love Appalachia, and he said to me, "There have been more things written about us that are nonsense than almost anywhere else in the world." And he just kept saying it, and talking about our mountains every time we were together. Even though he was blind, he knew where we were when we were walking on the farm, and he would relate to the landscape and he would point. He would get himself centered on one geographic feature and then he would tell me everything he knew about it. He talked to me constantly about the history, the culture, the language—the way things were. It was the best childhood anybody could have ever imagined, and even though it was World War II, courtesy of the Japanese, I got to spend World War II back home with the old folks.

From the moment I got up in the morning he was holding me, talking to me and telling me something, or setting me to some task. He did a lot of riddles and rhymes and taught me games, or to count, or he sang to me. At night, the last thing I would remember would be my head on that old man's chest and he would be telling me those olden-golden tales and I'd fall asleep heavy-like, the way a young'un will, in the middle of that story, and they would put me down in the bed. In the morning when I got half-awake, I'd crawl back up on Great-granddaddy's lap and he'd start about where that story left off while Grandmamma was gettin' breakfast. And I wanted to be like him worse than anything in the world, so in a way, I kinda did. He was obsessed with the time, and the place, and the people of the region where he was born, and that was what he passed on to me.

We have this thing in Appalachia saying the greatest compliment you can give somebody is to follow after them. That doesn't mean that you traipse along behind them necessarily, but that you are influenced in some deep way, and my grandfather had that effect on me. He was blind for fourteen years before I was born, and he was waiting for this little human tape recorder to come along. I was his seein' eye dog—his little grandbaby. He had just enough sight that if the sun would glint on my blond hair—he would put his hand out and walk along like people have seeing eye dogs, and off we went. And we would go everywhere and get into all sorts of trouble together. They couldn't watch us all the time—they had to allow him some dignity and some freedom, because he literally could not see.

[Voice very, very soft and measured in this passage] His blindness had come on so slowly that he had memorized his world. And in that big house up on that farm, unless I moved a chair an inch or two out of the way, everything was left in its exact spot and he could walk around that house and you would never guess he could not see. He memorized the porches, the yard, the few acres around the house where he could walk without a cane or any sign of being blind. It was amazing how well he did that, but you can't memorize your whole farm.

While Daddy was away fighting in World War II, Mother taught school and that was the only cash we had comin' in. Great-granddaddy had land—he had plenty of land, but everything else was rationed and everything was expensive. My grandmother's second husband, my Daddy—Eden Swanson, the one she married for entertainment [a lift at the end of this], he drove the school buses and did some maintenance on the buses, so they needed to be near the school so they could get rides. And gas was a bigger issue than they say it is going to be now, because it was rationed and the teachers would carpool out to the rural schools where they taught. That meant that in order for him to work on the school bus and in maintenance, and Mother to teach, that when school took up we had to move from the big house—the big farm house—into town, to the village of Chatsworth, where my great-granddaddy had built a house for each of his daughters. My grandmother and her sisters had houses on Locust Street, and it was terrifying for Great-granddaddy because he hadn't memorized the village of Chatsworth. All of a sudden, he's like an old man. Well, what to do?

Mama, his daughter, and my grandmother had to decide how we were going to handle this. You can't keep your father cooped up like he's an imbecile or something when there's nothin' wrong with his mind, and he wants to get up and go and do, and she's got the house to run, and meals to cook and bills to pay, and us to watch; Mother's teaching and Daddy was gone. We worked out a compromise [pause], she couldn't keep us in the house all the time, so every morning, about 9 o'clock, she would walk us down the hill on Locust Street, to U.S. Highway 411—the main-most highway between Knoxville and Atlanta ... and she would set us across the highway, because I'm too little to know anything about cars, and he can't see the cars ... so she would set us across it. And on the other side there would be the little dirt trail that would pass for a sidewalk for more than half a mile until we got to the edge of Chatsworth and then we'd have two and a half blocks of paved sidewalks—big deal!

And we would walk along that sidewalk toward town everyday; if it wasn't raining we were out there. And I would be holding his hand and we had a system worked out and if somebody was comin', I would pull once on his hand if we met a woman, and pull twice on his hand if it was a man ... so he would know how to do, you know, when to tip his hat. Now, I ask you, how does a child, I was four the first year and what, five the second ... know who somebody is ... what their station in life might be.... God knows who I told him to tip his hat to, and he thought he was doing the right and the gentlemanly thing. So we would be going into town, and if it was somebody who knew us, we'd stop there and talk on the sidewalk. When we got to town, we would get up on the sidewalk, and we'd go the first block of our two paved blocks of town and we'd get to the drug store on the corner and somebody would be watching, and the druggist would send them out, and one of the clerks would set us across the next street. And then we would go to the left and down and turn right until we came to the Westville store.

The Westville store was one of those magic places that every child should have this opportunity to visit, and you don't know when you are a kid how great it is. It was an old country emporium that had kind of grown like Topsy. In the center of it, there were places they said there were logs beneath those board walls in the center—I don't know, but there was a potbellied stove and around that potbellied stove there were rockin' chairs—there were seven, big and either mule-eared, or step rockin' chairs, and one little rocking chair for guess who? And we would sit there for two, two and a half hours, every day, and visit. Now they were Great-granddaddy's friends: there was Mr. Westfield who owned the store—he was older than Great-granddaddy—Great-granddaddy by that time was—well, here's to say, they were all somewhere between eighty-five and one hundred and two!

They sat there and rocked and they would spit "tub-bacca" on that potbellied stove. They wouldn't let me have that, but they had this stuff, I think it was sort of a forerunner of Kool-Aid—grape stuff in the store, and Great-granddaddy would buy me one of those every time we went into the store and I would sit there and spit my "tub-bacca" on that stove and I would learn words my mother would never want me to know. [Laughter] And then after just about two and a quarter hours, somebody would come over and say, "Mr. Tyler" and say what time it was, and it would be like 11:00 or 11:15 A.M., they would send us back home. We'd get up and go back, and somebody from the drugstore would go out and set us safely across the side street; we would walk on the same side of U.S. 411, and we would stand there and wait beside the highway until my grandmother came down to take us safely back across the highway to the house. We had a little routine goin' each day.

I knew I loved my great-granddaddy; he was the most special great-granddaddy in all the earth. I did not know he was going to influence my whole life and every choice I ever made in it, but that was what happened.

The first year we were living down there, the first winter, I was three and a half goin' on four, and I wanted a tricycle—a perfectly normal thing in ordinary times, but in World War II you could not get a tricycle, and I know they did look and they could not find a tricycle. And I know that Christmas mornin' I threw a stomp-down fit. I just said, "I'll be too big, I'll be too big for a tricycle by next Christmas!" And they agreed that they would try to get me a tricycle for my fourth birthday, in June. No tricycle—they couldn't find one.

So I put the word out to Santa Claus and all, and I know they must have made a tremendous effort, because by that time I was going to be four and a half and pretty soon my legs would be too long to ride a tricycle. But again, they could not find one, and Christmas morning I woke up and I just started to cry.

Now, I don't know how it was in your house, but I knew if anybody told me "no," that my court of last resort was my great-granddaddy, and I got right up in front of him [voice pitched high with a child's cry embedded in it] and I cried, "Great-granddaddy, I'm going to be too big for a tricycle. I never will learn how to ride a tricycle. Great-granddaddy—that's all I wanted."

I didn't want that ole dog; all I wanted was a tricycle. And he says, "Honey, I'll take care of it." And he started arguing with my mother. And he loved my mother, his granddaughter, and she was just about in tears, and she said, "Granddaddy, I tried. Granddaddy, if you think you can do better, you try." And he said, "Well, I will, bedab! I will." So he hired Katie Hollis from next door—her fourteen years old and not much sense, to come and do the writing for him. And he had letters written to all his former friends and associates in the mercantile business—he'd had stores all around the county in the past and knew a whole bunch of people.

The letters started to come back after Christmas—"deceased"; "store closed." Occasionally a son or daughter, a niece or a nephew would answer to let us know the older people were no longer alive or in business, and "besides, Mr. Tyler, we can't get a tricycle. You might be able, if you go to a welding shop to get enough pieces. You might try that."

And it was about this time of year, the third of March, and one day we came back from the Westfield store, and he said to my grandmother, "Clara, there's gonna be a picture-takin' man down to the Westfield store. Why don't you get me and this young'un gussied up tomorrow." Grandmamma loved doin' that, and we looked good ... he had on his best suit, his Stetson hat, his vest all buttoned up underneath; his shoes were shined—he looked sartorial. And I had on a yellow coat, a yellow hat, a matching muff and leggings. Oh, we looked good! And Mama thought we were going to get our picture taken....

We got to the corner by the drugstore, and the clerk came out to set us across the road right here [pointing to an imaginary spot on the table], so we could turn and go towards the store, and he said, "No, I'd admire to go across the other way—so set us across 411. I'd admire to go sit on that bench on the courthouse lawn." It was the prettiest courthouse in Georgia, and we went over there and sat. And every few minutes he'd stop and say, "Are they watching us?" Those people at the drugstore were watchin' us, wonderin' what on earth are those two up to? And he'd say, "Just sit back down and smile and talk," and I played with my marbles. After a while he kept looking his watch, taking the crystal off so he could feel where the hands were. He says, "Honey, let's get up and let's mosey down to the corner. Do you see a sign that says Bus Stop?" I said, "Yes sir." I could read, I was four and a half in a houseful of educators—you know I could read—so we got on the bus and we started to Dalton, which was about sixteen miles away. Back during the war, you couldn't get a seat on the bus and people were hangin' on to straps and had their produce and everything with them—it was a show. Somebody gave him a seat and I climbed right up on his lap and leaned against him and almost went to sleep.

In Dalton, he gave me the money like he was trying to train me to make change, so everybody could guess he was blind. He's holding on to my shoulder, and we go up to the ticket booth, and he says to me, "Now Charlie, count it back to me." So the woman counted the money to me, and I counted the bills back to him, and he put it all away and we got two tickets to Chattanooga—we were going to find Charlotte Ann a tricycle. Of course, by this time, my grandmother has noticed that we have not met her at the bottom of Locust Street. We're not home for dinner. We're on the way to Chattanooga.

Used to be, that was the most winding mountainy road up from Dalton. There were about nine stops between Dalton and Chattanooga and you'd wind around those. What I remember most about that day is all of the bedspreads hanging out—before Dalton was the carpet center; it was the tufted bedspread industries—all rebel flags and peacocks. We wound up through there and finally, got to Fort Oglethorpe, a big military installation just south of Chattanooga, and it was still open in World War II and in fact it had been enlarged, and so when we go to this little town, Ringgold, one whole block of the town had been made into this big shed roof, tin bus station with so much bus traffic going in and out. A whole block was devoted to bus traffic, and the bus driver said, "We will be here for twenty minutes and everybody ought to take a bathroom break and we'll go on to Chattanooga."

Now, I knew what to look for on a bathroom door [sotto voice] but ... it ... never ... occurred to me to look for something different to take my great-granddaddy into, and him blind as a bat. So we go into the women's room and it gets real quiet. He went into his stall and did his necessaries and I went into my stall and did my necessaries and he came out and I checked all the buttons on his vest—it was my job—and he was so particular about his appearance. He was a proud, sartorial man. We go over to wash our hands and a big woman comes in [whispering] and she is big! We know it's a woman because she's got on a skirt, but she's got a [guttural sound] real, deep masculine voice, and she looks at us and hollers, "What are you doing in here?"

And I said, "Peeing." And she turns around and steps on my foot and I screamed! Now, you know where he thinks he is ... and he thinks some man has attacked his great-granddaughter and he takes that white cane that he carries and he starts belaying it about, hittin' wooden stalls and glass mirrors and now all the women in there are squealin' and carryin' on and we wind up down to the *po-leece station*.

She's just as mad as she can be—she wants to press charges. Well the police in Ringgold, Georgia, don't particularly want to press charges, but what they do want to know is who we are and where we're supposed to be, because they're real sure we're not where we're supposed to be.

By that time my granddaddy Hyden Tyler is just mortified and whispers so embarrassed—he understands what's happened. And he won't give his name and he won't let me give my name and he's saying nothing and I'm saying nothing. Police in Ringgold are buying me ice cream trying to get me to talk. [Laughter] I sure did eat a lot of ice cream that day. By this time, my grandmother has had the local sheriff, her cousin, out looking for us. Usually he can find us in an hour or so but he came back and said, "Aunt Clara, I can't find hide nor hair of 'em. They're not in any of the places they could have gotten to by themselves."

Mother comes home about four-thirty in the afternoon—carpooled in from Tennessee, and she panics. The whole menagerie is breaking up. And they put out a call—we don't have a radio station in town—from the Dalton radio station. By that time it's good dark in March, you know. Some woman who had been in that bus station when we bought that ticket and that woman counted that money back to me—"that old man and that little blonde-headed girl?" She thought she knew who that was, the problem was she didn't have a telephone, so she's got to put on her coat and get her flashlight and walk about half a mile to somebody with a telephone, and get them to call Whitfield County sheriff's station and they've got to call Murray County and then, after that the bus stations. They started callin' each bus station from Dalton to Chattanooga and when they got to Ringgold, the sheriff was [laughter] darned glad to hear from them, 'cause he didn't want to put us in jail overnight and the town's full. You couldn't have gotten a room—everybody who had a spare room had it rented out to the military. He didn't know what to do, but he was so glad. And then we've got the other problem—gas was rationed and there's nobody to come and get us. One of the state patrolmen was in there and he offered to go as far as Dalton. We started rolling back to Murray County.

Now up to this point, it has been a terrible day, but Hyden is riding in a state patrol car. Now, he can't see it, but he knows what he's in. Now, he starts talkin' to this young man and of course, after a while they wind up about half related. You know, if you're in the mountains, you're going to be related. Oh, he knows this boy's granddaddy, and he said, "Now son, when we get to Chatsworth, it's unincorporated. There's a little sign as you go into town on the left. Let me know when we get to that sign." And the boy said, "Mr. Tyler, here's Chatsworth." And Great-granddaddy said, "Now son, son, would you do me the biggest favor? Have you got one of those sirens? And flashin' lights? Would you turn it on when you take me to the house?" And that boy turned on one of those flashing lights and turned on that siren and we went ridin' into the village of Chatsworth riding in style, much to the mortification of my prissy little school teacher mama, don't you know that?

Well, the upshot of that was they got really serious. They got some scraps and some pieces—what they could find, and they made me a big tricycle. I still have the last picture that my great-grandfather Hyden and I had made together, which was on my fifth birthday when he gave me that tricycle. He's taken off his suit coat, got his white shirt and he's bending over, his white hair is flyin' in the wind and I'm sittin' there in a little blue organdy pinafore. And I guess the reason they got real serious about it is they figured we'd get in some real trouble if they didn't—we'd hired people to take us driving before. This is the point at which Mother took the wheels off and put that old touring car up on blocks, or she had Edsel from the gas station do it, so we couldn't hire anybody to take us off on any more adventures. So any time we wanted to go anywhere after that, we'd have to go out there, climb into the car (with the garage doors open) and sit there in the semi-dark and pretend we were driving someplace.

I was working on my master's degree when I found Cratis Williams' dissertation, and I wanted to meet him. A few weeks later, the *Chronicle of Higher Education* advertised a job in the history department here, at Appalachian State University, and I talked Ross, my husband, into applying for it. We walked into the room—we got there in a snow storm and we'd been around campus all day, and Ross had just about decided to take the job. We were back over in the president's office in the old administration building that is no more, and still hadn't met Cratis, and he came into the room behind us. He must have done this [making a gesture for silence], because we didn't turn around. He just listened and after a few minutes—we had both been talking and he had heard our voices—Dr. Plemmons said, "Come on over here and let me introduce you to Cratis Williams." And I said, "Oh, you're the reason I wanted to come to Boone!" He did something that day that I will never forget: he placed each of us within twenty miles of the place that we were born by our accents. Cratis and I became, for all the difference in our ages—there was 32 years difference in our ages—we became best friends and we were best friends for seventeen, nearly eighteen years until he died.

I started the Appalachian Regional Collection at Appalachian State University in my misspent youth, and I was with it a little less than five years.

When I started, there was no budget; no money and no salary, but Cratis is the one who urged me to do it when nobody else on campus thought it was a good idea, but they let me do it and it is something I have been very proud of. When you do something like that, do a collection or write a book, it's sort of like you have given birth to a child, and you have a connection with it. I started it in 1969 and I was there until 1975 when I moved to the North Carolina Humanities Council. I did not have a library degree and had done it as long as I could as a subject matter specialist, which was Appalachia. Now the librarians have it, and it's in really good hands. It's done really, really well. And if you are looking for stories, you need to come to our big new library at ASU. It has a glass dome over the top and you can be there and see the mountains and watch it rain or snow—it's just beautiful, and it has rocking chairs and it's wonderful in there. Stories!

While I was building the library, I taught school, and people started coming into the collection and they were looking at genealogy and trying to find out things about their families. I'm married to an historian, so I started working with my husband Ross, and started putting it together, and I got the facts and figures together, and suddenly I've got shoe boxes—actually they're old library boxes filled with index cards front and back with stories I thought I'd work up some day. The ones I worked up first tended to be for other people. Families would come in and we had the facts right there on those cards and we could put the facts together for them. I could do that because I had all that information at my fingertips and I was working with it everyday. I would check the facts and organize it and get the chronology right—the dates and the places and what county it was, because counties merge and divide over time and change, what regiment it was, because a lot of families don't have those facts right, and then I put the story back together and helped them with it.

I do a lot of legends, and my card says Legend Lady, but I tell you this: truth is stranger than fiction, and you can't play with the facts of people's lives. Sometimes you just have to go with the flow. It's their lives and I'm not going to change it. I lived with an historian and I taught Appalachian history and I love history, and I'm not going to push history around just to make a story fit into a certain structure. I won't do it, so some of my stories may end up a little in the air. Some stories, especially personal narrative stories, don't always have a beginning, middle and an end. Usually, those are the deeper ones; they have the values.

When I first started putting the stories together from the collection, a lot of times I went to the family reunions and told it to them, and they just loved that. I enjoyed it too, so I just started making myself available to Brownie Scouts and the Cub Scouts, and the Girl Scouts, the Lions, the Moose and the Elks and ladies' sewing circles.... I don't really know how it happened, but Cratis Williams was a part of it, because he was a very popular speaker on Appalachia and that's what I began doing, too. We started working together and I started telling stories as a part of those public presentations. Cratis Williams reminded me in so many ways of my great-grandfather. It was like I got two chances for that kind of mentoring in my life.

When I began to develop the Celtic Hypothesis, and I was one of the first to talk about it, everybody was searching for where the Appalachian people came from and who the people really were—that was a lot of fun getting the ethnic groups and placing them on the map, and I figured it out in descending order—Scotch-Irish, the mountain Germans, Welsh, English, the Highland Scots, the French Hueguenots, and the [indigenous] Cherokees, who were the Indians who married out the most, and the Cornish, who were one of the last groups to be brought over. And then I had to figure out why they came and I looked at the subsistence patterns and the time period when this valley was settled, where the roads, the migration routes, through the Appalachians went ... you just get a feel for the beautiful landscape [her voice trailed off here as she reminisced about the past] and how they survived. They followed the old Indian tracks and herded cattle, hogs and turkeys. That way of life was destroyed by the War Between the States, and because of a deal between the government and the railroads, but it took a people unafraid of a wilderness to be able to look out there and see opportunity in the beginning, and it is because they were hunter-gatherers.

I have been an anachronism all my life and just really can't do with computers and modern things. I love old-timey things—I'm a folklorist and a storyteller. There's not much to my story, really. The most remarkable thing about my life was that it was just the last moment to be born into old-time Appalachia, and see it. My siblings, six, seven, eight years younger than I, have no clue. They're livin' there—two of 'em are, on the farm, but they don't know nearly as much about it as I do. They never rode a horse and wagon—I did. I tell people I'm a ninth generation Appalachian mountaineer, and consequently I can't be intimidated, and I don't often get fooled. You don't have to hold back, you can laugh larger; you can be more blunt—we have to be a little careful with middle-class women, because we're perceived as saying things.... I was always considered outspoken or eccentric but I was just being totally natural. And then too, there was such an awareness, just something about mountain people, of being tied to the land—being pulled to the land, and a lot of times that turns two ways: some people go in conventional, religious ways, and some of us—as I've indicated about my grandmother, who had a tremendous gift—she was such a good sender and I was just a good little receiving set—there's almost a spiritual connection for many of us with the landscape and the culture.

Cratis used to say to me, he'd say, "Girl, girl! Would you tell me what it is ... I do not see how people of our blood can live in a city. Pray tell, they live in this flat country—what do they rest their eyes upon when there are no mountains?"

Old time Appalachian people sort of felt that way and believed it, and it's just so lucky that by the skin of my teeth I was born in that older Appalachia. But what I do that means something is that I still go about and talk to people about the mountains.

James "Sparky" Rucker

Born in Knoxville, Tennessee, James "Sparky" Rucker grew up in Knoxville and was drawn to music from the beginning. He began playing guitar at the age of eleven and sang in church, school, and community choirs throughout his childhood. After graduating from the University of Tennessee, he taught school in Chattanooga before becoming a full-time folk singer. He was part of the folk music revival in the sixties and an active participant in the civil rights movement.

A natural storyteller, Rucker is descended from a long line of Church of God, Sanctified, Inc., preachers and law enforcement officers, and he grew up hearing his father, uncles, and other family members telling stories both in church and at home. When he realized storytelling was a natural accompaniment to his music, he became a storytelling musician, and he has been telling stories set to music ever since.

Rucker frequently performs in tandem with his wife, Rhonda Hicks Rucker, who is from North Carolina, and together they have performed for audiences in schools, conferences and festivals all over the country. They have also been the tellers-in-residence at the International Storytelling Center in Jonesborough, Tennessee, and their CD *Done Told the Truth, Goodbye!* features the husband and wife team telling stories together. They have one son, Jamey Rucker.

Rucker received the "Life Membership Award" bestowed on him by the National Association of Black Storytellers, and is featured on *Tall Tales of the Blue Ridge: Stories from the Heart of Appalachia*, a video produced by the Eastern National Park and Monument Association in 1992. He has appeared at numerous festivals, including the National Storytelling Festival in Jonesborough, Tennessee, the Festival of Storytelling on Martha's Vineyard, Motlow State Community College's Storytelling Festival, and the Texas Storytelling Festival, and contributed to *More Ready-to-Tell Tales*, an anthology of stories from many of the nation's best professional storytellers in 2000. His expert blues and bottleneck style of guitar playing makes him a popular teacher at folk music camps and schools such as Common Ground on the Hill in Maryland and the Augusta Heritage Center in West Virginia.

The Interview

I've been a traveler and a road performer full time since the early seventies. I taught public school in 70–71, and I had already begun my folk singing career prior to that. It was during the Civil Rights Movement—that's where I switched from being a rock and roll/rhythm and blues performer to folk music, and I've been doing it full time since the fall of '72—a long time.

Sure, I get tired of it and I get peopled out, and I get tired of the business aspect of it. The part I don't like is to have to deal with agents and that kind of thing, but the people you meet, and the people you stay with, and the other performers—I love them. That's the reason I do it—to see my friends and to travel.

I was a school teacher and did some stage acting in college, and I come from a long line of preachers, so I am more at home on the stage than I am off the stage, and if you let me talk, I'm happy. When God said let there be light, He said, "Sparky, would you get that switch for me?"

I was late getting married—I was 42 when I got married and 46 when my son was born, and my wife Rhonda began performing with me in '89. She took a hiatus to be a doctor after our son was born—the money you make being a folk performer is hit and miss and, mostly, not a whole lot even when you're hittin'—she went through three years of residency and five years of practice, and then decided to come back into performing. We started traveling together as a family in 2001, and have raised our son Jamey since he was in the fifth grade with homeschooling.

It's been an interesting thing—if you make it a family enterprise, it means two people are putting in the effort to make it work, and you don't have to leave your family to go on the road, which was really tearing me apart, especially after our son was born. Rhonda was in medical practice at that time, so at first I had Jamey traveling with me till he started school. It was like being a single parent. Here I was on the road with this baby from the time he was 10 months old until he started school. Then Rhonda was the single parent after Jamey started school while I was traveling. I started making my tours shorter and shorter and not traveling as far, because I didn't want to leave the family. I almost lost my career that way. If you're not out there continually touring, you can lose it ... you have to continually re-invent yourself if you are going to do this storytelling and music for a living.

Rhonda worked as a doctor just long enough to pay off our house, and then we went back on the road together as a family. Now we are cash-only family—we don't do credit. My wife is wonderful—she's practical and knows how to budget; I'm like this old hippie with my head in the clouds. I can create ways to make money, but I can't keep it. Somehow, to me, it's not important. When I was single and on the road, I learned how to cook. I knew I'd never starve, and when I stayed with people they supplied the food and I would prepare it, so I just kind of always believed "the Lord makes a way." Here I am 63, and like I said, I've been doing this full-time for forty some odd years ... and so far it works. I love it.

Speaking of being around some of the older musicians and learning from them, I was lucky to be a young person, and at the right time and place, and to be like a sponge. A lot of people would say, "I want to learn all of your stories;" but me, I just wanted to know these people! I figured if I learned something from them, it would be like getting the gravy. My wife calls it my "old man fix," but I just like elderly people. Now that I'm older, I know you want somebody young to teach, and I understand what it was like. I would ask the older folks about themselves and they would began to tell me about how it was when they were growing up ... and digging for roots in the mountains like goldenseal and ginseng.

The Rev. Pearly Brown, a blind street singer from Georgia, taught me how to play the bottleneck-style guitar; Babe Stovall, an old bluesman from Mississippi (his family came from the Stovall Plantation—that's where his name came from) who was livin' in New Orleans, taught me the blues. John Shines, and Robert Lockwood, Jr., and Buddy Moss. I got to know older guys like this when I was just startin' out as a folk singer. I was picked to be the younger performer to go on tours with all these wonderful people, so I got to meet Bessie Jones, who was a founding member of the Georgia Sea Island Singers because of that.

How I started storytelling was like this: when I was a folksinger, I realized that as a performer I couldn't just do song after song after song, and nothing else. When I was in a band it worked, but like I said, I've been a solo performer longer than touring with a partner, and I just realized I had to let people know where the songs came from; I had to take time to catch my breath so I started talkin'. I'm one of these kinds [of] people who do word association, so I would hear or say something that would make me think of something else, and I would do this "stream of consciousness" thing on stage, just like Jack Kerouac, and I began to realize that people were coming more for the talk than they were for the singin'.

My stories grow in front of my audiences. I will get the core of the story if it's a traditional tale, or one that I remember learning as a kid, and it will grow from there. I grew up in "the projects" where there were a lot of kids. We would play ring games, and tell each other stories that we had learned from our families, and then as I got older I realized that a lot of the tales I was reading I had already heard as a child. There were a couple of older people who told stories, too, like Bessie Jones—I knew her extremely well, and even toured with her, but then I would realize this was a version of a story I already knew and had heard all of my life, but she told it the way it was told in the Sea Islands. The difference between what was told there as opposed to East Tennessee—it was interesting to see how the stories had changed from place to place.

Every folk song has a story behind it, because it was written from people's experiences, and a lot of times we don't even know who wrote the song. It comes from something that happened in the Civil War, or something that happened to a king in England, or something that happened to a prince in Africa, or something that happened to a warrior. I started researching the stories, and that's when I realized I'd better start telling people the whole story before singing the song, and that's the way to create a bridge in their minds; that song will always trigger that story memory again. That's why Rhonda and I go into schools—they bring us into schools to tell the history of the Civil Rights Movement, or the history of Native American/African American interaction in this country, like the Seminoles—all those people who ran away from slavery who joined forces with the native people in those swamps, and formed their own tribe. What a unique experience—what happened in Florida was a very unique experience. Or what happened when the Buffalo Soldiers went west—when the country sent one suppressed minority out to suppress another.

I started telling these stories about how blacks, Indians and the Spanish conquistadors became Mexicans; three cultures coming together. Or how in New Orleans the various cultures came together and an entirely different culture grew out of that experience. What a unique country we live in!

There was an organization called the Southern Folk Cultural Revival Project. It grew out of the Civil Rights Movement. It was a touring group, which was composed of a lot of folk singers, of which I was a member. Later I sat on the board of directors. It was there that I first met Bernice Johnson Reagon, who had been an original member of the S.N.C.C. [the Student Non-Violent Coordinating Committee] Freedom Singers, and who later was the founder of that wonderful a capella singing group, Sweet Honey in the Rock. I also met Anne Romaine and her husband, Howard—they were instrumental in founding the S.F.C.R.P. [Southern Folk Cultural Revival Project], an offshoot of S.S.O.C. [Southern Student Organizing Committee], which toured from the 1960s through the 1980s. Pete Seeger, Gil Turner, the Georgia Sea Island Singers, Len Chandler, and Bob Dylan all came down to perform, and we realized we needed to take this folk culture around to southern schools ... to let them see both blacks and whites, on stage, performing together.

Like I said, I've traveled throughout a large portion of the world but nothing is like this country. It's one of the most amazing places I've ever been. I want to tell people about that, and help them understand that this is what we have here. That's what motivates me—that some kid is going to hear the things I am saying, and what I've learned is not going to die with me—it's gonna get passed on.

My wife's the one who started makin' me write. She said, "That stuff's going to die with you." I finally learned to write like I talk, which is a hard thing to do. I'm a scholar in terms of my research, and I was makin' stuff too scholarly when I wrote. It was too dry, but then I realized I could still do that in the footnotes. I could tell the story so people would read it, and stick the scholarly material in the footnotes so people will know where I got the information from. I don't want people to lose that way of finding things—of tracing back.

Families matter so much here in the South. I'm not sayin' they don't in other parts of the country, but they really matter in this Southern Appalachian culture, both black and white and Native American. Your family connections are who you are. People say things like, "Why, he's my third double cousin on my mother's side." My wife is from Louisville, Kentucky, and they are Midwesterners, and when I would tell her about my second cousins, she would say, "We don't even consider those people kin." And I would say "You don't?"

You never feel alone down here in the South because you know all of the connections in your family. That is common to West Africans where the culture has always been matrilineal, and so it is with the Native Americans as well. When you add in the Scots-Irish—all of those cultures knew what clan they were in, and that's why everybody in this area shares the same kinds of values even though they come from three separate societies. They had so much in common that when I started studying these cultures I began to understand that we have so much to share—a lot of common attitudes, mores and morals coming from three separate religious attitudes and yet it is all the same.

I grew up in Knoxville—the African American population there is smaller than in many other southern cities. East Tennessee was pro–Union during the Civil War and it affects so much of the present-day attitudes—and I didn't understand this as I was growing up—why things happened the way they did during the turbulent sixties. We had our differences and our civil rights protests—I was very much a part of that because I went to segregated schools all through high school.

I went to the University of Tennessee as one of the first blacks to go there—there were maybe ten of us. The graduate school was already integrated. Marion Barry, the former mayor of Washington, D.C., who was the

S.N.C.C. field secretary during the Civil Rights Movement, and who was later involved in many scandals during his tenure as mayor, was very much a part of the early movement then, and I can forgive him for what he has done as an old man, because of what he did for us when he was young.

In 1919 there were race riots all throughout the country and we had what was known as the "Red Summer." People don't really want to talk about it, but it happened—there was a huge race riot in Knoxville and a lot of people were killed. There were all these black veterans from World War I who wouldn't take the oppression any longer and fought back. There was a huge shootout and supposedly a lot of people were killed, including a man named Morris Mays who was lynched

James "Sparky" Rucker

for being in an interracial relationship, and this sparked the riot. Because of that, what happened in the 1960s was a lot less violent—there were still people who remembered that "Red Summer."

Don't mistake me—I used to get jumped on when I was a kid living in Lincoln Heights—one of the two segregated "project" tenement areas—I was born in the projects. For the first fifteen years of my life I was living in the closest thing to a ghetto that a southern city could have and attending all-black schools, but when we moved to Lincoln Heights it was adjacent to a "poor white" neighborhood. A major road called Beaumont Avenue ran between the neighborhoods. It was where they had all those little stores where you could go buy candy and etc. You could go to the store but you had to have a pocket full of rocks in case you got in a fight along the way.

There were always one or two white families that were still living in the black neighborhood and they were the people you trusted. On my mother's side of the family, not only did they get along, they were kin. My great-grandmother, on my mother's side, was a Virginia Carter, which means I'm "kin" to Robert E. Lee, Robert King Carter, and the singing Carter family. If you listen closely you can hear Robert E. Lee turning over in his grave!

The parent I was closest to [was] my mother. She was an artist, she sang, she sewed, she was a Girl Scout leader, and she read to us. If she had been younger she would have been more involved in the Civil Rights Movement. She was a wonderful mother and I miss her terribly.

I dream about my mother and father and they come to me and still give me advice in those dreams. I'm just grateful I got their family stories before they passed away. For Mother's and Father's Day, about five years before they died, I did family histories for both of them that included dates and other information, and that sparked even more memories from them and their siblings. I wrote down all the stories my father told me about my grandfather, a preacher and bishop of the Church of God, Sanctified, Inc., and I wrote down the stories my mother told me about her side of the family, so that now they are part of my stage presentation. I even use them "fictitiously" because I do these "preacher tales"—there is a genre for American southern preacher stories, and a lot of the stories I tell I put my grandfather or my uncle—who was also a preacher—in there as characters.

Like I said, I come from a long line of preachers [laughter] and I'm telling real stories in there about my uncle and my grandfather, and then that's the introduction to a "traditional tale" and it's also the introduction to the real story. It's also a way to pay homage to my grandfather whom I never knew. He passed away when I was but one year old. There are many stories about him being this Church of God, Sanctified, Inc., bishop who had twelve kids. My father was the youngest boy; he was the ninth of the twelve and I think he was probably my grandfather's favorite, because he's the one he chose to chauffer him around.

I tell my son, Jamey, that he has to look at his heritage—it's who he is. With his mother there's Cherokee and German heritage—it's an interesting mixture. We're all mixed together like that, and one of the things I wanted to do was to try to learn as much as possible about both of our families so that my son would know who he is. As a bi-racial child he would have those "Am I black or am I white?" things all the time. I don't know if he's resolved it, but I've told him he's both. He's an "old spirit" and I'm blessed that I was put in charge to teach him.

I'm very proud of this country and where I've come from, and I want this country to be what it claims to be; part of my job is to see that it happens. That's one of the reasons I don't just try to entertain when I'm on the stage—the teacher in me comes out. Teaching is a God-given skill—it's not something you can learn. You have to have it in you to be able to put a thought into someone else's head, and as a storyteller, I know how to create that picture, and to make people identify with me, and the characters I weave together into the story. We all have the same hopes, dreams, and aspirations, the same needs and wants, and that's what the storyteller puts out there. You have to put your audience into the story and make them feel it.

This gets me to that universal truth that it doesn't matter what name you call God; no matter what you believe, it all comes from that same spark. There is something that happened and everybody saw it, but they put their own spin on it. You can only understand things with what you already know. That's why when you read the four gospels, two of which were supposedly written by folks who were there when the event took place, anyway, when you read those gospels you get two different takes on it because they brought themselves into what they saw.

I just try to figure these things out and try to observe people. It makes me think about my parents who died within twenty days of each other after they'd been married almost sixty years. When one died, the other one just didn't want to be left alone. I love watching elderly couples, even if they snap at each other, they love one another and couldn't get along without each other.

I was raised with that old "hippie attitude" that everything belongs to everybody. I'm just passing through this life, we are just here temporarily—we're stewards of this earth. I firmly believe this. That's why I get so angry when I see people destroying this planet. We treat this planet like we have someplace else to go.

After I taught in public school, I found a job that was an example of what we called "Vocations for Social Change" because of who I am, and where I have come from. I've tried to make a living and be true to myself. After I gave up teaching school, I said I have to find a way to make a living where I can be my own boss; I can't work for somebody else. I've been blessed that I found a way to make a living. Like I've always said, I knew I'd never be rich, but I've got to do what I've got to do and make a living.

That's one reason I waited to get married—I had to find somebody who would fit into my lifestyle and contribute to it. My wife, Rhonda, works with me now, and she is a wonderful musician and songwriter. At first she was my accompanist, but now she is singing with me and learning to be a "front person." Let's face it, I ain't gonna be here forever, and I want her to be able to do what she wants to do when I'm gone. It's important.

Doc McConnell and I started out at about the same time in the late sixties. When he was first startin' out as a folk singer, and so was I, he was just beginning to do the medicine show thing, and every now and then he'd get me to come up and sing. We didn't know we were storytellers—we just ran our mouths all the time.... That's the way it is with mountain folks—we come from an oral tradition and everything comes out as a story. That "long line of preachers?" They were storytellers; so are teachers. I'm just glad people are finally realizing it's important to remember these old stories and traditions.

I remember when I first met Connie Reagan-Blake and Barbara Freeman in the late '60s. They were librarians and they came to the Folk Festival of the Smokies. They had been doing things in their library that were wonderful and I said, "You guys are great! You ought to be doing this for a living," but nobody was doing professional storytelling back in those days. I was impressed with the tandem telling they were doing because I had never seen it before. They were just experimenting with it and it was wonderful. And just look what happened with it. Had they not started telling stories, the whole Jonesborough thing might not have happened. The people gathered and decided to try to document this wonderful treasure we have here in this area of the world, and it has spread throughout the culture.

A bunch of African American writers came up with the term "Afri-lachian." They recognized that there are close to one million blacks living in Southern Appalachia, and that's a culture.

A lot of the people that I know who are into being "Afri-lachian" are not performers; they are educators, social studies–type people. Two of them wrote a book together: Ed Cabell out of West Virginia with the John Henry Foundation; he's living in North Georgia now. And then there is Dr. William Turner, Bill, he's up in Berea now. They are both very good friends of mine and I respect both of them—they are great educators and we all have sort of taught one another in the understanding that there is a unique black culture in Appalachia. It's not southern, it's not New York black—it *is* what it *is*.

It is stories like Taily Poe, which come out of the Appalachian black tradition; it's the songs, like "Down in the Valley to Pray," that came out of the black tradition, but now has spread throughout Appalachia. "Get Along Home, Cindy, Cindy" comes out of Appalachia, but it's black! I understand this is our country, too—John Henry, John Hardy. And it's something that had been pushed into this big category called Appalachian, but it's not, it's a unique area—it's African and it's Appalachian, so they created that term "Afri-lachian."

I don't know of any black folks from *this* area that object to the term. Henry Louis Gates is from Afri-lachia; Nikki Giovanni—she and I grew up in Knoxville together; Maya Angelou is an Afri-lachian, and Bill Withers is from West Virginia. There is uniqueness to the black people who grew up in this area.

For instance, there were the black coal miners who joined forces with the white coal miners to fight off the "outsiders" who came in to exploit the mountains, and the feud with the Hatfields and McCoys that made the rest of the country aware of the resources we had here. I still get angry about it when I drive through and see the "mountain-top removal." Those mountains have been here since the beginning of time—and now they're just gone!

The majority of slaves were from West Africa—Yoruba in fact, and their religion mixed with Catholicism to become what is known as "Voodoo." There were these spiritual beings, which are similar to angels, called Orisha. One of these is named Eshu or Legbe and he is the guardian of the crossroads. The Christians say he is the one who became the devil at the crossroads, but he is also a trickster and very much like Br'er Rabbit and Anansi, who also became Aunt Nancy, who is like a voodoo person. A lot of the Orisha were people who had lived and came back as "helper spirits" or "higher beings"—I don't know how they make those distinctions—it's a part of my culture and yet it is *not* my culture.

In speaking of Richard Chase's re-publishing of Joel Chandler Harris' Uncle Remus Tales, the thing I have against that work is that he left the songs out; he only used the stories. They were just tales Harris had collected that were sometimes published serially in *The Century* magazine, and later brought out as books by Joel Chandler Harris or by his estate, but when Chase collected the things he quite often did not reprint the songs Harris added to his tales. A lot of these tales had songs that came with them. Bessie Jones would tell a story, and if there was a song connected to the story she would sing it, like an old preacher telling his sermon would break out into a song that somehow reflects the sermon he's giving; it's a natural part of storytelling to have a song. Chase was so academic; he was a wonderful collector but he made editorial decisions that I wish he hadn't, because unless you find one of Harris' original books—like I've got one, *Daddy Jake and the Runaway* that I found in a used bookstore—there's songs connected to some of the stories.

Joel Chandler Harris took exactly what he had written in the magazines and put them together and made collections of the stories. Especially *Daddy Jake and the Runaway*, after he'd already introduced Uncle Remus as the vehicle to tell the stories, he finds an old African that's there on the plantation—Daddy Jake. He has things in there that are scarier; the stories ... some have voodoo attached to them. There are a couple of women that are on the plantation that are African, as opposed to having been two or three generations in this country, that tell him stories.

When you listen to some of these tales, you realize they are older and still have this "African connection." The story of when "Br'er Rabbit Goes to See Aunt Nancy" (Anansi)—all of these animals are going to pay homage to Aunt Nancy and something about her doesn't feel right. Br'er Rabbit sneaks around and looks in the window and she's there, and she's got this big ole apron on, and he notices her eyes are red. All of a sudden she turns, and where the apron has not covered her he sees these spider legs [chuckle, then laughter]. Then I thought, "Ah, there is a connection between Aunt Nancy and Anansi."

I had heard of Aunt Nancy, but hadn't been able to find any stories until

I found this one Harris collected. Then come to find out, there's this place called the Laura Plantation in New Orleans that's now a tourist plantation—an old Creole plantation where Harris had gone when he was young and collected tales. They have collected some of the Br'er Rabbit stories from there—they are in French, and translated and they have published them. They are different than the ones that Joel Chandler Harris and Zora Neale Hurston collected from Florida and Southern Georgia. You can find versions of Anansi, and the other trickster stories, in this country, and you can find the West African connection in a lot of them. Some of the details are changed, but the cores of the stories are the same story. Just like the Cherokee have all those rabbit tales that are mixtures of African and Cherokee tales. That's when I began noticing the similarities, but they go so far back in time you just don't know where the original story began. It's interesting—which came first, the Indian story or the African story? They are so far back in time you just don't know.

Let's face it: once the radio, recordings and printed books came along, it really interrupted the flow of oral storytelling. We are probably one of the last generations who have a connection to people who are illiterate that told the stories. It's real important to document what we've learned, because it's going to be gone. I'm glad I have such a good memory of all those old people that I knew from my church, and that I started learning some of the stories that they told me. Even if they are just personal stories, I'm writing them down.

Right now, I've got on my personal computer stories about the Boyd Street Church of God that I went to—tellin' about the people—anything I can remember about them I'm puttin' in there, because these were important people in my life. I didn't know it at the time, but a lot of my attitudes came from going to that church and those old people. There were people that went to my grandfather's church that had been slaves. There were people during that time who marched in the Armistice Day parades, and that had been Civil War soldiers that were still alive when I was growing up. So we're right at that crux of time: one generation before us went from mules to the moon!

When I was growing up, groceries were still home-delivered; people still came by in horse-drawn carts selling vegetables out of the back of the wagon that came through our neighborhood. I still remember the ice-man delivering big blocks of ice, and those cold chips that melted in my mouth. My grandmother, when I was growing up, didn't have a refrigerator, she had an ice-box and we made ice cream for Sunday dinners. Also, you remember the old coke machines and you had to kind of push it through this maze and by the time you got it, it was cold because it had been in there a while? There's stuff people don't know about anymore, and I was right at that age when things were starting to change, and I realized I needed to talk about these things. That's part of what I'm doing.

I've already got a book ready telling those stories and it's called *The Preachers in the Pulpit*, which is a line from an old blues song by Bo Carter.

When Rhonda was doing her medical residency, we moved to Lexington, Kentucky, but when she finished, I said I had to be closer to home. I travel, but when I'm home, I have to be here, in the mountains and near my parents. This was perfect, and I got to be emotionally close to them in the last years of their lives. You are lucky if you get to have no regrets over the relationships with your parents, and I was fortunate that even in the sixties, when everybody else was rebelling against their parents, that I had a good relationship with mine. In fact, my mother took me to my first civil rights demonstration when I was eleven or twelve years old, and my dad was a cop with the Knoxville Police Department!

I was lucky to have a good relationship with both of my parents, even my father, who was skeptical about me, and what I was doing with the education he had sweated so hard to provide me, but after he came to one of my concerts, he became my biggest fan. You know that old thing about fathers and sons—getting the approval of your father is so important, and I had it.

I am a gypsy and the mountains are my grandfather. There are several places that do that for me, but the Appalachian Mountains are sacred. Not just because the way the Cherokee felt about it—they really are special. That's one of the things that sold me about the place where we live. It's in an old subdivision where the trees are tall and old, and there are mountains right behind us. We are in the foothills of the Smokies and I can see the high mountains in the distance every day. The only other thing that makes me feel this way are the giant redwoods out West. Those mountains have been here so long, and the stories they can tell ... the Appalachian Mountains have been here since Pangaea.

I feel lucky to have been born here and to have that heritage—Davy Crockett, Daniel Boone, Sequoia and Simon Kenton. My great grandfather Daniel Rucker, the father of the bishop who was born on the Mordecai Rucker plantation in McMinn County, Tennessee; my grandfather, John Lindsey Rucker, the bishop of the Church of God, Sanctified, Inc.; my grandmother, Luola Cunningham, and her mother, Eliza Cunningham Fore, who was born a slave, sold on the auction block and walked chained behind a wagon from Williamsburg, Virginia, to Athens, Tennessee. She gained her freedom at the end of the Civil War and raised three daughters. I've got so many roots—my great grandfather Jessie Thomas, a freeborn black man who was a handler of mules who didn't get to see his fourteenth child born because he was confiscated and forced to be a teamster in the Civil War and didn't survive the war—all that is a part of my heritage and a part of these mountains.

My father's people are from Athens, Tennessee, and my mother's people are from Dandridge, Tennessee—all of my roots are within sight of that mountain. Pinto beans and cornbread, turnip greens, fiddles and banjoes—it's a wonderful area to be from. Everything I'd ever want is here.

Betty Smith

Betty Smith is an Appalachian ballad singer, author and playwright who has amassed an extensive collection of Southern, Appalachian and British ballads, folksongs and hymns, and has sought to preserve the ancient tradition of storytelling through song.

The child of a musical family, Smith has performed, taught and shared the traditional music of the South for over thirty-five years in classrooms, concert halls, workshops and festivals. Recorded by Folk Legacy Records, June Appal Records and Bluff Mountain Music, she also wrote curriculum for Open Court Publishers and Children's Music Workshop, and was part of the 1997 Smithsonian American Sampler Series.

Her one-act play, *A Mountain Riddle*, was produced by the Southern Appalachian Repertory Theatre (SART) on the campus of Mars Hill College and received the Paul Green Multi-Media Award in 1999. She and her husband Bill helped organize the thriving Atlanta Area Friends of Folk Music and several festivals, including the Chattahoochee Festival, the Byard Ray Festival and the Bluff Mountain Festival.

In 1982, Smith was awarded the Bascom Lamar Lunsford Award for significant contributions to the folk traditions of the Southern Appalachian Mountains, and she received the Bascom Lamar Lunsford Award in 2002 for her leadership efforts to preserve and encourage traditional Southern Appalachian culture at the 75th Mountain Dance and Folk Festival. She is the recipient of numerous ballad and dulcimer awards, including the Minstrel of the Appalachians Award at Mars Hill College in 2005, and was awarded the honorary doctor of humane letters degree from Mars Hill College in 2008.

Smith sat on the board of the John C. Campbell Folk School in Brasstown, North Carolina, for ten years, and continues to teach dulcimer skills and traditions classes at the school. Her numerous dulcimer workshops have included Western Carolina Dulcimer Week, Winter Dulcimer Weekend, Augusta Heritage, Swannanoa Gathering, Pine Mountain, and the Hindman Settlement School.

Betty Smith is the author of the acclaimed biography *Jane Hicks Gentry: A Singer Among Singers*, published in 1998 by University Press of Kentucky and awarded the Willie Parker Peace History Book Award by the North Carolina Society of Historians. The Appalachian Writers Association presented her with the 1999 Award for Contributions to Appalachian Literature; in 2001 the North Carolina Folklore Society gave her the Brown-Hudson Award for contributions to the study and appreciation of folklife in North Carolina.

Other honors include the Alumni Distinguished Service Award by the University of North Carolina at Greensboro in 1994; recognition by the North Carolina Society of Historians as Historian of the West in 2000, the California Traditional Music Society, the Memphis Dulcimer Festival and the Dr. Gene Wiggins Award for long and significant contributions to traditional music in North Georgia.

The Interview

I went to Vancouver, British Columbia, to a United Nations housing conference in 1977, and they were having music there from all over the country. A woman was supposed to meet me at the airport and I said I would have a blue-check dulcimer bag over my shoulder. Well, the place cleared out and there were just the two of us standing there. So, I walked over and asked, "Are you lookin' for Betty Smith?" And she said, "Are you Betty Smith? You don't look seedy enough to [laughter] be a folksinger." This was when that's the way folksingers were supposed to look—seedy: they had holes in the knees of their jeans and their hair needed a wash and then they thought they looked like folk singers.

So I said if you come down where I live, you won't see any folk singers that look like that. Mr. Lunsford [Bascom Lamar Lunsford] always said it's a social occasion when you go to make music, so you wear the best you have. If they're overalls, they are clean and pressed, and the boys in the band—they wear white shirts and dark pants, and sometimes they even wear string ties. And I said, what you're callin' folk singers aren't folk singers. [Laughter] They want to be, but they're not.

My mother's mother was a singer—we all sang. We all sang, and my mother played piano by ear—she put everything in F—I couldn't sing in F, but I sing in D an awful lot [laughing].

I learned some of the ballads from my grandmother, but not as many as I should have, because she died when I was just sixteen; I didn't really start singing those songs until I was an adult. It's almost as though I was meant to do ballads, but I had to grow into the ballads as I got older.

One thing I like about ballads is the way they tell a story, but they don't tell the whole story—this is not a novel, it is a short story and they have to tell you things so you will understand what happened. If they told you everything you couldn't sing but one ballad in an evening. Like in "Little Margaret," she's lookin' out the window and she sees him walking by with another woman, and it says she threw down her ivory comb, she threw back her long yellow hair, but the next thing you see is she's standing at the foot of his bed and she's a ghost. When he goes to find her, she's in her coffin. One old ballad singer said, "You know, she jumped out the window!" It doesn't say that, but he thinks that's what happened, so that's what happened. But you understand by the time you get through, that she saw him and she died of love and jumped out of the window or whatever you want it to be, and then he sees her and he's sorry. She asks him how he likes his snow white pillow, and how he likes his sheets, and how he likes that fair young girl. He says he likes the one standin' at his bed feet and he goes to find her. That's typical—there are certain themes that go through the ballads. If you forget something, you can fill it in with something you know from another ballad. A lot of it is folklore anyhow. In "Little Margaret" it says he kissed her lily white hand, her cheek, and then he kissed her clay, cold lips. If you kiss a dead person, you die; and he falls in her arms asleep. It means he died when he actually kissed her.

At the end of "Barbry Allen," the rose and the briar grow together. She is the one who is not being fair and he dies of love, and then she dies when she realizes how unfair she was. He told her he didn't really care about those other women, but she didn't believe him. In the end they are buried in the same churchyard and the rose grew around the briar. The themes are universal, and in some countries it might be a story and in another, a song. They change from one culture to another, like the Jack Tales. He's not going to be Jack in Germany, maybe he's going to be Hans, or in Scandinavia or wherever.

Sometimes people say, "Why do you sing those bloody old ballads?" And I say, "You read the newspaper, don't you?" And then they will say, "Don't they make you sad?" and I say, "No! It's not happenin' to me." Lyric songs tell what's happening to you. A love song is a lyric; a hymn is a lyric—it's how you feel about something. You're not singing about how you *feel* about something when you sing a ballad, you're telling a story when you're singin' a ballad about whatever. It doesn't have to affect you personally, if you're telling it. You might sound like it is sometimes, but it is different from trying to express yourself with something like a personal story. Ballads are more like journalism—they are about somethin' that happened. Some things happen to people wherever they are—there are universal themes that go through the stories and ballads.

Olive Campbell is largely responsible for saving many of the ballads before radio and recordings changed everything. The first time that Olive Campbell heard a ballad sung here was when she and her husband John were on one of their first junkets in the southern Appalachian Mountains, and they were in Hindman, Kentucky, doing research at the Settlement School. It was wintertime and it was snowing outside and they said, "Would you like to hear a ballad?" She was from New England—they knew ballads in New England—and she said, "Of course," and a young girl by the name of Ada Smith sat down on a low stool by the fire with a little banjo and sang "Barbry Allen." It was different from how she had ever heard it, and it just turned her life around. She had never heard that modal sound before, and that changed her life and started her on the search for the ballads and songs. She actually was the first one who did any kind of real research on the ballads in the southern mountains. She doesn't get the credit for it that she ought to.

After that, wherever she went, she would write down the songs she heard; she would try to write down the tunes, but even though she played piano, she wasn't really that good at it. Sometimes she would have to go back again, but she got down about 225 songs and ballads, just writin' 'em down.

Betty Smith

It was a very hard job, but she took them to her old professor at Tufts College, and then took them to a man at Harvard who told her how important what she had collected was.

She heard about Cecil Sharp, an Englishman who'd collected in England, who was in the Boston area—he was into dance, as well as music—working on *A Midsummer Night's Dream*. She took about 75 of her pieces—people have said she only collected 75—oh no, she didn't! She probably took seventy-five songs to him, but she collected 225. We found 'em in the collection at the Cecil

Sharp House in London—we couldn't find 'em [the songs she collected] in this country, but we found them there.

Anyway, Olive Campbell took herself off to Boston where he was staying at the home of a Mrs. Storrow, who was apparently a wealthy woman, because one of the streets in Boston was called Storrow. The lady was supporting the work he was doing, but anyhow he had gout, and I don't think she wanted to let Mrs. Campbell in, but she did, and then he started to get better, because he thought this was very important work. He was the one who knew how to write down the tunes—he also understood the modes—he was the best that there's ever been at that. He spent forty-six months in these southern mountains, collecting the songs. People said, "How did he get along with mountain people?" He got along with them because he liked them and respected them, not for any other reason. He and Olive both really respected the folks they were collecting from. They were different from some of the collectors who came later, too. There was a lot of backbiting and jealousy that went on, but not with them. They respected the people they collected from—and each other.

People said, "Why didn't Olive go with him [Sharp]?" but during this period of time, she lost two babies, and she just couldn't travel with him, but her husband, John Campbell, got him around. It was John who took him to Hot Springs. He came first to Madison County because this was one of the best places to get the songs; it is in what they call the "Laurel Country" along the Tennessee–North Carolina border, and it's where Jane Gentry, who I did the book on, did more songs for him than any other singer in this country.

The *English Folksongs from the Southern Appalachians* is the best collection there's ever been from any region and could never be done again. It was done before radio, before recording. It was even done before the boys came back from World War I. Sharp's assistant came back in the forties and she found things had changed because by that time we had radio and recordings.

I will never forget this woman in Berea where I learned "Isabel and the Elfin Knight" from. She was only seventeen when Cecil Sharp came through there, and she sang for him. She wasn't known as a singer—she was secretary to the president of Berea College and even her children didn't think of her as a singer, but she knew the songs. She was eighty-five years old when I met her, and all of these songs were coming back to her because Loyal Jones and I wanted to hear them. That's just one of hers that I really latched onto.

A lot of the ballads we sing today came across from the British Isles and if you got here and you didn't remember the story the way you heard it maybe from your parents or your grandparents, you could still make up that story because you would know what happened in it. I don't know how many were written, or how many they brought over and were just perpetuated, but I do think they kind of made up songs around local happenings. They knew songs like that old English ballad where the girl gets killed ... and then in this country it is the "Banks of the Ohio," it's the "Knoxville Girl." You don't know why he killed her but he did. The English version may have told you, but here, there might have been some Presbyterian grandmothers who took out some of that stuff.

When you think about it, it's the community that decides what is going to be sung or told. You don't tell or sing things that are not acceptable in the community, and so they were bound to change when they came to this country. A lot of songs, like "Omie Wise" and "Knoxville Girl," I've had people tell me when I'd sing that song in Knoxville, "I know that song and I remember when it happened," and they remember it from their own setting. Often, they knew one of those ballads already, say, they learned it from a broadside either in England or in this country, and they just adapted it, gave it another name or another place, and used the same melody. Mrs. Gentry sang three songs to essentially the same tune. They weren't note for note, but they were the shape of the same tune. I bet she didn't even realize it because they were different kinds of ballads. One was a love song and the others are really bloody.

Cecil Sharp wrote down Mrs. Lizzie Roberts' version of "Black is the Color of My True Love's Hair." She lived in Hot Springs, and her husband ran the ferry. This was after the great flood of 1916 and the bridges were all gone and so there was a ferry across the French Broad River, and Sharp crossed the river and the ferryman told him if he wanted some ballads to go see his wife. She sang that song for him and he wrote it down. I've always felt, and I could be wrong, that John Jacob Niles, who also collected Appalachian folk music, kind of re-wrote that song to fit his own voice; he did that a lot since he was a composer. I like the way Mrs. Roberts sang it [she sings the Roberts version, and then the Niles version].

My dad sang—he knew ballads and he sang shape-notes; he knew about all the shape-note song leaders because he had been doing that for years. There were good stories about all those people, but I didn't write it down, and I didn't tape it. It was the whole history of that world that I don't have because I didn't do something about it when I should have. You listen to the stories and you think about it ... my children are telling me, "Please write it down," and I say, "But you know that story," and they'll say, "Not like you do!"

I've got all these letters that my dad wrote my mother when they were courting about the singin' contests, saying, "We went up against Pleasant Garden...." But I don't think they got prizes, they just had these singings. I know that he sang in a group and that he didn't play an instrument, but others played instruments. Often I think why I didn't tape my dad more? But you know, you just think people are going to live forever. On one of my recordings, I have him singing: Bill Morris took an old tape with my dad singing on it; cleaned it up and put it on there. We couldn't use the whole song, but I said I'd just like to hear his voice on there, you know, and I was playin' and he was singin'.

In the sixties I started hearing a lot of folk music and I said, "Oh, I know that!" This was the time of the big folk song revival and I said, "It never really died." That's what it's all about—that's what oral tradition is! You know a song because you used to hear people sing it, or you knew somebody who sang that—that's how you know that.

When I first started singin' in public, I didn't have the nerve to walk up, like people do at festivals, and say, "Can I be on your program?" Instead, I wrote Mr. Bascom Lamar Lunsford, and sent two songs to him—I'll tell you what they were—my aunt came to see me one time and she said, "You sing 'Barbry Allen' more like Mama than anybody,"—that was my grandmother. I don't remember learnin' that from her. I have just always known it. She said, "Of course you did. You were the oldest grandchild and that was her baby-rockin' song and you got more rockin' than anybody else did!" I figure with eight children on the farm, you picked the longest song you could think of to rock to, 'cause it might be the only time you sat down that day. But I sent Mr. Lunsford that one and then the other one that I sent him was the "Ballad of Omie Wise."

My dad is from Randolph County, and my grandmother is an Adams from Randolph County and they lived right there where the "Ballad of Omie Wise" took place. I have a second cousin, Thelma, she's gotten to be in her nineties ... and she lived right across Highway 220, or whatever that road is, that goes through Randleman you know, and that was one of the first ballads I knew. My dad—they all knew the "Ballad of Omie Wise" because that's where they grew up. And so, this new book came out that kind of said that Omie was "no better than she ought to be," and probably had some other illegitimate children. Anyhow, it was supposed to have been a diary found in California and I told Thelma, this new book—I told her all about it, and Thelma said, "That is not so." Since 1807 they have been protecting her, this beautiful young girl who was done wrong and murdered by Jonathon Lewis, and Thelma said, "No," because her whole life she had heard the story. So, that was the other song I sent him.

And Mr. Lunsford, well, he told me he had a piece of the door frame off of my great-grandfather's old house [laughter] and I said, "William was my grandmother's father!" I never understood how he got that, 'cause I used to go there with my grandmother, you know. I never understood how he got that door frame, but anyway, I sent that letter to him and he said to come to the festival.

Joe Bly was the emcee at the Asheville festival for years. Joe Bly's a storyteller, and Joe, if he didn't know you, sent you to the left side of the stage and you went on early. For years the festival started along about sundown, and it went on the radio at seven o'clock so if he didn't know you, you went on before seven o'clock. And Joe would say, "She [Betty, mimicking Bly, who was talking about her] was only there on the left side of the stage one year and then she got to be on the other side!" [Laughter] He would always tell that story [chuckling].

We all sat on the stage—our children, our husbands or whoever. It was really an ideal thing. Mr. Lunsford had a platform built out from the stage, and the dancers used that. Nowadays, all they do is move microphones around all the time and it takes forever to get all set up. No, they didn't do that. See, with the platform, they didn't share the stage, but it was really nice and people sat all around the stage and you could see faces ... they tend to cut the lights out in auditoriums you know, but you could see faces of people sitting on the floor all around the platform. I kind of liked that back then you know, I thought it was a kind of a nice way to do it, but things get modernized.

I learn more by ear, I mean, I always have, but I took violin when I was growing up. It's good for you and you do learn to read music that way. I was in the school orchestra and I really liked it, but what I liked to sing is stuff that is traditional—things that my dad sang and that my grandmother sang. I never really thought about that music too much until I was plumb grown, you know. I should have been listening better.

I just have this thing about playin' by ear. I think it's great to be able to read music and I think sometimes you have to; you do learn a lot about reading music when you use tablature. You have to pay attention to time and you have to know what a half note and a quarter note ... you gotta be noticin' and I just think that to be a complete musician you ought to do both.

Some things I hear ... like when I first got my psaltery, I thought, "What am I going to do with this?" I had no teacher and no books—no nothing. That's not the way I learn music anyhow. I did play the violin and I can read music, but I've never been that kind of musician. A professor at Georgia State, Professor Sally Monsour, when I was working on my master's, she said something I've never forgotten: "Did you write a curriculum for Open Court Publishers?" When I answered, "Yes," she said, "You listen to me, and don't you ever forget it: there are all kinds of musicians and all kinds of ways of doing music, and you're what I call a natural musician, and you keep right on doing what you do, and don't ever feel bad about saying what you do."

When I taught dulcimer at Western Carolina University during dulcimer week at the college, I would make a recording and a list of all the songs that we were going to work on that week. I sent it out to all the students ahead of time; and I said "I don't want you to try to play this—I just want you to listen to it as many times as you can every day until all the songs are in your head." You'd be amazed at how much faster that goes with beginners—it just does! One year I had these two nurses, they were just something, and I always said that if I got sick, I'm goin' to Gainesville, Georgia, 'cause they work in the hospital. They were so much fun and one of them we were startin' to play a piece, and she said, "Oh, that's what I brush my teeth to." [Laughter]

The dulcimer is a modal instrument and it's the kind of instrument that goes well with ballads. It's a diatonic instrument—it does not have all the half-steps that a guitar or a banjo does. Almost all folk music, and it does not matter which country it is, is done on a five-note scale. The way modes are different than scales is this: if you say that this song is in the key of D, there's a certain pitch, and that's where it is done.

A mode is an arrangement of notes, just like a scale, except it doesn't matter what the pitch is because it's not based on pitch at all like scales we use now. We tune into Aeolian which is minor, Dorian which is mountain minor with a sharp note in the scale, and Mixolydian, which has a flatted seventh note like "Old Joe Clark." That's what old-timers called it—Old Joe Clark tuning, or the minor is Shady Grove tuning. They tuned their instruments where they could play certain songs; the banjo players did it, too.

I taught for a long time at Mars Hill College and at some point, the folks at John C. Campbell Folk School asked me to come teach there, and I've been teaching there ever since.

When I teach the dulcimer classes—I sing the whole day long, 'cause I think people do better if they sing the songs they are trying to learn. I say, in some of my class descriptions, that we'll sing with the dulcimer, because I think if you sing the melody that you'll be able to play it. There are people who teach it by numbers, and you do have to use numbers, because you have people who can't read music and you have to use tablature, but I think that is a very hard way to learn a song—to read numbers and to go from one fret and go to another without any sense of what it sounds like, 'cause you move so slowly you get no sense of what that song is really like. If you hear it, and you get it in your head, you just know when it goes up and when it goes down.

I do programs for the North Carolina Humanities "Road Scholars"; I do a program on Jane Gentry [Appalachian singer and storyteller from Madison County, North Carolina], and another program called *Women in Traditional Song*—the women in the songs and the women who sang the songs. I can talk about the women who sang the songs, how they look in the stories, because they play all different roles. In some, the woman is the protagonist and has the pen-knife—she's the "brown girl." Because of the role they played in life on the frontier and in the early days, and because of the way their lives were, why did they remember certain songs? Which ones did women keep alive?

One that I do because I like the story is "The House Carpenter" or the "Demon Lover." In that ballad, the old lover comes back and she leaves her husband and her baby and goes off with him. That is not what women did in the Calvinist tradition—you don't go off and leave your husband and your baby, but in the end, she's punished when her lover's ship sinks and she has to be punished in that tradition.

Of course there are bad women out there, but then there are women who are victims: they may be murdered, they may be abandoned, but it all comes out in the ballads—women playing different roles in life. There are a few where nobody is the victim, but the story—things have to happen in a story. Everybody can't be nice and have a good attitude. For instance, there is "Young Hunting," where she is not a nice person. She wants him to spend the night with her, and he won't do it, so she uses her pen-knife. You can imagine that maybe women who had no choice back then—there was nowhere to go if things were not like she wanted them to be, there was nothing she could do about it, but she might sing about somebody that did. It might have been a form of escape. For instance, you can imagine that Jane Gentry was always busy—she had a hard life, and the ballads may have helped her deal with it.

I used Jane Gentry's stories and songs in my classes when I was teaching back in the seventies. You see, I had already found her, and then I wrote a book about her [*Jane Hicks Gentry: A Singer Among Singers*, University Press of Kentucky 1998]. I have enough material left over from that book to do another one just on Maud Long's [Jane Gentry's daughter] eleven Jack tales—they are long Jack tales, and the thirty-five songs that I couldn't fit into the first one.

Ms. Gentry was a ballad singer from Madison County, North Carolina, and I would give anything to have met her. She died about the time I was born, so maybe we passed each other; her family says that I know more about her than they do.

I missed some things because they had a big flood in Hot Springs. James, her grandson, ran the hardware store right there in Hot Springs. The filing cabinet where he had all his clippings from his grandmother and all his family stuff washed away when Spring Creek flooded and washed away half of the store. And I thought, *oh, no—what all was in there?*

Sharp had a diary that was at the Cecil Sharp House in England, and I said to them, "Every time you see Hot Springs, or Jane Gentry on something in the collection, could I have it?" I wanted the book to tell what she was like and I wanted it to show how important was that incredible repertoire of songs and stories, and riddles and rhymes she knew, and I put all those in the book.

The thing that has happened with the book is that I knew that I would probably have to have a university press print it, because no other press would let me put all the songs and the stories and the rhymes and all that in it, and the University of Kentucky Press let me do it. There aren't very many contextual studies of singers or storytellers. You either get a biography, or you get a collection of songs or a collection of stories, but you don't get them all together. In my book, you get to know the woman who sang the songs and told the stories, and how they fit into her life. For instance, her children said they always knew where their mother was because she sang all the time. I don't know if I sang as much as she did, but I like to sing.

Jane Gentry was really born on Beech Mountain in Watauga County. There weren't a lot of families on Beech Mountain back in those days, so a lot of them married into the Hicks and Harmons, Presnells and all those old families—there just weren't many people to marry in those days.

Her mother was a Harmon and her father was a Hicks—she was old Counce Harmon's granddaughter—she is the only one of those who've been collected from, who learned directly from him. All the others—Ray or Orville, will say my great great, great, however many great grandfather's, but he was her grandfather and she lived right there until she was twelve and her father moved the family over to Meadow Fork, which is just a few miles from here. Bill [her husband, sitting behind us] said, "It's just across the mountain, about a mile and a half," and so Old Counce came over here. You know he had 19 children and three of them moved out to the Meadow Fork area, and so when I was lookin' at the census, I saw that old Counce was over here one year, which means he was over here when they did the census. That's a long way to just go see your children.

I got some of the best stories about her from the writings of a man by the name of Irving Bachelor. He was the Sunday editor of the *New York World* under Joseph Pulitzer. He thought she was the most wonderful woman he ever met, and he actually wrote a book based on the stories that she told him, but the book and all of the copies were burned in a house fire and he never—I think it was a thing that was so upsetting to his wife, and all that, that he never got that book re-written. After that, he wrote short pieces about Jane Gentry, and he wrote an article about her in the *American Magazine*, a very popular magazine at one time, and he wrote a piece called the "Happiest Woman I Ever Knew." That was one thing about her that in spite of everything she could have used not to be happy, she was. Old Counce was that way too, apparently, and she probably got that from him. She had a terrible back and you would think she would complain about it, but one time she said, "I've just learnt to feel badly and keep cheerful." One of the best stories he wrote about her, he wrote about them coming across the mountain when they moved, and he wrote about her marriage and how they walked twenty miles to Marshall in the rain, and she said that they were happy, walkin' twenty miles in the rain—they were just happy. There was one daughter that said she always had an apron on and it had some trim on it—tatting or pulled lace. People don't do that who have plenty of time! Said people would walk into her kitchen ... and you wouldn't notice you were peeling apples or stringing beans or something, and they wouldn't notice 'cause she would be singing or tellin' stories, you know. One of those singers from over at Beech Mountain said that's how they kept their children on the job.

One woman I interviewed was ninety years old at the time, and she was a live wire. She said, "I remember when Jane Gentry came to the Asheville Normal School and she told us about that man that came to see her to get her songs." She didn't remember his name, and then she said he told her—and this is one story that I was so glad to get—he told her the first time he came to see Mrs. Gentry, that if she wanted to, she could set in one room and sing and he could sit in the next room and write down the songs. And she told him that if he could stand to look at her, she could stand to look at him. [Laughter] I figured it had been over seventy years since she heard her [Gentry] say that! Nobody's going to remember what I say after seventy years!

Jerry Wolfe

Jerry Wolfe is a storyteller of Cherokee descent. He was born in Cherokee, North Carolina, and spoke only the Cherokee language, although his mother had taught him some English, until being sent to the government school. There, forbidden to speak Cherokee, he learned to speak English, but spoke his own language with the other children at every opportunity.

He learned about storytelling at the feet of his father, who taught him many of life's lessons through story. Today, he tells the traditional Cherokee stories in both his native language and in English, but according to Wolfe, "they are not the same in English. Much of the rhythm is lost and some of the humor. It's not as much fun."

Wolfe enlisted in the U.S. Navy in 1943 and was a part of the invasion of Normandy, "D-Day." The father of five children, he and his wife returned to Cherokee to live permanently in 1949, where he became a noted stone mason. He taught the craft of block and stone masonry with the Job Corps for twenty years. He then worked independently for many years after that, and his stonework is a part of many of the buildings around Cherokee.

"Look all around here, and you will see my hand in it," said Wolfe, whose personal favorites were the stone fireplaces he built. "Today's workers don't work like we did—we did it by our skill and took pride in the work."

Now retired, he works three days a week at the Museum of Cherokee History in Cherokee, where he leads groups through the museum and teaches through story.

The Interview

I am Jerry Wolfe of the Eastern Band of the Cherokee in Western North Carolina, and I am from the land of the Cherokee.

Most of our old storytellers are gone. Of the next generations coming along, very few of them took interest in learning the traditions and the culture of the Cherokee people. I heard the stories coming up, and listened to my dad tell the stories about stickball games, and stories about the animals like chipmunk and snake—I heard them all as a young boy.

The stories that we know are not really legend stories; they are old and they are true stories. They are spiritual in nature, and we conserve and preserve them. They fit in with the animals of the forest and the fowl of the air and all of the living creatures. When you hear the story and then look at the behavior of that animal, it is in there—it's collected—it's all together. A lot of truth comes out of those stories. They are real. There is one story that will illustrate this: for all of the animals that have markings, there is a reason and a story behind those markings, and they are true stories.

> Often we picture the animals as talking to one another at a gathering. One is the little chipmunk. Many years ago the animals that were edible and those who were not edible gathered because they had a "beef," and each one had a say about the hunters. The hunters came into our forest and killed our brothers and our sisters, mothers and fathers. "They don't care," they said. "The hunters don't care, and they never put anything back for payment into the forest," and that was their concern. It went on and each animal had his say about the hunters. Finally, the big bear, the big one of our forest—he was the chairman of the meeting, he looked up at the ledge of the council house and there sat the little chipmunk, not saying anything. The big bear looked at chipmunk and said, "You haven't said a word in this meeting," and the chipmunk looked back at him and said, "The hunters don't bother me, and besides the hunters need meat on their tables to feed their families." This made the bear mad and he grabbed that chipmunk with his big paw, and with his other paw he scratched him down the back. Where he scratched him down the back, to this day those stripes are still there—seven stripes.

The old Cherokee people when I was growing up didn't call it a chipmunk or ground squirrel; they called him "seven stripes" in our Cherokee language (speaking in Cherokee). So that's how he got his seven stripes in that meeting, and the big bear scratched him down the back—four claws and in-between—seven stripes to this day. We have two names for it in Cherokee and two names in English. That's the kind of stories we have—reality comes out of those stories.

> The copperhead snake was made into an ugly snake, the copperhead was. He's sneaky, too. The copperhead is the kind of snake that will bite you, but now, he was not always like that. In this Cherokee village was a troublemaker, and this troublemaker would go around to all the homes and houses and cause trouble—carry news, tell lies—all those things. And so the people of the village were concerned with the woman and they decided they needed to get rid of her. They went to one of their leaders in the village and he said, "I have a man who is very knowledgeable of doing things like that," and he went to see him. The man studied a long time and finally said he had a solu-

tion to the troublemaker. "Before we do," he said, "we will go into the mountains and find a big bull snake which is non-poison. It's a scary-looking snake, but it's not poison. We will bring it in, and I will make a concoction and feed that concoction to the bull snake and he will become poison. What we will do put this snake out where this troublemaker walks and this big snake will tag her on the leg. When he tags her on the leg, she will surely die." They were in a log cabin discussing this, but during that discussion, just outside where they couldn't see him, was this snake listening to what they were saying. This man took the concoction he had made up—it was real poison, and sat it on a shelf and they went looking for the bull snake. When they caught it, they were going to bring it here and feed the poison to the snake and make him poi-

Jerry Wolfe

son. While they were gone, the snake that was listening crawled in and up the shelf to the container and he drank the poison. He went and lay out for the troublemaker. When they came along, he did the job and she died. Well, when they returned with the bull snake and took the poison down, there was no poison there. Just about that time the copperhead came crawling in and he was so happy. He said, "Hey, I went ahead and did the job for you people. You didn't have to go out and catch this snake, because I did the job." The man who had made up the concoction said, "You will be hated all your life; you will be dreaded all your life and you will be a thief all your life. You did wrong; you were not supposed to drink that and that's the reason you will be hated and dreaded for the rest of your life by all people, because you are a sneaky snake and a thief." That's why the copperhead is the way he is.

When I was a boy, we'd sit around at night—there were no telephones, no televisions—and there would be a big fire going. My dad would talk about ballgames—the Cherokee love to tell stories about the old games from back to when. And he would tell us about stickball and the happenings at the ballgames, and tell all kinds of stories and I would listen to him. He would tell stories about Bird Town, Big Cove Town, and Wolf Town—all of the townships had a ball team and they played against one another. It was big to the people. The way he described it, just about everybody on the boundary would gather to watch that game.

Stickball is an old tradition of the Cherokee people and dates "back beyond." It is a very physical game, and it was being played when the settlers came, and the settlers saw them play it here, in Cherokee. The shamans, or "conjure men" were the coaches, and they had great knowledge of the mind and often foretold who would win. If the conjure man lost four games in succession, he was doomed to die—he had been over-powered by the other shaman.

After the crops were gathered in, the people had time for the games. They took their sticks to the water often as they traveled to the games. There were ball dances at the playing grounds, and the male dancers danced all night; they didn't sleep a wink. There were two fires, but one was special for the ballplayers, it was a sacred fire. The players danced all night and when they took a break, they went to the water, dipped their sticks in the water and drank.

The old men started talking and telling what was going to happen, and sometimes they took a bear claw and crisscrossed the arms and chests of the players to draw a little blood—this was to get rid of tired blood and to prevent cramps. There were reasons for everything that was done, but much of this is no longer done today.

The women danced the last dance, and that was at daybreak. Then the shamans took black beads to represent the enemy—the opposing team, and at the end of the dances, dug a little trench in front of the fire and sowed them there, and the women danced on top of them, which meant stomping the opposition.

The women brought quilts and blankets and other things they had made to bet with at the games. They all walked down to the games so they had to bring the goods they were going to bet with, so sometimes they wore layers of clothing—seven or eight dresses stacked one on top of the other. When they reached the fair grounds, they took the extra layers off and used them to make their bets. Sometimes they would tie their other items together and put them into a pile. Whoever won the bet got the items in the pile. The men brought horses, mules and oxen, knives and rifles to bet with. The government of North Carolina frowned on the people for betting and they were against it, saying we were gambling, and they tried to ban it.

The women—the grandmas played stickball back in the 1870s and they were banned from playing because they got too rough with each other. They went out for blood when they played. In the games that were coming up in 2000, some of the young ladies came to me saying they wanted to break the ban, and make history—make stories. It sounded good to me; it was 130 years ago when they were banned. Of course, the grandmas were young women when it was banned. Anyway, they practiced (and it is a rough game) and they practiced out and practiced out, and they came in with sprained ankles and elbows, and all skinned up where they had just practiced. The Big Cove and Wolf Town women wanted to play against each other, and one of the managers came to me and said, "We *don't* want to go out there like our grandmothers did. We *do* want to play a good hard game, but it's going to be fair. We're *not* going out to kill each other." So our 2000 Cherokee Fair came along and they met on the playing field—about 15 people on each team, and there were speeches made and a prayer was said before the ballgame; we always have prayer before any kind of event takes place.

The goal is to make twelve points—the team that gets those points is the winner. The umpire tosses the ball up and they bat it with those sticks (straight sticks with a rigid, woven loop at the end). At the game, as the ball went up on the far side, I saw a woman go up with it and she was picked up and body-slammed on the ground. Then I looked around and they lay all over the field; it was bad. It was the roughest game I've seen, I guess. Those women were really getting at it [he said with a grin]. They told me it was going to be a mild game—I'd hate to see a rough game! They came out to play in 2004, but they were told, "No more!" They were too rough.

The only way to get a real picture of the games is to hear it in our language. Much of the color is gone when I try to tell the stories about them in English; they just don't come out the same.

We have children's immersion classes in Cherokee, where our children are taught our language and customs, and it is near the museum. They begin at age five and many of those kids have gone beyond English; they are becoming strong in the Cherokee language. I learned it at home. My mother finished fifth grade, which was a high grade in those days—it was the late 1890s when she finished school, and she said, "I was offered a job as teacher because I had a fifth-grade education." My father never had any schooling a day in his life, and he spoke the language. I would hear it and ask, "What was that word?" he had spoken, and he would tell me. I learned it like that. Then my mother told me she was going to teach me English, because "it will help you when you go to school." It really happened that way, because my peer group couldn't speak English; they couldn't speak a word of English. Some spoke broken language, but at school, we couldn't speak our language. The government had a lot to do with our school back then, and even our land. After we changed our leadership, and different men came in, each new group that came in knew more about these things, and how to hold the tribe together. The man we have in charge today is a graduate of Western Carolina University. He's very intelligent and well-educated, and that's what we need—we have 14,000 people living here. You have to be Cherokee to live here, but there has been a lot of intermarriage, but the back-folks, their memaws and papaws, are full Cherokee.

Index

abuse 78, 199, 202; *see also* ballads; Silver, Frankie
addiction 76–77; *see also* coal mining; community plays
advocacy 90, 103; *see also* mountaintop removal
Aeolian 201
African American 14, 59, 130–131
Afri-lachian 133, 188
Allen, Harriett Bias 134
Allen, Richard 128
alternate roots 61
American Indian 19, 20, 24–25, 27–28, 30, 42, 168–169, 183
American Revolution *see* Revolutionary War
Anansi/Aunt Nancy 189–190
ancestors 5–6, 20, 34, 38, 130, 191
ancestral home 39
Andersen, Hans Christian 36
Angelou, Maya 188
Appalachian Regional Collection 176; *see also* Appalachian State University
Appalachian Regional Commission (ARC) 63, 70
Appalachian State University 85; *see also* Appalachian Regional Collection
Appalshop (Appalachian Film Workshop) 86; *see also* Richardson, Bill
aprons 100, 111, 204
atom 37, 45
Atomic Frontier 36, 40

Bachelor, Irving 202
Baker, Dan 86
ballads 6, 11–12, 80, 110, 114, 146, 156–157, 194–204

banjo 13, 82, 118, 192
baptism 83, 110, 166
barefoot 35, 38, 63, 108, 155; *see also* walking
Battle of King's Mountain 79
Beech Mountain 138, 144, 203–204
Beloved Woman 169; *see also* Nunceahi; Ward, Nancy; Wild Rose
Bible 36, 65, 67, 75, 125; biblical 117
Birchwood Center for the Arts 149, 158
birthright 38
Black Arts Movement 127
Black Power Movement 127
blood 27, 46, 56, 208
Blue Ridge 77, 163
Blue Ridge ghetto 152
Blue Ridgers 148
bluegrass music 13, 77
Bly, Joe 200
Bowen, Guinn 116
Bowie, Linda 2, 151
Boyd Street Church of God 190
Br'er Rabbit/Buh Rabbit 65, 125, 129, 189–190
briar patch 147
broadside ballads 12, 198
broadside television 69–70
Brother Blue 132, 134, 137
Brothers Grimm 60, 95; *see also* Grimm's Fairytales
Buffalo Soldiers 183

Cabell, Ed 188
call to storytelling 18, 23, 37, 46, 48, 57, 70, 86–87, 92, 102, 104, 114, 134, 146, 153, 178, 182
Campbell, John 197

Index

Campbell, Joseph 47–48, 60
Campbell, Olive 196–197
cancer 11, 18, 45, 63, 69, 111
Carlson, Chief (Navaho) 30
Carson, Kit 30
Carter, Bo 191
Carter, Mother Mary 120, 132, 134
Caudill, Henry 63
Celts 35, 178; heritage 34, 37, 39; hypothesis 178; mythology 58
Chase, Richard 48, 146, 155, 189
Cherokee 17, 22–24, 26, 37, 43–44, 47–48, 50, 186; Cherokee-Appalachian 39, 42–43; Cherokee Nation 34; culture and heritage 16, 28, 34–35, 42, 43–44, 36–37, 48, 50, 163, 209; forbidden language 209; land of 205; language immersion 209; reservation 16; see also Eastern Band of the Cherokee; Museum of Cherokee History
Chief Carlson, Navaho 30
Chief Dragging Canoe, Cherokee 79
Chief Joseph, Nez Perce 28, 29
Chief Wilma Mankiller, Cherokee 43
Choctaw 36
Chota 166; see also sacred places
Church of God, Sanctified, Inc. see preacher tales
circle 44, 97, 107
circuit riding preachers 95
Civil Rights Movement 126–127, 181
Civil War 10, 11, 95, 183, 151, 183–184, 190
Clinchfield Railroad 78; see also railroads
Clingman's Dome 84–85
Clower, Jerry 116
coal mining 76, 89, 188; see also mountaintop removal; strip-mining
Cobb Mountain 98
coming home 9, 14, 21–22, 33–34, 107–108, 144, 151
community plays 73–74, 80, 91
Corn Mother 43–44
Cornish 178
Corriere, Jules 76
Cothren, Martha 29
courtship 107, 111, 140–143
creeks 168
Crockett, David 106
culture 35, 42, 52, 54–56, 80–82, 86, 91, 113, 139, 146, 178, 184; Appalachian subculture 107; mountain 33, 42, 54, 118

D-Day 106, 205
Damron, Allen 104
dams 36, 81, 150
Danish Folk School 70
Davis, Kooki 135

death 51, 99–100, 127, 140, 133, 158
Deedy, Carmen 19
desegregation 127
divine 103–104
Dorian 201
Dragging Canoe, Chief (Cherokee) 79
drugs 76
Dunbar, Paul Lawrence 126

East Tennessee State University 36–37
Eastern Band of the Cherokee 16, 205; Texas Remnant 163; see also Cherokee
Ebbing and Flowing Springs, Tennessee 35–36
Eckstine, Billy 123
Elderhostel 48, 50
elders 9, 21, 85
England 5–6, 10, 87
English (language) 85, 96, 209
Eshu 189

family stories 11, 15, 23, 65–67, 84, 88, 94–95, 125, 130, 134, 152–155, 165–166, 186
fiddle 13, 82, 118, 192
finding voice 87, 91–92, 114, 122; see also repression of voice
fish 54, 96, 145
floods 81–82; see also dams
folk schools 48, 70, 194, 196, 201
folk tellers 106; see also Freeman, Barbara; Reagan-Blake, Connie
folk wisdom: remedies and traditions 9–10, 56, 82, 111, 114, 182
Fontana Dam/Lake 81, 150
Fort Oglethorpe 174
France 40–41
Free Africa Society 129
Freeman, Barbara 106, 116, 146, 188
French Huguenots 178

Gaillard, Frye 153
games 16, 24, 27, 41, 84–86, 67, 126, 174, 182, 206, 208; see also stickball
Gates, Henry Lewis 120, 188
Geer, Richard 72, 76
genealogy 177
Gentry, Jane Hicks 156, 193, 197, 202
German 40, 95, 168, 178, 186, 195
German Americans 107
ghosts 92, 96, 140; see also haints
Giovanni, Nikki 188
Gipe, Richard 76, 102
going back 10, 88–89; see also memory
going home 9, 13, 106–107, 136, 144, 151; see also coming home
Grandmother Corn 43–44

Index

grandparents 9, 11, 12, 34, 35, 49, 52, 62–64, 71, 83, 97, 100, 117, 124–125, 132, 151, 165, 169–176, 185–186, 191, 199
Great Smokies *see* Great Smoky Mountains
Great Smoky Mountains 21, 22, 83, 121, 133, 135–136, 191
grief 15, 18, 30, 50–51, 59, 102, 108, 113, 127, 133, 140
Grimm's fairytales 95; *see also* Brothers Grimm
GRITS: Girls Raised in the South 122

haints 9, 92; *see also* Ghosts
Harmon Council 138, 144, 146, 203
Harmon family 156, 203
harmonica 117
harp 107, 140; *see also* harmonica; jaw harp; visions
Harris, Joel Chandler 129, 189
Hatfield and McCoy's 188
healing stories 88–89
Hembree, Mike 149
Heng, Chhi Chhi 135
herbs: and plants 182
heritage 32, 34–35, 37, 52, 64, 69, 107–108, 113, 118–119, 179, 186, 191–192; mountain 33, 42, 54, 118; southern 136; *see also* Celtic; Cherokee
Hicks, Ken 105
Hicks, Orville 203
Hicks, Ray 22, 116–117, 138–144, 155–156 203; *see also* Lipman, Doug
Hicks, Stanley 155–156
Highland Scots 178
Highlander Center 69, 70
hillbilly 14, 38, 55, 90, 151; *see also* stereotypes
Hindman Folk School 194
home 14; home place 108; *see also* ancestral home
homesick 144
house 63
Houston, Sam 106
Howard University 127, 134
HUD's Truck Stop 33
Hughes, Langston 126
Huguenots 85, 178
humor 7, 15, 83, 107, 115, 141, 143, 147
Hurston, Zora Neale 125, 190

ice man 118–19, 190
identity: personal 37–38
"In the Tradition" (National Black Storytelling Festival and Conference) 120
Indian corn 165
integration 126

International Storytelling Center 93, 144
Ireland 95
Irish 96, 97
Ishi of the Yahi 30, 31
isolation 92, 149
Italian American 107

Jack tales 48, 50, 82, 146, 156–157, 195
Jackson, Andrew 30
jaw harp 117
Jinks, Joy 72
John C. Campbell Folk School 48, 157, 193, 201
John Henry, John Hardy 188
Johnson, James Weldon 126
Johnson-Allen, Martina 135
Jones, Absalom 128
Jones, Bessie 182–183, 189
Jones, Loyal 197
Jonesborough, Tennessee 6, 11, 35, 116, 134, 138, 144–146
Joseph, Chief (Nez Perce) 28, 29
Jung, Carl 132

Kennedy Center 18, 80
Kingdom of the Happy Land 59–60
Ku Klux Klan 128

land: and culture 177–179
landmarks 34, 136, 161, 163–164
Laura Plantation 190
Legbe 189
Legend Lady 162, 177
Levi-Strauss, Claude 163
life force 43, 44, 47
linguistics 7, 42, 53–54, 80, 85, 108, 111–112, 117, 122–124, 146, 151–152, 156, 159, 162
Lipmann, Doug 22; *see also* Hicks, Ray
Little Deer 44, 45; *see also* Spirit Deer
little people 10, 167
Long, Maud 202
Long Island Memorial, Kingsport, Tennessee 36
Lunsford, Bascom Lamar 193–194, 199–200

magical people 165, 167; *see also* little people
Manhattan Project 35
Mankiller, Chief Wilma (Cherokee) 43
McConnell, Doc 145, 187–188
McCrumb, Sharon 77, 176
memories/memory 10, 88–89, 106, 110, 114, 163
Mills, Billy 20; *see also* Olympics (1996)
Mitchum, Robert 57

INDEX

Mixolydian 201
Mooney, James 21
Mother Earth 26
Mother Mary Carter *see* Carter, Mother Mary
Mount, Lisa 72
mountaineer 10, 14, 117, 157, 163, 178
mountaintop removal 89, 188
Museum of Cherokee History 205
Museum of the American Indian 16, 29, 244
musical influences 11, 13, 114, 123, 130–131, 164, 182, 188, 194, 198–199
mystery 42, 45, 60, 69, 83

Nancy Ward, Beloved Mother 169
National Association for the Advancement of Colored People (NAACP) 126–127
National Association of Black Storytellers 120, 132, 135
National Folklife Center 18
National Heritage Day 24
National Public Radio (NPR) 41, 162
National Storytelling Festival 93, 105, 121
National Storytelling Network 93
Native American 16, 27–29, 119, 184; storytellers 16; *see also* American Indian
nature 36, 135, 161, 187; respect for 42
Niemi, Loren 93
Niles, John Jacob 156–158, 198
North American Indigenous Women's Association 20
Nunceahi 167; *see also* Ward, Nancy
Nunnehi 167–169; *see also* Little People

Oakridge 36, 38, 40, 45
O'Brien, John (*At Home in the Heart of Appalachia*) 55
old-time music 114–115
Olympics (1996) 20; *see also* Mills, Billy
oral history 63, 75
oral tradition 37, 190
Orchard at Altapass 77
Orisha 189
Overhill, Cherokee 34, 36
Overmountain Men 79

parents 35, 40, 51, 42, 84, 93–94, 100–101, 121, 185–186, 192, 198–199; caring for 64, 71, 99, 102, 121
Parks, Rosa 127
Philadelphia Folklore Project 120
play writing 11, 72–75, 87–91
Poesie Première 32
polygamy 77–78
porch 51–53, 57, 81, 97–98, 109
Portelli, Alexander 71

Pottel, Connie 105
preacher tales 186
psychic 165; *see also* seeing/sight; shine/sight
Pulitzer nominations 148

raconteurs 67, 95–96
railroads 78, 136, 178
Reagan-Blake, Connie 106, 116, 144–145, 188
Revolutionary War 61, 77, 95
Red Summer (1919) 185
repression: of voice 85–86
Richardson, Bill 86
ritual 88, 91, 166, 88, 91, 208
rivers 79, 83, 97, 136, 148, 150, 166, 198
Road Company 70
road scholars 201
roadside theater 70, 87
Robertson, Ben 152
roots 34, 81, 102, 113, 119, 192
Ross, Gayle 105–106
Rucker, Rhonda Hicks 180–183, 187
Rudolf, Erick 111
Ruthstrom, David 104

sacred fire 208
Sacred Medicine Wheel of the Lakota 27
Sacred Mother 169
sacred places 164, 191; *see also* Chota; Long Island
sacred ritual 35, 83, 88, 91, 108, 110, 166, 208
sacred story 26, 27, 103–104, 206
St. Luke's Press 37; *see also* Tickle, Phyllis
Scotch-Irish, Scots-Irish 33, 52, 96, 110, 178, 184
seeing/sight 9, 165; *see also* shine/sight
segregation 121, 126, 184–185
Selu 32, 43–44; *see also* Corn Mother
Sequoyah Museum 21
setting 14; stump setting 46
Settlement School 193
Sevier, John 79; *see also* State of Franklin
shaman 61, 208
Shakespeare 19, 65
Shannon, Gretchen 135
Sharp, Cecil 196–198, 202
shine/sight 9; *see also* seeing/sight
Silver, Frankie 77–78
slavery 129, 131, 188
Smith, Ada 196
Smith, Jimmy Neil 146
Smithsonian 193
Smithsonian Festival of American Folklife 134, 162

INDEX

Smoky Mountains *see* Great Smoky Mountains
snake 8, 24, 35, 155–156, 206–207
snake oil 27
Sobol, Joseph 114
South Carolina Storytelling Network 109
Southern Folk Cultural Revival Project (S.F.C.R.P.) 183
Southern Order of Storytellers 17, 19
Southern Student Organizing Committee (S.S.O.C.) 183
spider 7, 74–75
spirit 44, 63, 73
spirit deer 41, 44
spirit guide 25
spirituality 21, 27, 103, 187, 206
Spoleto 80, 87
State of Franklin 79; *see also* Sevier, John
stereotypes 45–46; *see also* hillbilly
stickball 24, 206–208; *see also* games
story catcher 14–15, 36, 114
story collecting 11, 74, 177
story teachers 23, 24, 92, 186
story weaving 37; *see also* web of stories
StoryCorp 128
storytelling: as theater 50, 80
strip mining 89
Stropnicky, Jerry 76–77
Student Non-Violent Committee (S.N.C.C.) 183, 185
Swannanoa 6, 194

Talawa 169
Tellico Dam 36, 148–149
Tennessee Valley Authority (TVA) 32, 40, 81, 149–150
Tickle, Phyllis 37
Tingle, Tim 105
Till, Emmett 127
Tomb Rock 161
Torrence, Jackie 134
Trail of Tears 30, 105
trash 53, 56, 158
trickster 65, 129; *see also* Br'er/Buh Rabbit

Tsali 19
Turner, Dr. William 188

Uktena 50
Ulmann, Doris 157
Uncle Remus 65, 129, 189
underground panther 90; *see also* advocacy
Union Grove 156
United States Information Agency 32
urban bushwomen 87

visions 140; *see also* harp
vocal cadence 42

walking: barefoot 35, 63, 155; *see also* barefoot
walking sticks 144
War on Poverty 63, 70
Ward, Marshall 146
Ward, Nancy 69; *see also* Beloved Woman; Nunceahi; Wild Rose
Watson, Willard 156
web of stories 34; *see also* story weaving
webbed mind 36
wee folk 9
West Africa: Yoruba 188
Western Carolina University 53
White-Cherokee 77, 79
Wild Rose 166–167; *see also* Nunceahi; Ward, Nancy
Williams, Cratis 176–179
Wilma Mankiller, Chief (Cherokee) 43
witches 10
Wolf Clan 45, 164
Women's Rights 77, 78, 91, 101, 126, 187
World War II 93, 170–172, 205

Yeats, W.B. 104
Yellow Mountain Trail 79; *see also* Sevier, John

Zeta Pi Beta 120, 134

Milton Keynes UK
Ingram Content Group UK Ltd.
UKHW040249011124
450293UK00012B/97